SOUTH AFRICA: DESIGNING NEW POLITICAL INSTITUTIONS

edited by
Murray Faure
and Jan-Erik Lane

SAGE Publications
London • Thousand Oaks • New Delhi

This edition first published 1996

Chapters 1, 3, 5, 6, 7, 8, 11 and 13 previously published as a
Special Issue of the *Journal of Theoretical Politics*, Volume 8
(1996), no. 2

SAGE Publications Ltd
6 Bonhill Street
London EC2A 4PU

SAGE Publications Inc
2455 Teller Road
Thousand Oaks, California 91320

SAGE Publications India Pvt Ltd
32, M-Block Market
Greater Kailash - I
New Delhi 110 048

British Library Cataloguing in Publication Data
A catalogue record for this book is available from the British
Library.

ISBN 0-7619-5302-7 hbk
ISBN 0-7619-5303-5 pbk

Typeset by York House Typographic Ltd, London
Printed by The Cromwell Press Ltd, Melksham, Wiltshire

SOUTH AFRICA:
DESIGNING NEW POLITICAL INSTITUTIONS

CONTENTS

THE CONTRIBUTORS

SUSAN BOTHA lectures on politics in the Department of Political Sciences at the University of South Africa. ADDRESS: Department of Political Sciences, University of South Africa, PO Box 392, 0001 Pretoria, Republic of South Africa [email: bothas@alpha.unisa.ac.za].

DIRK J. BRYNARD is Professor and Head of the Department of Public Administration at the University of South Africa. He graduated from the University of Pretoria in Public Administration and Political Science. His fields of specialization are administrative justice, the ombudsman concept, public management and management of change. He is currently engaged in research on justice and fairness in public administration. ADDRESS: Department of Public Administration, University of South Africa, PO Box 392, Pretoria 0001, Republic of South Africa [email: brynadj@alpha.unisa.ac.za].

ROBERT CAMERON is a Senior Lecturer in the Department of Political Studies at the University of Cape Town. He obtained Masters and PhD degrees from UCT in Public Administration, specializing in local government. He is also a member of the Western Cape Demarcation Board for local government boundaries. ADDRESS: Department of Political Studies, University of Cape Town, Private Bag, Rondebosch 7700, Republic of South Africa [email: rob@socsci.uct.ac.za].

MURRAY FAURE is Professor of Political Science in the Department of Political Sciences at the University of South Africa in Pretoria. He has co-edited and co-authored a number of books, including *Die Westerse Politieke Tradisie* (*The Western Political Tradition*), *Die Moderne Politieke Teorie* (*Modern Political Theory*) and *Suid-Afrika en die Demokrasie* (*South Africa and Democracy*). He has published articles on the philosophy of social sciences, methodology, comparative politics, the theory/action problem and electoral systems.
ADDRESS: Department of Political Sciences, University of South Africa, PO Box 392, Pretoria 0001, Republic of South Africa [email: fauream@riscl.unisa.ac.za].

DEON FOURIE commenced the teaching of Strategic Studies at the University of South Africa in 1975. He has published in South Africa, Europe, the USA, Latin America and the United Kingdom. He has chaired or served on various official committees dealing with defence problems including the Defence Secretariat Working Group of the Joint Military Coordination Council during 1994. He serves as a Citizen Force officer and until 1995 was Director, Part Time Forces at SA Army Headquarters with the rank of brigadier. ADDRESS: Department of Political Sciences, University of South Africa, PO Box 392, Pretoria 0001, Republic of South Africa [e-mail: fouridfs@alpha.unisa.ac.za].

PIERRE HUGO is a graduate of the universities of Stellenbosch, Bristol and Zimbabwe and teaches African Politics at the University of South Africa. He is currently engaged in a comparative study of the politics of intellectuals. His other areas of publication, in the form of articles and five co-authored or edited books, have *inter alia* dealt with African political issues, affirmative action, qualitative research methodology, ethnicity, white right-wing ideology and sexual racism. ADDRESS: Department of Political Sciences, University of South Africa, PO Box 392, Pretoria 0001, Republic of South Africa [email: hugopj@alpha.unisa.ac.za].

DIRK KOTZE is a senior lecturer in the Department of Political Sciences at the University of South Africa. His main interests are South African politics, development issues, ideologies, the national question and the use of political cartoons for political communication. He is involved in research about the SACP's interpretation of the national question. For the last two years he has been involved in negotiations regarding the transformation of local government in the Pretoria metropolitan area. ADDRESS: Department of Political Sciences, University of South Africa, PO Box 392, Pretoria 0001, Republic of South Africa [email: kotzedj@alpha.unisa.ac.za].

HENNIE KOTZE is head of the Department of Political Science at the University of Stellenbosch. He has written more than 50 articles in academic journals, is the co-author of three books and has contributed several chapters to other books. He writes on a regular basis for popular magazines and newspapers. ADDRESS: Department of Political Science, University of Stellenbosch, Stellenbosch 7600, Republic of South Africa [email: hjk@maties.sun.ac.za].

JAN-ERIK LANE is Professor of Comparative Politics at the Université de Genève. He is Professor Extraordinarius at the University of South Africa and has taught at Cape Town University. He is co-editor of the *Journal of Theoretical Politics*. His many publications include *The Public Sector* and (co-authored with Svante O Ersson) *European Politics: An Introduction* and *Politics and Society in Western Europe*. ADDRESS: Science Politique, Université de Genève, 102 boulevard Carl-Vogt, CH-1211 Genève 4, Suisse.

ANDRE LOUW is Associate Professor in the Department of Political Sciences, University of South Africa. A graduate of the universities of Cape Town, Cambridge and Leyden, he teaches political philosophy. ADDRESS: Department of Political Sciences, University of South Africa, PO Box 392, Pretoria 0001, Republic of South Africa.

MARIE MULLER is Professor and Head of the Department of Political Sciences at the University of Pretoria. She has published mainly on aspects of South African foreign policy and external relations and is currently co-editing a book on *Change and South African External Relations*. Dr Muller is on the editorial board of *The South African Yearbook of International Law* and *The South African Journal of International Affairs*. She is active in professional associations in South Africa and serves on the Advisory Board of the Centre for the Study of Diplomacy at Leicester University, UK. ADDRESS: Department of Political Sciences, University of Pretoria, Pretoria 0002, Republic of South Africa [email: mulleme@libarts.up.ac.za].

KIERIN O'MALLEY has an LLB from the University of Stellenbosch and a BA Honours in Politics from the University of Cape Town. He teaches in the Department of Political Sciences at the University of South Africa and is an Advocate at the South African Bar. He has written widely on federalism, nationalism and ethnicity in the Third World. ADDRESS: PO Box 15, Parliament, Cape Town 8000, Republic of South Africa.

LOUWRENS PRETORIUS is Professor and chairperson of the Department of Sociology, University of South Africa, and Research Associate of the Centre for Policy Studies. He has lectured in Political Science at the universities of Durban-Westville, Stellenbosch and South Africa, and managed research for the Urban Foundation. His publications and other research contributions deal mainly with relations between interest organizations, political parties and the state in South Africa, but include work on the politics of poverty and on ideological discourse. ADDRESS: Department of Sociology, University of South Africa, PO Box 392, Pretoria 0001, Republic of South Africa [email: pretol1@alpha.unisa.ac.za].

ROBERT SCHRIRE is Professor and Head of Department of Political Studies at the University of Cape Town where he is also the Director of the Institute for the Study of Public Policy. He has published widely in the fields of public policy analysis and South African politics and his most important recent publications include *Adapt or Die: The End of White Politics in South Africa*, and the edited volume, *Critical Choices for South Africa: An Agenda for the 1990s*. ADDRESS: Department of Political Studies, University of Cape Town, Private Bag, Rondebosch 7700, Republic of South Africa [email: schrire@socsci.uct.ac.za].

JOH VAN TONDER studied at Potchefstroom University, South Africa where he obtained his PhD in 1976 and also lectured (1963–84). He did post-doctoral studies at the University of Michigan (USA) and The Arnold Bergstreasser Institut (Freiburg, Germany) (1977–8). He entered government service in 1985 as Chief Director of the Constitutional Development Service. In 1994 he returned to Potchefstroom University as Professor and Head of the Department of Political Sciences. He has published over 80 learned and popular articles. ADDRESS: Department of Political Sciences, Potchefstroom University, Private Bag X6001, Potchefstroom 2520, Republic of South Africa.

1. INTRODUCTION

Jan-Erik Lane and Murray Faure

Institutional design versus social forces – this is the theme for this collection of articles on the transition of the Republic of South Africa (RSA) from the era of apartheid to a democratic constitutional state. The dismantling of the old regime and the coming of a new one in South Africa is an archetypal case of negotiated transition of a regime. What is unique for the RSA is the strong emphasis upon constitutional mechanisms, i.e. for getting the constitutional rules right and the setting up of institutions for the implementation of a large variety of constitutional provisions. This is the reason why this collection devotes much attention to the new albeit interim constitution of the RSA.

Nevertheless, the South African system transition has involved more than merely redesigning institutions. What made the process highly uncertain, involving the occurrence of large-scale political violence, was that it was driven by deep-seated cleavages between various groups. They are groups with a history of animosities dating back almost to the arrival of the first Europeans in 1652, when the recently appointed commander of the Cape, Jan van Riebeeck, arrived from Holland. The social forces mobilized by the key elites were so strong that they at times threatened the entire process of negotiating a system transition, especially so during the weeks just prior to the country's first fully democratic elections at the end of April 1994.

The critical question for the future of the RSA is whether the new institutions so carefully designed match the driving social forces in a highly divided society. What is in place is only a temporary constitution, which includes unsettled issues between the major players and the chief social groups. The process of constitution-making is still under way, with the hope that a 'final' constitution will be in place from 1999.

The RSA leaves the transition phase and enters the consolidation stage with several highly divisive issues unresolved, in particular the question of the nature of the state itself: whether there is to be a unitary or a federal framework for the RSA.

The prospects of a successful consolidation phase depend upon the willingness of the key players to reach agreement on constitutional matters. But, to a large extent, they also reflect the development of the economy and its capacity to counteract poverty and unemployment. There can be little doubt that these factors exacerbate the frequent occurrences of political violence as well as violent crime in South Africa. After a period of tranquillity following the 1994 election, the occurrence of political violence and crime has returned to very high levels, especially in the province of KwaZulu-Natal where conditions may be likened to a low-intensity civil war.

The population of South Africa may be classified according to race or according to ethnic community as defined mainly by language. Table 1 shows the racial distribution.

The population of South Africa has increased sharply over the past decade and is expected to continue to grow to over 60 million people by 2010. The rapid population growth among blacks has changed the numerical proportions between the four races in South Africa. At the same time South Africa has received a large number of illegal immigrants; the exact number is not known. The official migration statistics show a slight net gain for the early 1990s as the number of immigrants has outnumbered the number of emigrants. Several of the latter were highly skilled, giving rise to a debate about the occurrence of brain drain in South Africa.

The racial distribution of the population varies considerably from one part of the country to another. Table 2 shows the regional distribution for 1993 when the total population was estimated at 41 million people.

Not only is the regional distribution of the Asian and Coloured populations highly uneven, the first concentrated in KwaZulu-Natal and the second in the Western Cape, but the white population tends to be concentrated in the provinces of Gauteng and the Western Cape. The most densely populated province is that of Natal with some 8.5 million people, whereas

Table 1. South African Population Statistics: Race (millions)

	Total	Blacks	Coloured	Asians	Whites
1970	21.8	15.3	2.1	0.6	3.8
1985	29.5	21.2	2.8	0.8	4.6
1990	37.5	28.2	3.2	0.9	5.0
1995	40.7	31.1	3.5	1.0	5.7

Source: Race Relations Survey 1985/86: 2; Race Relations Survey 1991/92: 2; Race Relations Survey 1994/95: 5.

Table 2. Regional Distribution of the Population of South Africa, 1993 (%)

Province	African	Asian	Coloured	White
Eastern Cape	87.6	0.2	6.6	5.6
Eastern Transvaal	88.7	0.4	0.6	10.3
KwaZulu-Natal	82.4	9.3	1.3	7.0
North West	91.1	0.2	1.1	7.6
Northern Cape	31.3	0.2	52.4	16.1
Northern Transvaal	97.1	0.1	0.1	2.7
Orange Free State	84.1	0.03	2.7	13.2
PWV (Gauteng)	63.0	2.2	4.1	30.7
Western Cape	17.2	0.8	58.4	23.6
TOTAL	76.4	2.5	8.5	12.6

Source: Race Relations Survey 1994/95: 5.

about 6.8 million live in Gauteng.

Diversity in South Africa is based on race, but it is also the result of the existence of several ethnic communities, which are based chiefly upon language. Table 3 shows the distribution of people according to their home language.

Table 3. Ethnic Communities in South Africa, 1993

Language	Number	Proportion (%)
Zulu	9,106,000	22.4
Xhosa	7,444,000	18.3
Afrikaans	5,919,000	14.5
North Sotho	3,704,000	9.1
English	3,428,000	8.4
Tswana	3,155,000	7.7
South Sotho	2,593,000	6.4
Tsonga	1,489,000	3.7
Siswati	1,269,000	3.1
Venda	683,000	1.7
Ndebele	290,000	0.7
Other	1,636,000	4.0

Source: Race Relations Survey 1994/95: 12.

It will readily be seen that Zulu speakers constitute the largest ethnic community in South Africa. But the political implications of the language divisions are far from straightforward. One political party, the Inkatha Freedom Party, has attempted to mobilize Zulu nationalism, but nevertheless the African National Congress (ANC) has received widespread support in the province of KwaZulu-Natal where the majority of Zulus live.

In addition, it should be remembered that many South Africans speak more than one language and also that some of the African languages are closely related. For example, Siswati, Zulu and Xhosa are all three Nguni languages.

Religion also constitutes a source of cleavage in the deeply divided society of the RSA. Table 4 shows the distribution of various religious creeds among 31 million South Africans.

Table 4. Religious Affiliation in 1991 (%)

Christian	
African independent churches	17.3
Dutch Reformed	10.4
Roman Catholic	7.6
Methodist	5.9
Zion Christian	4.9
Anglican	3.8
Apostolic	3.1
Lutheran	2.5
Presbyterian	1.3
Other	9.7
Hindu	1.3
Islamic	1.1
Jewish	0.2
No religion	1.2
No response	29.7
TOTAL	100.0

Note. The figures do not include people living in the former so-called 'independent' homelands of Bophuthatswana, Ciskei, Transkei and Venda, comprising almost 7 million people.
Source: Race Relations Survey 1994/95: 10.

Religion has not been the rallying point of political mobilization to any great extent, although there is an African Christian Democratic Party. Among many rural and even urbanized people traditional animist religious practices still occur.

South Africa has an industrialized and urbanized economy with several modern economic institutions. The overall urbanization rate is 65 percent, yet the literacy rate stands only at 62 percent and life expectancy is 63.4 years. Urbanization has taken place only recently for a very large number of people. There are signs of the emergence of a post-industrial economy, although the state remains a third world country as measured by gross domestic product (GDP) per capita. The contribution of the tertiary sector to GDP in 1993 was larger than that of the combined primary and secondary sectors. The overall structure of the economy appears in Table 5.

Table 5. Structure of the South African Economy (current prices in Billion
Rand)

	1990	1994
Gross domestic product	265	422
Gross national income	266	424
Gross domestic saving	54	76
Private consumption	160	256
Government consumption	53	91

Source: South African Reserve Bank (1995) *Quarterly Bulletin*, March.

With such a pronounced population growth, it is vital that the economy
should have a growth rate which at least matches the population increase in
total output. However, the growth rate in the economy has barely matched
that of the population increase in the early 1990s.

Indeed, the economic growth rates have fallen dramatically over the last
decades. Between 1960 and 1969 the average growth rate was 5.6 percent.
From 1970 to 1979 it was 3.3 percent and between 1980 and 1989 it
amounted to 2.0 percent. In the early 1990s economic growth has swung
from being negative in 1991 and 1992 to around 2.0 percent for 1993 and
1994. This means that the growth in total output is insufficient to offset
population growth, which amounts to about 2.4 percent a year.

The critical problem in the economy is the high unemployment rate,
particularly among young blacks. Inflation may also be cited as a severe
problem, as the South African economy has typically had inflation rates
above 10 percent per year. The average inflation rate was 15 percent in the
1980s, but has reduced to 10 percent in the 1990s. Interest rates are typically
very high in South Africa, and are about 15 percent. The political consequences of substantial unemployment need to be emphasized. The growth
in employment has continually been much lower than the overall growth in
output. At the same time there has been considerable labour unrest, even
after the transition in the system.

While unemployment is a fundamental problem for the country, it is
alleviated to some extent by the existence of a hidden economy. In the early
1990s when the total labour force amounted to about 13.4 million people,
those with formal jobs numbered 8.0 million and those without formal jobs
amounted to 5.4 million. Of the latter, the informal sector comprised 2.8
million and the unemployed numbered almost 2.4 million, i.e. about 18
percent of the South African labour force. At the same time it should be
noted that unemployment is much higher among blacks in the huge townships than it is among South Africans who are not blacks.

Another major concern is the unequal income distribution with a Gini-
coefficient of about .63, one of the highest in the world. Table 6 shows the

Table 6. Distribution of Pre-tax Income, c. 1993 (% Shares of Deciles)

Decile	African	Coloured	Asian	White	All
1	0.6	1.1	1.1	1.0	0.4
2	2.1	2.5	2.6	2.8	1.1
3	3.2	3.7	3.7	4.3	1.7
4	4.2	5.0	4.9	5.5	2.4
5	5.4	6.6	6.7	6.8	3.3
6	6.9	8.9	8.3	8.1	4.6
7	9.1	11.1	10.0	9.7	6.8
8	12.2	13.7	12.8	12.0	10.9
9	17.6	17.8	16.9	15.4	18.8
10	38.7	29.6	32.9	34.2	50.1

Source: Human Science Research Council (1995) *A Profile of Poverty, Inequality and Human Development in South Africa.*

distribution of income by stating how much the poorest and richest deciles can claim.

There has been considerable discussion about whether the new government's policy should emphasize growth or redistribution. It appears that the major new policy for development, the Reconstruction and Development Programme, attempts to do both.

A further main concern is the continuing boycott of payment for public services in the townships. Since the inequality of income in South Africa is among the most pronounced in the world, it may be argued that there is scope for redistributing money from the top of the income scale. However, consideration should also be given to the fact that the taxation base in South Africa is not broad and that income tax rates already stand at 45 percent. Any redistribution policy reducing the degree of inequality of income would have to involve substantial lump sums not only from high-income white households but also from those middle incomes. These are the only earners whose incomes are sufficiently high to be capable of extensive taxation. Table 7 shows monthly household income data.

The state budget already contains several redistributive items of expenditure, although the bulk of public expenditure goes to allocative items. Table 8 indicates the breakdown of the state budget. It should be noted that the provinces and local governments have not been given taxation powers.

The 1995/96 budget is projected to allocate more than R150 billion. This amounts to some 31 percent of the GDP. The 1990/91 budget allocated about 29 percent of GDP. The bulk of the state expenditures are allocated to education (R32 billion), health (R17 billion) and to defence and the police (about R11 billion each). There is therefore some redistribution in South Africa, including so-called social pensions and child allowances. But these are limited to a maximum of some R17 billion. Finally, R29 billion is

Table 7. Gross Household Income, 1993

Rands per Month	African Proportion	Asian Proportion	Coloured Proportion	White Proportion
1–499	34.5	3.7	17.0	1.5
500–799	18.6	4.5	10.1	2.2
800–1399	28.4	19.2	22.6	6.5
1400–2499	11.8	20.0	20.9	12.0
2500–3999	4.3	21.7	16.4	18.7
4000–5999	1.5	18.0	7.9	21.1
6000–7999	0.4	8.8	3.4	16.0
8,000–	0.3	4.0	1.6	22.0
Average rands (R)/month	996	3,261	2,050	5,602

Source: *Race Relations Survey 1994/95*: 493.

needed for state debt service. This amounts to almost 19 percent of the budget or nearly 6 percent of GDP.

In total, the country has almost 2 million public employees. In a population as large as that of South Africa – more than 40 million people – that should not be considered high. Given the high level of unemployment, however, the number of public employees amounts to some 15 percent of the economically active population. Had the unemployment figures not been so exceptionally high, the relative size of public-sector employment would have been regarded as low. Compared to public-sector employment in western Europe, the South African public sector cannot be considered as particularly large. Several countries in western Europe reach a proportion of around 30 percent. Most public employees are to be found in normal state institutions, i.e. central government (30 percent), provincial and local government (approximately 25 percent) with a further 20 percent active in the former special apartheid institutions, the so-called 'homelands'. Given the excellent infrastructure in South Africa, it is no surprise that many people

Table 8. Structure of the State Budget

	1990/91	1995/96
General Government Services	7	11
Protection Services	18	27
Social Services	34	72
Infrastructure and Development	11	16
Interest Payments	12	29
TOTAL	82	155

Source: South African Reserve Bank (1995) *Quarterly Bulletin*, March.

work in state enterprises, equivalent to about 25 percent. The number of academics must be considered small, particularly so if higher education is considered as a development mechanism for the future upliftment of a population that will most probably grow to over 60 million by 2010. The number of students enrolled at universities is only about 210,000 with an additional 126,000 working their way through the University of South Africa (UNISA) correspondence system.

The demand for public-sector expansion will be very strong in the new South African state. Development requirements will call for more resources to counteract poverty and its correlates in a wide sense. Public-sector employment will be seen as a route for reducing the substantial income inequalities between various groups. And the political forces that trust the state more than the market will presumably hold the majority of positions. In addition, the structure of public employment will be affected by the way competencies between the central government and the new provincial governments are allocated.

Yet, there is widespread awareness about the negative consequences of a process of public-sector expansion that is too rapid. A widely debated question is whether affirmative action programmes should be employed in the recruitment of people to new positions in the public and private sectors. What should be done with the parastatal corporations? Transnet and Telkom as well as other public corporations employ large numbers of people. There has been much public discussion about the introduction of privatization as the new government tries to undo many of the restrictions on the South African economy put into place in the past. Thus, it has been proposed that trade barriers be lowered substantially in order to increase competition in the economy. It is also hoped that the policy of liberalization of the economy will boost exports.

The economic policies of the new government need to take account of South Africa's connections with the international economy because the South African economy is an open one. Total exports, including service receipts, amounted to R105 billion in 1994 and imports, including payments for services, cost R107 billion, leading to a R2 billion deficit on the current account, which was compensated for by capital movements. The new government has lifted some of the restrictions on the currency, abolishing the two-currency system used to prohibit capital flight. The rand, however, has depreciated over several years, as South Africa's foreign liabilities are larger than its foreign assets while at the same time the deficit on the state budget is substantial.

The political transformation of South Africa has focused sharply on institutions. What is being attempted is the introduction of a strong constitutional state with numerous institutions, safeguarded by judicial bodies including the Constitutional Court, the Supreme Court, various commissions and an ombudsman. However, political transformation is taking place alongside the implementation of the constitutional state. The case of the RSA indicates that there are limits to what constitutional policy-making can do to resolve conflicts among social groups and between elites (Hesse and Johnson, 1995). Constitutional engineering has no doubt changed the mode of political interaction from confrontation and large-scale repression to bargaining and mutual respect; but that engineering is itself the focus of much conflict. Despite the erection of a strong constitutional state, there is no solution in sight to the problem of the interpretation of the nature of the South African state itself: unitary or federal, centralized or decentralized. Federalist and anitifederalist forces collide not only over the definitive national constitution, but also over the possibility of regional constitutions. At the end of the day, constitution-making *reflects* social forces more than it *governs* them; constitutional developments might in future mirror, rather than shape, the political struggle in the RSA. The situation is highly volatile. Attempts to stem the RSA's high and rising level of crime have been largely unsuccessful, and political violence continously rocks KwaZulu-Natal. The prize of democratic stability may be in sight, but it is not yet grasped.

The developments in South Africa are interesting because they raise questions about the feasibility of a negotiated process towards democracy as well as the possibilities and limits of constitutional engineering of regime change. However critical it is for the right institutions to be established, the prospects of the South African regime transition depend much more upon the social forces at work and upon the way in which the various political elites will manoeuvre in relation to those forces.

If constitutionalism is the first major feature of the new regime in South Africa, then consociationalism is the second. The key players from the large social groups, in Arend Lijphart's (1977) interpretation, share executive powers. Whether the consociational mechanism, recommended for the RSA by Lijphart himself (1985), will prove a lasting conflict-resolving mechanism is too early to tell. Ethnic mobilization of the different *zuilen* or camps, although strong, is far from complete, as both Mandela and de Klerk try catch-all strategies, whereas Buthelezi mainly attempts to catch the Zulu vote. All three players are of considerable age; it will be interesting to see how the second generation of leaders will position themselves in relation to consociationalism, or making concurrent majorities in the late 1990s.

Social forces or institutional mechanisms – which of these are to be given decisive weight when calculating the probability of democratic stability in the RSA? Thus far, constitutional engineering has accomplished much, but can it mitigate the conflicts in the social structure beyond the short run (Sartori, 1994)? The predicted immense population growth can only fuel the clashes between economic interests, especially if the economy fails to absorb the millions of unemployed in the black townships, despite the fact that the South African economy is mainly founded upon an urbanized and industrialized country, which makes the RSA different from the rest of the countries on the sub-Saharan continent. Interpreting South African society one must remember that the majority of the population live in urbanized areas within industrial or post-industrial settings. The proportion working in agriculture is much smaller than in the rest of Africa. Racial and ethnic conflicts are closely connected with distributional conflicts, although the severity of the former is often reinforced by a wish to settle old scores.

The RSA has achieved democracy, but it is still searching for stability. Without sustained economic growth, the economy cannot deliver the resources that could settle the distributional conflicts. If the intensity and extent of ethnic conflict increase, then the institutional fortress protecting the Rechtstaat will not hold, unless expanded into real federalism. But if the economy brings real opportunities to most South Africans, then the institutional dams and canals within the unitary RSA will control the overflow of social and political conflict, violence and crime.

Postscript

On 8 May 1996 the final constitution was adopted by Parliament in Cape Town by all players except the IFP, abstaining. Next day the GNU broke up, as de Klerk and the NP left the cabinet, regretting the absence of rules about a consensus government. There were other differences between the final and the interim constitutions, but the positive specification of some exclusive competencies for the regions, as well as the lack of a constitutionally derived grand government, are the major changes. Does this reflect the growing tensions among the groups, adversarial politics replacing consensus building? Or is it a sign that ordinary opposition politics in a constitutional democracy is really feasible in South Africa?

REFERENCES

Hesse, J. J. and Johnson, N. (eds) (1995) *Constitutional Policy and Change in Europe*. Oxford: Oxford University Press.
Human Science Research Council (HSRC) (1995) *A Profile of Poverty, Inequality and Human Development in South Africa*. Pretoria: HSRC.
Lijphart, A. (1977) *Democracy in Plural Societies*. New Haven, CT: Yale University Press.
Lijphart, A. (1985) *Power Sharing in South Africa*. Berkeley: Institute of International Studies, University of California.
Sartorti, G. (1994) *Comparative Constitutional Engineering: An Inquiry into Structures, Incentive and Outcomes*. Basingstoke: Macmillan.
South African Institute of Race Relations (SAIRR) (1986) (1992, 1994, 1995) *Race Relations Survey 1985/86* (1991/92, 1993/94, 1994/95). Johannesburg: SAIRR.
South African Reserve Bank (1995) *Quarterly Bulletin*, March.

2. THE SALIENT FEATURES OF THE INTERIM CONSTITUTION

Joh J. van Tonder

Introduction

Constitutions tend to reflect societal dynamics in general and, if this is true in the South African case, the most prominent salient feature of the negotiated interim South African constitution is obviously that it embodies a transition from authoritarian rule to democratic infancy. However, broadly speaking the constitution is also a product of and reflects:

- a transitional spirit
- conflict resolution
- forced coalition
- unresolved conflict
- compromise
- and an eclectic approach.

This chapter will therefore not only deal with the prominent aspects of the interim constitution (Act 200 of 1993) but with its origins in the negotiating process (1991–1994) and with its introduction, as well as pondering its potential effect on the final constitution (which at the time of writing is being drawn up).

Referring to the Constitution of South Africa Act 200 of 1993 and its amendments as an 'interim' (in the meantime) constitution reflects an ambivalence underlining, on the one hand, the fact that it is a complete and comprehensive constitution in the fullest sense of the word, while on the other that there is still an ongoing process towards a final constitution. Thus, while the 'new political order' has taken shape it is not yet the final form and result of the negotiation process that began with the Convention for a Democratic South Africa (Codesa) in 1991. However, constitutionally speaking, a salient and remarkable feature of the South African process up to the present phase has been that the whole transition – transition in the full Huntingtonian sense of the word – took place within the parameters of constitutionality.

Since this chapter is about a negotiated interim constitution, or more correctly a constitution that is the result of a process of negotiation, some reference to this salient and ongoing feature is necessary. The status of the constitution, and some basic values that allude to its nature, will subsequently receive brief attention. Constitutional Principles (34 of them), representing a unique framework binding future constitutional development are discussed. Fundamental Rights, a separate chapter in the constitution, are a new and very important feature. The parliamentary and provincial systems and the controversy as to the classification of the constitution cannot be overlooked; neither can the transitional features of the Government of National Unity, including a perspective on the political dynamics.

A Negotiated Constitution

The interim constitution was the product of a comprehensive negotiation process that took place between up to 26 political parties in a society which, in Arendt Lijphart's terminology, could be classified as deeply divided. The thrust for the outcome thus far was derived mainly from a pact of necessity between the two major parties, the African National Congress (ANC) and the National Party (NP). (The Inkatha Freedom Party was an uneasy third.) However, the role, input and influence even of minor parties contributed to the process and outcome.

Deep divisions in this conflict-ridden society still exist, and this fact has left little room for constructive visions of a 'solution'. However, closer observation of events seems to suggest a society with an inherent interdependence (Hanf et al., 1981; Horowitz, 1991; Adam, 1977) among its heterogeneous components. This 'understanding' of itself allows it to pull back from the edge of the abyss to the comparative safety of 'consociality' and nationality, leaving ample room for conflict resolution. The fact is that South Africans do not 'hate' each other: they only need to learn to like and love each other as fellow countrymen. Since the basic facts of societal diversity and division are not going to change dramatically or substantially in the near future, the 'solution' will remain with process and consociality – a process in search of consensus (consential), a balance and a consensus of forces through convergence – because therein lies the only way to progress and nation-building in this country. In this regard, leadership – a quality not lacking in South Africa – will be crucial.

The balancing of forces and managing of the transition will be facilitated by the relatively successful learning experience of the last five years. The durability of the democratic constitutional and political results thus far will depend on more than constitutional and political developments. According to John Burton (1987:16), deep-rooted conflict involves 'basic human needs' such as security, recognition, identity and human development. These are not negotiable and the new system will have to work towards meeting these needs unconditionally if constitutional and political continuity is to be ensured. This will depend on socio-economic developments.

Process, compromise, consensus and many other concepts have come to be accepted as inherent to the transition and democratization process in South Africa. This constructive negotiation process is based on approaches and experiences developed over the last two to three decades and expanded on by scholars like Burton (1987), Fisher (1983) and Zartman (1985), all of whom visited South Africa. Such a negotiation process has been possible because all parties have been exposed to longer or shorter courses on these principles and the practices involved.

In practice this led to a process contrasting remarkably with the traditional adversarial negotiation methods and style such as had been used to bring about South Africa's 1910 Constitution. The nature of the 1910 settlement was exclusive, made up of a number of loose compromises leaving unbridgeable divides for future generations to face. Thus the 1910 settlement was short on process and long on implementation – among other reasons, because the political process was not completely indigenized. The 1993 settlement, by contrast, used modern negotiating tools that were consultative in approach, inclusive, comprehensive, focusing on solutions, rectifying historic issues and facilitating nation-building through consensus and an open or transparent process: long on process and short on implementation. The 1910 compromise process was guided by the dictum 'Let things develop' as against the present approach of 'Let's develop things'. Today's consensus approach is in stark contrast with the aims, motives and circumstances surrounding the 1910 Convention. Then the Westminster framework was a given and very little latitude existed. The approach of the National Convention (1908–1909) was to reach a set of compromises within the parameters of British colonialism. For this reason the compromises were not only between 'Boer and Brit' but between South Africa and the consolidation of British colonial interests. They included a compromise that deprived the majority of South African citizens of their political rights, because British interests in an approaching war dictated compromise rather than meeting basic human needs. In contrast, the present process, concentrating on basic human needs, could not afford to compromise the interests of *any* South Africans because this would jeopardize lasting solutions following from consensus.

The negotiated settlement of 1993, which for the first time enabled *all* South Africans to participate in a democratic national election, had a number of unique features. It opted for internal, indigenous debate instead of calling in foreign experts or powers to facilitate the process (but in the final stage before the April 1994 election the IFP demanded foreign mediation); it accepted the fact that the outcome would be achieved through a process rather than a single short takeover or settlement; it fearlessly addressed the holy cows of the past, and it reached a promising degree of understanding of the rules necessary for settling political differences. A process including local content and quality was available at a cost of probably adding too much to the constitution. *The Bold Experiment* (Giliomee and Schlemmer, 1994), *The Small Miracle* (Friedman and Atkinson, 1994) and *Birth of a Constitution* (De Villiers, 1994) are the titles of some of the first scholarly books on a settlement reached on the basis of a complex, innovative, consensual negotiation process.

Timothy Sisk (1994:66) correctly summed up that the negotiation process, and the election and inauguration of the first government 'mark a triumph of democratic transition in a deeply divided society – an anomaly to be sure' that 'will be closely studied for many years to come by students of regime change, political economy, democratization, ethnic and racial politics, negotiation and conflict resolution'.

The landmarks of this consensus, and the salient aspects of the interim constitution, which can probably best be typified as a socially engineered hybrid with eclectic and composite characteristics, are:

- a sovereign constitution;
- a set of immutable constitutional principles and basic values;
- fundamental rights as a chapter in the constitution;
- a constitutional court;
- an electoral system of proportional representation;
- a government of national unity – the executive;
- a constitutional assembly to finalize the constitution;
- 11 official languages;
- a new flag and two anthems;
- nine provinces, each with legislative and executive functions; and
- a system providing for comprehensive local government.

A Sovereign Constitution

Section 1(1) of the Constitution of the Republic of South Africa declares South Africa to be one sovereign state, while section 4(1) stipulates that the constitution shall be the supreme law of the republic. Both these sections have wide implications. Sovereignty of the state and the new constitution sets aside all the legal (and geographical) divisions created by apartheid and, read with Schedule 7, repeals the 1983 Constitution and all laws (nearly 60) related to the old order. Section 4(1), on the supremacy of the law, represents a dramatic deviation in South African constitutionalism. It creates a constitutional state or *Rechtstaat* which, read with chapter 3 on fundamental rights, affects a justiciable constitution.

In Sartori's 'constitutional engineering' terms, 'constitutions are, first and above all, instruments of government which limit, restrain and allow for the control of the exercise of power' (1994:198). Naturally a constitution must allow and be predicated towards a system of government that makes governing possible. Government should have agreed powers and limitations on that power through structural and procedural provisions that cannot be altered other than by special procedure, all of which the constitution provides for, as will be expanded on later. However, being a justiciable constitution, with provision for fundamental rights, and a rigid constitution (section 62), which also includes a set of immutable constitutional principles (see pp. 16–18), the constitution has also to provide for a Constitutional Court (section 98). Described as 'a court of final instance over all matters relating to the interpretation, protection and enforcement of the provisions of this Constitution' (section 98[2]), it thus has an effective veto right. The Constitutional Court in itself is a totally new concept in South African constitutionalism and a salient feature over and above the sovereignty of the constitution. The court will, in time, become a political court comparable to the North American example. If it refuses 'political' issues it will put the constitutional process at risk.

The nature of the constitution is not, however, fully described in terms of its sovereignty and justiciability. It has been pointed out that former South African constitutions were outstanding examples of formalism and that the new one, by contrast, qualifies as a normative constitution (Olivier, 1994:56). This brings the constitution into the realm of constitutionalism as it is understood today, especially so during the latter half of this century. Some of these norms have already been referred to; however, I now offer a short discussion of values, also reflecting the transition in its deeper sense, since I believe in the dictum that structure follows values.

Basic Values

The preamble to the constitution recognizes the 'need to create a new order' in South Africa. The constitution in various chapters and sections reflects the extent of this undertaking. The 'new order' is also closely linked to values alluded to in the constitution. It is obvious that a democratic dispensation should provide for common citizenship, voting rights, regular elections, equality between people of all races as well as between men and women, equal rights and freedoms, human rights, democracy, rule of law, transparency and freedom of information, and so on. However, although all of these are clearly embodied, being principles and norms catered for in the constitution, it is also important to keep in mind that this constitution represents and caters for a transition, a transition from an apartheid state and its constitution to a dispensation that must address formally the legacies of the past. Therefore the constitution includes some value-based provisions for specific arrangements and/or restitution through commissions. Examples are the Commission on Gender Equality (section 119); restitution of land rights (section 121); the Human Rights Commission (section 116); the Public Protector (ombudsman) (section 110) and, last but most important, the Constitutional Court which, through its jurisdiction, will interpret and pronounce on issues of human rights and thus contribute to the further development of values and norms.

A more definitive meaning of most, if not all, values included in the constitution will be derived from what South African society and its courts ascribe to them over time. Hopefully it will happen in a way that strengthens the legitimacy of the transition and of the new governmental dispensation towards consolidation and a new democratic tradition. The 'rainbow nation' is not there yet, but the goals have largely been set.

Value consensus in the new South Africa implies reconciliation, which must allow for a climate of bargaining and compromise or consensus. Everything in the end will depend on the ability to *live with the reality of conflict* while at the same time, from existing interdependence and communalities, developing the ability to live as equals in a country with a growing political culture of moderation, cooperation, accommodation and meaningful practical common values – for example, values such as democracy increasingly having the same meaning for the various sectors of this heterogeneous society. Value consensus will also imply living with the reality of a functioning constitutional court, with leadership accepting the due process of law and controlling the risks of majority dictatorship.

Constitutional Principles

Many constitutions contain a few general or specific fundamental principles catering for rights to be protected, such as relations between central and state governments, the form of state or the relations between state and citizens. Spain's (1978) constitution is an example of this, while in the case of India and Ireland more elaborate provision is made for principles of state and policy. In some cases the preambles of the constitutions, containing such ideals and principles, develop a mythical, almost sacred status of an immutable nature, even though they do not legally form part of the constitution.

The 1993 Constitution of the Republic of South Africa contains, apart from the ideals and principles in the Preamble, an impressive list of 34 relatively detailed principles (in Schedule 4) which on the one hand reflect the values that governed the constitutional negotiations and on the other constitute an immutable outline for the future constitution. These principles were developed after Codesa II (Atkinson, 1994a:94–5).

The concept was indirectly built into the Record of Understanding of 26 September 1992 between the ANC and the NP. Subsequently, the Inkatha Freedom Party (IFP) and other members of the COSAG alliance (Concerned South Africans Group [of parties], later the Freedom Alliance) demanded further detailed constitutional principles about the future dispensation, even demanding that it expressly refer to federation as the form of state (De Villiers, 1994a:39–41). The 34 principles are entrenched and the Constitutional Court therefore has the function of certifying the new provincial constitutions and the final constitution as being within the parameters of these principles before they can become legally functional.

Apart from those constitutional principles referred to earlier, the following (highly summarized) should be noted.

- Separation of authority between legislative, executive and the judicial branches of government with checks and balances (section 6) and guaranteed independence of the judiciary with jurisdiction to safeguard the constitution (section 7).
- Government being representative and responsible and established through regular elections on the basis of proportional representation (section 8). Recognition of diversity of culture and language (section 11), also of collective rights of minority groupings in civil society (section 12). Three levels of government, i.e. national, provincial and local (section 14), all based on democratic representation (section 15).
- Exclusive and concurrent powers for provincial governments (sections 12 and 21); special procedures and majorities to change provincial boundaries (section 18); powers allocated with income and in accordance with entrusted functions (section 20). National government will not encroach on provincial functions (section 22). Framework for local government powers and functions to be set out in the constitution with details provided for in provincial legislation (section 24).
- Fiscal powers and functions related to the three levels of government to be outlined in the constitution (section 25) with a Financial and Fiscal Commission, in which both central government and provinces are repre-

sented, being responsible for allocations (section 27).

- Provision for the independence of a Public Service Commission, a Reserve Bank, an Auditor-General and a Public Protector (ombudsman) shall be made and constitutionally protected (section 29), with a public service broadly representative of the South African community, non-partisan, career-orientated and efficient (section 30).
- The right to self-determination of any community sharing a common cultural and language heritage whether in a territorial entity or any other recognized way but within the framework of the right of the South African people as a whole to self-determination. Such forms of self-determination are allowed if there should be substantial support within the community concerned (section 34).

How salient are these principles and their entrenchment over the short, medium and longer term? To answer this question, one has to bear in mind the background against which these principles developed. Firstly, there is evidence indicating that, in the face of an inevitable ANC majority in a constituent assembly and the unpredictability of what 'final' constitutional course it could take, minority parties felt the need for some framework, outline or limitation on that process. Thus, before making a concession, they needed detailed commitment to democratic principles and constitutionalism. The ANC was prepared to make this commitment and from there the set of principles developed.

Secondly, it is a unique development that will, at a minimum, have an influence on South African political culture and the character of its democracy in the years to come. It sets norms and ideals – the outline of which, however, could probably have been clearer and more succinct.

Thirdly, in the short term, the principles will be strong guidelines in the development of the final constitution. After that, the Constitutional Court in its certification process will be the first test for the meaning, relevance and staying power of these principles as well as a test for the credence the court attaches to these principles. However, it is in the ambience rather than the letter of the principles that one would seek their long-term significance.

Lastly, to the extent that the principles are the result of the minority parties' fear and suspicions of the process of democratization and transition within the body politic, they have already contributed to lessening anxiety. Hopefully the principles will become a positive and proud legacy of our constitutional traditions – an outline of a worthy model and an instrument for others to follow. Here and now, however, they are a crucial and salient part of the process of transition. Without them South Africa would neither have reached its present stage, nor be able to make headway with the intricacies of the new dispensation.

Trias Politica and Checks and Balances

While the 1993 Constitution is a modern constitution, it also embodies classical features such as a partial separation of powers, and checks and balances to prevent arbitrary exercise of power. In both instances it compares well with other modern democracies. It can be outlined as follows:

- Legislative authority is vested in a parliament of two houses which controls its own affairs and which can legislate within the framework of the constitution (chapter 4, sections 36–67). This includes setting up committees (standing and special) which will be accessible for evidence by individuals and interest groups to a much greater extent than in the old era. Duly accepted laws of Parliament have to be signed by the President (section 82[1] a and b). The National Executive, consisting of the President, his or her deputies and the Cabinet, is dependent on majority support of Parliament and its functions are fully outlined in the constitution (chapter 6, sections 75–95).
- The Constitutional Court and the divisions of the Supreme Court can declare *ultra vires* any executive action that violates provisions of the constitution. Provision for a Public Protector (ombudsman) (sections 110 and 114) with wide investigatory powers also acts as a control on the whole system. Lastly, the Human Rights Commission (sections 115–118) provided for in the constitution can on its own initiative or on receipt of complaints – also with regard to the executive – provide citizens with the necessary assistance to obtain redress.
- Motions of no confidence in a parliament can be taken vis-a-vis the President forcing him or her to resign (section 93[2]), in which case a new president has to be elected within 30 days (section 77[3]b). Such a motion in the whole cabinet (President included) implies that 'the President shall, unless he or she resigns, dissolve Parliament and call an election' (section 93[1]). Such a motion in the cabinet leaves the President the choice of resigning, reconstituting the cabinet, or dissolving parliament and calling a general election (section 93[3]).
- An independent judiciary, subject to the constitution, is specified (section 96[2]) with ample provision to ensure that judges can only be removed from office by the President on grounds of misbehaviour, incapacity or incompetence after this has been 'established by the Judicial Service Commission and on upon receipt of an address from both the National Assembly and the Senate praying for such removal' (section 104[4]).
- The *trais politica* principle also applies to two elements of the provincial system of government, namely, the legislative and the executive.
- Ample separation of powers and checks and balances comparable to

other modern democracies is thus well provided for; its value and relevance will have to be proven and tested over time.

Fundamental Rights

Without doubt the most salient and important aspect of transformation, constitutionally speaking, is to be found in the entrenchment of fundamental human rights with the constitution being sovereign and the courts, especially the new Constitutional Court, having the last word. This represents a new and dynamic power-regulating/limiting factor in South Africa which, it is hoped, will have far-reaching normative, political and cultural effects in the maintenance, development and growth of the new South African state and society.

Chapter 3 of the 1993 Constitution contains justiciable fundamental rights. It is not, however, a full or comprehensive bill of rights, especially since second- and third-generation rights receive limited or no constitutional protection. However, chapter 3 has opened up a new area – a dispensation that will almost certainly move towards a more comprehensive bill of rights. The rights outlined in sections 7–35 can be categorized as basic rights, basic freedoms and socio-economic rights. Summarized, with the relevant section indicated in brackets in each case, they amount to:

- *Basic rights* – equality before the law (8) with no discrimination in terms of race, gender, sex, ethnic or social origin, colour, sexual orientation, age, disability, religion, conscience, belief, culture or language (8[2–4]); which includes affirmative action (8[3]a); right of life (9); human dignity (10); freedom and security (11[1–2]); freedom from servitude and forced labour (12); privacy (13); religion, belief and opinion (14); access to justice (courts) (22); access to information (23); administrative justice (25a–d); political rights (21); rights of detained, arrested and accused persons set out in detail (25[1–3]).
- *Basic freedoms* – expression (15); assembly, demonstration and petition (16); association (17); movement (18); residence (19); citizenship (20).
- *Socio-economic rights* – economic activity (26); labour relations (27[1–5]); property (28[1–3]); environment (29); rights of children (30[1–3]); language and culture (31); education (32).

Chapter 3 protects the rights of individuals and legal bodies, and is relevant in the area of public law which gives protection against abuses of state power. Whether this also applies juristically, i.e. to an artificial person or a body corporate, is still uncertain. However, as Du Plessis points out, 'it was agreed that the chapter should operate vertically only, but that provision be made for seepage to horizontal relationships' (1994:93). Thus this chapter is enforceable against the state and its organs with some horizontal implications for private institutions and persons.

The process of drafting the chapter on fundamental rights while keeping cognizance of the diverse views among and within the parties involved was no easy task, and necessitated protracted, detailed arguments and give-and-take through various stages and reports of the Technical Committee. The process created the first instrument of this nature in South African constitutional and legal history. The result does not go far enough, but it provides ample basis for further development through practice, courts and possible extensions in the final constitution. It can be stated with conviction that chapter 3 of the 1993 Constitution represents a breakthrough, a first in the human rights direction, that is sure to grow into a culture of rights in this new democracy. This, of course, is in stark contrast to the old dispensation that resisted implementation all along. The pendulum has now begun to swing to the other side; hopefully it will not over-swing and unbalance a salient feature of the new order.

Some Features of the Parliamentary and Provincial Dispensation

The 1993 Constitution provides for a Parliament with two houses, a National Assembly consisting of 400 members (section 40) (half the members from provincial party lists) and a Senate of 90 members (section 48). Members of the Senate are indirectly elected (10 each) by the nine provincial legislatures. The provincial governments as regional administrations will also cater for the third tier of government, that is at the local or municipal level. The constitution provides for autonomous local government (sections 174–80). Representatives on all three levels of government will be democratically elected through a system of proportional elections (party list system) except in the case of local government where a mix of proportional and ward systems will apply (section 179).

Before addressing more detailed aspects, a few salient and contentious aspects must be highlighted to give some perspective on the new parliamentary dispensation. The 1994 Parliament, no longer sovereign as in the former era, also has less power, since the provinces have more status and functions than under the 1983 Constitution. The tug of war as to centralization on the one hand and maximized autonomy in the fullest federal sense on the other, has been a highly controversial political issue right through the negotiation process. Historically, federalism was on the agenda of the convention that led to Union in 1910; regrettably, decentralization to the four provinces of *that* dispensation became the paraclete, ending in an authoritarian, centralized system with very limited devolution.

The 1993 Constitution provides for provinces with specific and concurrent powers, also laid out as follows in the Schedule on Constitutional Principles:

xvii (1)   The powers and functions of the national government and provincial governments and the boundaries of the provinces shall be defined in the constitution. [This is the case in the interim constitution, although it includes a provision to finalize a few unresolved details.]

xvii (2)   The powers and functions of the provinces shall not be substantially less than, or substantially inferior to those provided for in the constitution.

xxi (6)   Provincial governments shall have powers, either exclusively or concurrently with the national government, *inter alia* –

  (a)   for the purpose of provincial planning and development and the rendering of services; and

  (b)   in respect of aspects of government dealing with specific socio-economic and cultural needs and the general well-being of the inhabitants of the province.

Read together with the 29 Legislative Competencies of Provinces outlined in Schedule 6 of the constitution, it is abundantly clear that the new dispensation has decentralized functions in the form of provincial governments alongside central government. Furthermore, the Senate, composed of members nominated by the parties in the provincial legislatures, represents the provinces in the central government. The Senate also has specific protective roles vis-a-vis the provinces: bills 'affecting' the boundaries of provinces require separate passage by both houses (section 61), and bills 'affecting' the boundaries of a specific province or the exercise of its powers or functions must be approved by a majority of that province's senators (section 61). This, however, must be read with section 98(2)c which can invoke judicial review of the interpretation of 'affecting'. If the Senate develops into a 'sanguine' body in the new system it will have to be on the basis of catering for and representing provincial government and its status and interests at the national level. Second chambers have little other justification and are increasingly being dropped in preference of unicameralism (Sartori, 1994:183).

The constitution delineates the boundaries of the nine provinces as outlined in Schedule 1 and further provides for a full-time Commission on Provincial Government (section 163). With regard to boundaries, this commission will bring recommendations regarding 'the finalization of the number and the boundaries of the provinces of the Republic' (section 164[2]a) to the Constitutional Assembly. Each province will have a member appointed to the commission by the president with the concurrence of the premier of the province (section 165[3]); the provinces will have majority representation in it (section 163). The objectives and functions of the commission are wide-ranging and provide for recommendations to the Constituent Assembly (section 161), government and provincial government (section 164[1]b). Subsequent to the implementation of the constitution a political forum for regular consultation between the premiers of the provinces and government has been arranged. Lastly, the constitution provides for a Financial and Fiscal Commission (section 198) with the 'objects and functions ... to apprise itself of all financial and fiscal information relevant to national, provincial and local government, administration and development and on the basis of such information, to render advice and make recommendations to the relevant legislative authorities ... regarding the financial and fiscal requirements of the national, provincial and local governments' (section 199[1]). The commission will consist of 18 members representing government, provinces and local government and its appointment procedure and the qualifications specified ensure that it will be an independent specialist commission (section 200[1–4]).

The provincial dispensation is new in many ways. It has to set up administrations and sort out functions between itself and national departments, at the same time consolidating functions and administrations. In the case of the Northern Province, four previous regional administrations have to be consolidated under one executive and administration.

Three remarks are necessary to bring the provincial system into some perspective. Firstly, it is asymmetrically composed – a fact that can cause political problems and therefore the last word has not been spoken. Secondly, since the provincial system is a new dispensation rationalizing and consolidating many aspects, it will take time to become well established. Thirdly, it is well entrenched in the constitution and its schedules, and can be taken as here to stay. How its relations with central government are to be constitutionally finalized remains to be seen. In terms of the accepted 'principles', its status and functions will obviously be more meaningful than mere decentralization.

A salient aspect of the 1993 Constitution on which opinions and evaluation differ is 'whether or not it will be possible to keep this model in the "middle" of the road' (Leonardy, 1994:149). Positions other than the 'middle' beg the question of whether we have here a constitution that qualifies as a federation or a union, and will it maintain such classification? Erasmus (1994:16) is of the opinion that 'in terms of purely technical criteria, it may well be concluded that some federal characteristics are present'. Kriek (1994:2) argues that the new dispensation is a federation if M.H. Riker's 'most rigid definition of a federal state' is applied. Shubane (1994:240) comes to the conclusion that the constitution 'does not lend itself to simple characterization either as federal or unitary. It embodies features which represents both systems. It can be tilted in either direction.' Welsh (1994:96–7) argues that the crucial determinant will be 'the extent to which provincial forces mobilize to force greater federalism'. Elazar (1994:36) matter-of-factly states that 'it is hard not to conclude that the interim South

Africa Constitution is federal within the general accepted definition of the term'.

Schlemmer (1994) argues that effective regional government and greater scope for regional autonomy is necessary from an investor, business confidence and economic point of view. He calls, among other things, for urgent consideration of the establishment of larger subregions within larger economically viable provinces, and more precisely defined powers of central government in the Constitutional Principles in order to avoid 'a policy hegemony throughout the country' (p.259). He refers to the present trend as a 'quasi-federation' that cannot 'achieve the stability which regionalism, if properly introduced, can deliver' (p.254).

The salient aspect here seems to be that there are differing, even opposing views on the nature of the state or system and that at best it will achieve more clarity in the final constitution, given the provisions that exist. However, at worst the prognosis is that the 'middle of the road position' has no potential effectively to serve South Africa's constitutional, political and economic needs, and that more time and fundamental consideration are necessary to bring about a structure and composition of state more responsive to existing realities.

In the meantime the process of writing the final constitution is under way, since the 1993 Constitution provides that Parliament (the two houses sitting together) should also form a Constitutional Assembly (section 68). This unicameral body should, within two years from its first session, approve a new constitution (section 73) by a two-thirds majority of all the members of the Assembly. Provision is made for various mechanisms and procedures if it fails to pass the constitution within the allotted time (section 73 [3–13]). It must be noted briefly here that the Constitutional Assembly, its process, hearings, theme committees and participatory openness, represents a unique and salient feature on its own.

The nature of the new state or constitution after the current debate is unlikely to deviate much from the existing situation (given party constraints, the more politicized circumstances of *this* process, and the constraints of the 'principles' of Schedule 4). If it does, it will in all probability be less federal (if it is now federalist), or more unitary with less decentralization of power (if it is now unitary). The point here is that the conflict among the parties in this regard succeeded in producing not consensus, but compromise. Compromise has brought about *vociferous dissension* from the Inkatha Freedom Party and subsequently put severe strain on the Government of National Unity. It has also contributed to the continuance of violence, bordering on a form of party or civil war, in the province of KwaZulu-Natal and even some areas outside the province. Yet there is no obvious solution – only ongoing challenges and opportunities. However, avenues to a more equitable way of agreeing to differ are being pursued by all the parties; it is hoped that the IFP's fears of ANC hegemony, and the ANC's appetite for control of Natal, can be contained.

A Government of National Unity

Provision for a Government of National Unity (GNU), as it is popularly referred to, must be seen in the context of transition, in particular allaying white fears, satisfying the power-sharing demands of (especially) the National Party and to some extent meeting the demand for constitutional continuity. The process leading to this approach developed after the collapse of Codesa II (May 1992) and culminated in the signing of the Record of Understanding between the ANC and the NP on 26 September 1992 (multiparty negotiations restarted in March 1993). It was later complemented by an ANC document 'Negotiations: A Strategic Perspective'. This document accepted that the balance of forces and the interests of the country would require a government of national unity (Welsh, 1994a:94; Atkinson, 1994b:94).

Since the executive or cabinet is the most prominent feature of most governments, the fact that the new South African constitution prescribes a cabinet of national unity makes it all the more the focus of the new dispensation. This 'government' in any case amounts to a paradigm switch compared to the previous authoritarian one-party 'government', the more so if there is reference to the concept of coalition when referring to the new executive. This salient feature of the new interim dispensation, coupled with the PR system for elections, deserves a closer look, not only because it is unique in South African terms, but also because there are not many examples elsewhere with which to compare it. It is a constitutionally prescribed coalition against a background of particular circumstances. It is not, however, unrelated to relevant theory with regard to the prevailing, deeply divided society. But first a brief outline on the nature of the executive.

The heading 'The National Executive' (chapter 6 of the 1993 Constitution) covers this branch of government in 20 sections (sections 75–95). Comparatively speaking, South Africa has a formalized enacted parliamentary executive with a clear hierarchical structure. According to Albert Venter, 'The Constitution moves closer to the German model of Chancellor government, in which Parliament gives its imprimatur to the leader of the executive' (1994:177). The prominent status of the President in the Cabinet also brings to it a 'presidential' character and, the incumbent being head of state and government, places the office somewhere between Westminster and the Fifth Republic of France. However, the executive (president and cabinet) is a parliamentary executive, with the exception that the president is not a member of the legislature.

The cabinet for the first five years after the first election (27 April 1994) under the interim constitution (section 38) consists of the president, two executive deputy presidents, one each from the largest and second largest parties in the National Assembly (section 84 includes more specific details), 27 ministers (section 88) and an equal number of deputy ministers (section 94). Subsection (2) of section 88 provides for the coalition composition for which parties with at least 20 seats (5%) would qualify for cabinet posts on a formula based on a proportional quota derived from representation, number of participating parties and the available cabinet posts. The president has to consult with deputy presidents as well as party leaders before appointing a minister. Cabinet meetings are chaired by the president or in his absence in rotation by the deputy presidents. Section 89(2) requires quotation here, since it provides that the cabinet 'shall function in a manner which gives consideration to the consensus-seeking spirit underlying the concept of a government of national unity as well as the need for effective government'.

This, then, is where the GNU enters the consociational and coalition debate. Before giving attention to this it must be pointed out that the same idea and implementation of proportionality and prescribed coalition applies to the composition of the executive councils of the nine provinces (section 149[2]). In this case parties with a representation of 10 percent can qualify. To return to consociationalism, Venter (1994:178), referring to the pre-scribed decision-making mechanisms of the cabinet (section 89[2]), con-cludes that it is compatible with consociationalism in Lijphart's definition (1977:24). Lijphart's eight well-known conditions (1984:23–30) for consocia-tional democracy

> ... aim at restraining majority rule by requiring or encouraging: the sharing of power between the majority and the minority (grand coalitions), the dispersal of power (among executive and legislative, two legislative chambers, and several minority par-ties), a fair distribution of power (proportional representation), the delegation of power (to territorially and nonterritorially organized groups), and a formal limit on power (by means of a minority veto). (1984:30)

The constitution does not provide for a veto at cabinet level – a considera-tion in consociational theory but not regarded as an inherent requirement. Although the (party list) PR system was now used in South Africa, the result was effectively a referendum along ethnic lines, not consociational and segmental proportionality. However, this could in due course be rectified or countered with minor adjustments to the PR system. 'Effective govern-ment', by its composition and its consensus-seeking spirit, should in most cases forestall open dissensus so that ministers do not debate their differ-ences outside the cabinet (the GNU has nevertheless experienced this on several occasions).

The important point about consociationalism here, however, is not whether the South African situation fits the Lijphart equation (it is perhaps fortunate that it does not, because then a formula 'solution' could have been imposed that in my view would not have succeeded). The crucial point here is therefore rather that a mandatory transitionary coalition outside consociational theory was opted for. The limitations and risks involved, as well as the alternatives, are well argued by Sartori (1994:69–75) and will not be pursued here. The current situation in South Africa cannot be explained in terms of paradigm positions; a more eclectic approach is necessary, leading to an independent perspective and synthesis.

The duration of the GNU has been an issue during negotiations and 10 years was suggested as a reasonable period. At issue here is a transitional and political consideration, but in scholarly circles especially, there is concern that this deeply divided society with its complex ethnic, language, racial, socio-economic and class divisions will not be able to contain and manage inherent conflict in a new open democracy with majority government. Many of these objective realities will not change in South Africa, being inherent phenomena, but the subjective dynamics are moving in a direction that, although with many uncertainties, evinces hope for the future. As of 27 April 1994, constitutional principle and prescription have been implemented in the form of 'consensus' government. Despite a number of crises it is surviving and governing relatively effectively – in any case, way beyond the (dire) expectations of many seasoned observers.

According to Vernon Bogdanor (1983:277): 'One of the pressing tasks of political science, surely is to attempt to discover the conditions under which coalition governments are likely to lead to consensus and progress and those under which it will result in immobilisme.' Given South African circumstances, and its recent convergence and consensus capabilities, there is a compelling motivation to explore the options and conditions in this field.

The possibilities of coalitions are theoretically unlimited. They are rarely specified in a constitution and survival or success is largely dependent on the needs of the country as interpreted by political parties and their leaders – not on elections, because 'Elections do not choose governments, they alter the power relations between the parties' (Bogdanor, 1983:272).

According to Dreijmanis, the Austrian case after the Second World War

> ... demonstrated that the maximization of a coalition partner's power is not always necessarily the main goal, nor is coalition formation an isolated single event. The need and the desire to cooperate in order to achieve national unity, independence, and economic reconstruction were matters far too important in the early years ... to entrust to a single party. (1982:257)

The challenge of circumstances led to coalition governments in Austria from 1945 up to 1966 and to some extent until today. Our challenge to meet the needs of our plural society is similar, and the ANC, NP, Democratic Party (DP) and IFP, if only for the sake of national interest and economic development, will have to consider taking this road.

Two critical factors on which parties could find a basis for an inclusive government or a coalition or a government of national unity beyond the five-year prescription are: first, the shared perception of the overriding need for national unity for South Africa to be able to survive[1] – internally and externally, socio-economically and even physically; second, the deep impact the process has had on the majority of our people. The leading participants – the majority of South Africa's leaders and political elite – know what effort will be needed but also that it does bring success. Therefore party leaders will have to continue to develop a cooperative spirit among their followers and also between autonomous political parties. Efforts in this direction can keep open a window of opportunity for this society that might close later.

Schlemmer, writing after Codesa II, argued the need for cooperation:

> Given the ... deep structural imbalances and conflicts in the society which have to be addressed and the contradictory pressures and demands on government, this period of change may require special elements. One such element which is often debated is a 'social contract' or 'pact' between major parties, to allow political opponents to suspend competitive antagonism sufficiently to allow co-operation in the solving of major national problems. (Schlemmer, 1991:63)

I believe it also to be a consideration for the post-1999 phase and agree with Sartori's insight that 'PR and coalition governments may help the "difficult societies" in muddling through and hanging together' (1994:61)

One cannot be overconfident about the GNU not splitting up. Apart from the issues that could give rise to clashes to the point of parties withdrawing from the 'coalition', we also have an ethnically divided leadership. Ethnic divisions, generally speaking, do not run as deep as many outsiders believe. However, because a functional national consciousness is only now being developed, some pockets of ethnicity, coupled with opposing party political loyalties, do constitute risks. More problematic are rival party clashes within the same ethnic group, as is the case at present among the Zulu people.

On the whole, divisions in South African society have begun to shade into a new era of nationhood, over-arching loyalties and increasing interdependencies. In the final analysis, this can develop positively only if factors like rising poverty, unemployment, socio-economic decay, violence and

---

1. A fact which has allowed the executive to overcome at least four major crises since April 1994.

crime can be arrested and then decreased by positive economic growth. Only then can the frail base of tolerance, cooperation, trust and acceptance be expanded and made dynamic, replacing the focus on differences and contradictions. In this country what unites must always predominate over what divides. Finding what we can agree on is more important than our differences.

A New Party System?

Can our party system give support? From a party-political point of view it could be argued that our party system may get by with a classification of 'moderate pluralism' but ideologically and on parliamentary divisions and numbers this can be rejected as opportunistic. Taken with the transitional process, and maintenance of continuity at the leadership level, the passage of time might narrow the classification gap from extreme pluralism to limited pluralism, thus avoiding the slippery slope of our party system becoming polarized and eventually a hegemonic party system where smaller parties are admitted as subordinate parties, leaving the party in power unchallengeable hegemony. Sartori, still the acknowledged expert through his monumental contribution in this field, has recently pointed out that indications are that South Africa's party system leans towards the pre-dominant category. By definition this implies a more-then-one-party system in which rotation does not occur – the same party manages to win, over time, an absolute majority of seats in parliament. It allows other parties opportunity for dissent, opposition, etc. and is therefore not a dominant party system (Sartori, 1976:196; 1994:109). In this sense Sartori's recent classification of South Africa's party system keeps it in the realm of party pluralism and thus the chances for coalition government, if national or other interests should persuade leaders in that direction, remain open and feasible. However, this is almost too close for comfort to a dominant party system with majoritarian authoritarian government. It is early days yet and if pressed my prognosis would be that the party system will, in time, become more balanced and thus more plural. A lot will, however, depend on party diffusion and competing leadership which, over the medium term, will probably take a further 'small miracle' to maintain sufficient convergence. The new constitution's transitional Government of National Unity will also have to be especially sensitive towards the accommodation of regional parties or national parties with a strong regional basis. At this stage of the political and constitutional development isolationist or secessionist tendencies can, as elsewhere in Africa, have major disruptive effects that a brittle new system can ill afford or survive.

The Road Ahead: the Stakes Involved

We find ourselves in a position where the dynamics of a functioning governmental system are developing a new political culture that at one moment illuminates the vision of the 'high road' and the next moment casts a shadow that scarcely allows a view of the 'low road'. It is rather like the man with his head in the freezer and his feet in the boiler who registers a comfortable average around his midriff. Fortunately the state is not a man. The present executive is on a course that is bound to influence the executive of the final constitution – I believe positively. This process of finalizing the constitution, the structure of our system, will in the future be guided by a number of other dynamic components including:

- our perceptions of our ability to succeed – the vision of the future;
- the guiding influence of the agreed Constitutional Principles;
- the precedents that will develop through our Constitutional Court;
- the growing party system;
- the evolving political culture;
- how we further see our national interests;
- how we see our nation and its unity;
- how we accept and use our plural reality;
- how we make use of the new opportunities for participation; and
- what we make of an existing negotiation culture.

The rest of the world is watching and visiting (as scholars and tourists) South Africa with keen interest. It is good to be back and part of the world, getting acknowledgement, investments and participation in international events. South Africa is and will continue to be dependent on economic growth and expansion of employment possibilities. It needs investors and incentives but also continued moral, political and financial support. And if there is a need for conditions to be met, let them be tabled openly – it can only have a positive influence. The point here is that the 'game' is on. It can be a win–win game *only if* the key external supporters, especially those who encouraged, nay, demanded change, now actively continue to help the process develop from transition towards consolidation of democracy.

'The degree to which the United States, Canada and western Europe have a stake in the South African future should not be underestimated,' according to Larry Diamond of the Hoover Institute (1994:75). He defines the stake as 'partly economic and strategic but most importantly it is cultural and symbolic'. He argues that against the background of its own history, the United States – and he could have included western Europe and other countries as well – 'cannot afford to have democracy and racial reconciliation fail in South Africa.' At stake here is certainly much more than South Africa!

The next few years will determine whether South Africa is going to become a winner for democracy in this sub-continent and continent – or be an African state plodding on in mediocrity. Constitutionally the salient aspects that have been outlined hold promise that South Africa, as a laboratory for the world, can find answers to intricate political problems through political settlement that most people never thought possible. With political will, leadership and support – also from outside 'stakeholders' – the challenging road to a better future will be negotiated.

BIBLIOGRAPHY

Adam, Heribert (1977) 'When the Chips are Down: Confrontation and Accommodation in South Africa', *Contemporary Crises* 1:417–35.

Adam, H. and K. Moodley (1993) *Leading all South Africans in the Negotiated Revolution.* Johannesburg: Jonathan Ball.

Almond, G. and G. Powell (1978) *Comparative Politics.* Boston, MA: Little, Brown & Co.

Atkinson, D. (1994a) 'Brokering a Miracle? The Multi-party Negotiating Forum', in S. Friedman and D. Atkinson (eds) *The Small Miracle* (South African Review Series 7). Johannesburg: Ravan Press.

Atkinson, D. (1994b) 'Principle Born of Pragmatism? Central Government in the Constitution', in S. Friedman and D. Atkinson (eds) *The Small Miracle* (South African Review Series 7). Johannesburg: Ravan Press.

Bogdanor, V. (ed.) (1983) *Coalition Government in Western Europe.* London: Heinemann Educational Books.

Browne, E. and J. Dreijmanis (eds) (1982) *Government Coalitions in Western Democracies.* New York: Longman.

Burton, J. (1987) *Resolving Deep-Rooted Conflict: A Handbook.* Lanham: University Press of America.

Cloete, G., L. Schlemmer and D. Van Vuuren (1991) *Policy Options for a New South Africa.* Pretoria: Human Sciences Research Council.

De Villiers, B. (ed.) (1994a) *Birth of a Constitution.* Kenwyn: Juta.

De Villiers, B. (ed.) (1994b) *Evaluating Federal Systems.* Dordrecht: Martinus Nijhoff.

Diamond, L. (1994) 'Civil Society and Democratic Consolidation: Building a Culture of Democracy in a New South Africa', in H. Giliomee and L. Schlemmer (eds) *The Bold Experiment: South Africa's New Democracy.* Halfway House: Southern.

Dreijmanis, J. (1982) 'Austria: The "Black"–"Red" Coalitions', in E. Browne and J. Dreijmanis (eds) *Government Coalitions in Western Democracies.* New York: Longman.

Du Plessis, L. (1994) 'A Background to Drafting the Chapter on Fundamental Rights', in B. De Villiers (ed.) *Birth of a Constitution.* Kenwyn: Juta.

Elazar, D. (1994) 'Form of State: Federal, Unitary, or ... ', in B. De Villiers (ed.) *Birth of a Constitution.* Kenwyn: Juta.

Erasmus, G. (1994) 'The New Constitutional Dispensation: What Type of System?', *Politikon* 21(1):5–19.

Fisher, R. and W. Ury (1983) *Getting to Yes. Negotiating Agreement Without Giving In.* New York: Penguin Books.

7376

Friedman, S. and D. Atkinson (eds) (1994) *The Small Miracle: South Africa's Negotiated Settlement* (South African Review Series 7). Johannesburg: Ravan Press.

Giliomee, H. and L. Schlemmer (eds) (1994) *The Bold Experiment: South Africa's New Democracy*. Halfway House: Southern.

Hanf, T., H. Weiland and G. Vierdag (1981) *South Africa: The Prospects of Peaceful Change*. London: Collins.

Horowitz, D.L. (1991) *A Democratic South Africa? Constitutional Engineering in a Divided Society*. Cape Town: Oxford University Press.

Huntington, S.P. (1968) *Political Order in Changing Societies*. New Haven, CT: Yale University Press.

Huntington, S.P. (1981) 'Reform and Stability in a Modernizing, Multi-ethnic Society', *Politikon* 8(2):16–26.

Huntington, S.P. (1991) *The Third Wave: Democratisation in the Late Twentieth Century*. Norman: University of Oklahoma Press.

Huntington, S.P. (1994) 'Democracy and/or Economic Reform?', in H. Giliomee and L. Schlemmer (eds) *The Bold Experiment: South Africa's New Democracy*. Halfway House: Southern.

Kraybill, R. (1992) 'Defining and Addressing Basic Human Needs Through Negotiation', in *Conflict and Negotiations Document 4*. Germany: Herbert Quandt Foundation.

Kriek, D.J. (1994) 'The New Form of State in South Africa: Is it a True Federation?', *Institute for Strategic Studies Bulletin* No. 3.

La Palombara, J. and M. Weiner (1972) *Political Parties and Political Development*. Princeton, NJ: Princeton University Press.

Leonardy, U. (1994) 'South Africa's Constitutional Provisions on Devolution and Federalism', in B. De Villiers (ed.) *Birth of a Constitution*. Kenwyn: Juta.

Lijphart, A. (1977) *Democracy in Plural Societies: A Comparative Exploration*. New Haven, CT: Yale University Press.

Lijphart, A. (1984) *Democracies: Patterns of Majoritarian and Consensus Government in Twenty-One Countries*. New Haven, CT: Yale University Press.

Olivier, P. (1994) 'Constitutionalism and the New South African Constitution', in B. De Villiers (ed.) *Birth of a Constitution*. Kenwyn: Juta.

Sartori, G. (1976) *Parties and Party Systems*, Vol. I. Cambridge: Cambridge University Press.

Sartori, G. (1994) *Comparative Constitutional Engineering. An Inquiry into Structures, Incentives and Outcomes*. New York: New York University Press.

Schlemmer, L. (1991) 'Between Intention and Inevitability: Policy Pressures on Government', in F. Cloete et al. (eds) *Policy Options for a New South Africa*. Pretoria: HSRC.

Schlemmer, L. (1994) 'Regionalism in South Africa: Opportunities Missed?', in B. De Villiers (ed.) *Birth of a Constitution*. Kenwyn: Juta.

Shubane, K. (1994) 'Provincial Institutions', in B. De Villiers (ed.) *Birth of a Constitution*. Kenwyn: Juta.

Sisk, T.D. (1994) 'Review Article: Perspectives on South Africa's Transition: Implications for Democratic Consolidation', *Politikon* 21(1):66–75.

Van Tonder, J.J. (1992) 'The Process of Negotiating South Africa's Future', unpublished paper delivered at the Frankfurt Institute for Pedagogical Research, August.

Venter, A. (1994) 'The Executive: A Critical Evaluation', in B. De Villiers (ed.) *Birth of a Constitution*. Kenwyn: Juta.

Watts, R. (1994) 'Is the New South African Constitution Federal or Unitary?', in B. De Villiers (ed.) *Birth of a Constitution*. Kenwyn: Juta.

Welsh, D. (1994a) 'The Making of the Constitution', in H. Giliomee and L. Schlemmer (eds) *The Bold Experiment: South Africa's New Democracy*. Halfway House: Southern.

Welsh, D. (1994b) 'The Provincial Boundary Demarcation Process', in B. De Villiers (ed.) *Birth of a Constitution*. Kenwyn: Juta.

Zartman, I.W. (1985) *Ripe for Resolution: Conflict and Intervention in Africa*. Oxford: Oxford University Press.

3. THE NEW SOUTH AFRICAN CONSTITUTION

Dirk Kotzé

1. Introduction

The transition in South Africa has not manifested itself merely in the form of political democratization, but entails also state-building, including constitution-making. Democratization in several African states has been introduced by a 'national conference' whose objectives were mainly to implement a multiparty system, associated with a limited, procedural definition of democracy, identified with Samuel P. Huntington (1991), Robert A. Dahl and others. It is closely linked to the conditionalities of the World Bank and International Monetary Fund (IMF) for access to international financing by their African clients. Normally, it does not involve an extension of the franchise, but rather departing from a one-party system or military rule to a civilian, multiparty regime and economic restructuring based on a neo-conservative agenda.

Julius Nyang'oro (1993: 7–9) observed that national conferences served as forums for the discussion of political futures, the formation of new governments which include opposition members and the introduction of a multiparty system. Those conferences did not take long to complete their tasks (between nine days and three months) and were mainly characteristic of former French colonies (Benin, Togo, Niger, Madagascar, Côte d'Ivoire, Cameroon and Burkina Faso). In contrast with the former British colonies (such as Ghana, Zambia, Nigeria, Malawi and Kenya), the French colonies were not characterized by a strong civil society that acted as a pressure agency for transformation. In the former British colonies long-standing pressure for democratization via pressure groups such as trade unions continued, while in the absence of such groups a national conference was convened. Significant is the fact that in South Africa, a former British Dominion, civil society has been well-institutionalized, albeit repressed and harassed, but still a national conference – the Convention for a Democratic South Africa (Codesa), the Multiparty Negotiating Process in the form of the Negotiating Council at the World Trade Centre and the Constitutional Assembly (CA) – has met to negotiate the transition.[1]

The results of democratization were a regime change (Zambia, Malawi, Benin, Cape Verde and Lesotho), a confirmation of the regime (Mozambique, Angola and Kenya) or a failure of the process (Nigeria, Algeria and, partly, Angola). In all instances, they did not amount to a radical restructuring of the entire state and constitution.

The transition in South Africa, in contrast to democratization in the other African states, entails an extension of the franchise to the majority of the population. It does not entail an introduction of multipartyism, but an increase in the level of political contestation as a result of the unbanning of the liberation movements. It has also not been linked to the conditionalities of the World Bank and IMF, but rather to international tendencies such as the demise of Latin American and eastern European authoritarianism. It involves a radical restructuring of the state and a new form of constitution-making. Two of the areas most dramatically affected are the state bureaucracy and the creation of nine new provinces, which involves the dismantling of the former homelands and their integration into the new state. In addition, the form of state is also contested by three political tendencies in particular: a centralized state propagated by the African National Congress (ANC), a highly decentralized, federal state propagated by the Inkatha Freedom Party (IFP) and a divided state which includes a homeland (volkstaat), by the white right wing.

2. Transition and Constitution-making

The transition in South Africa manifested itself in two processes: the first was the erosion of the governmental power of the National Party (NP) in an evolutionary manner to create a situation of co-determination or power-

---

1. The negotiations up to 1994 were conducted in two distinct phases. The first was the Convention for a Democratic South Africa (Codesa) that convened at the World Trade Centre in Kempton Park, northwest of Johannesburg. Two plenary sessions were held, namely Codesa I (December 1991) and Codesa II (May 1992). After the deadlock between May and September 1992, the second phase, known as the Multiparty Negotiating Process, resumed between January 1993 and January 1994, when the interim constitution was finalized. The negotiations were conducted at the same venue. Hence, those negotiations have become known as the World Trade Centre or Kempton Park negotiations.

sharing in transitional institutions such as the Transitional Executive Council in order to 'level the political playing field'. The second process is to negotiate a new constitution. Serious differences of opinion had to be overcome regarding the procedure that ought to be followed. On the one hand were the NP and IFP which favoured a process conducted by nominated persons who represent their parties based on the principle of equal status. On the other hand, the ANC and Pan Africanist Congress (PAC) proposed an elected Constituent Assembly as the appropriate negotiating forum. A compromise was reached that a two-phase approach would be followed: first, a nominated negotiating forum in which all parties would have equal status, to negotiate an interim constitution and prepare for a democratic election; second, an interim period for an elected CA to write the final constitution.

A significant feature of the first phase was that the negotiations not only occurred in the formal forum of the World Trade Centre, but also outside it. After the walk-out by the IFP and conservatives and the formation of the alliance of Concerned South Africans Group (Cosag) and later the Freedom Alliance (FA), a dual process developed. The FA was extremely effective in bargaining for a double ballot in the 1994 elections, for more powers granted to the provinces, for a constitutional recognition of the Zulu monarchy and for a constitutional entrenchment of the right to self-determination. Such a dual process in the second phase seems unlikely. The second, interim period of the transition started with the national and provincial elections on 26–8 April 1994 and will last up to 1999 when the final constitution should be implemented. The interim period has a number of characteristics:

- An interim constitution which resembles the Zimbabwean precedent since 1980 of a constitution applicable for a specified period to foster a transition and a spirit of national reconciliation.
- The Government of National Unity (GNU), based on the Second World War, multiparty British government and Joe Slovo's proposal of a 'sunset clause', which is a compulsory coalition of all the major parties with more than 5 percent support represented in Parliament. According to the Minister of Constitutional Development and Provincial Affairs the successes of the GNU are its ability to create an atmosphere of national reconciliation and cooperation, a decrease in political violence and financial discipline. However, its challenges are to address the expectations created by the transition and to translate the Reconstruction and Development Programme (RDP) into practice; to improve economic growth; to finalize the restructuring of provincial and local governments; to consolidate the democracy at all levels; restructuring of the civil service; and violence (Meyer, 1995).

- A fixed five-year term guaranteed for the civil service. One of the final agreements reached by the NP and ANC at the World Trade Centre was that the civil service should be guaranteed job security up to 1999. It not only resulted in the continuation of the civil service that supported the NP and implemented its policy of apartheid, but also the bureaucracies of the 10 former homelands. Due to the pressure to usurp the civil service as the main reward for its election victory, together with the call for structural changes in the form of affirmative action, and the fact that the civil service is one of the most visible symbols of the state, the ANC faces an impediment which is impossible to resolve short of massive financial expenditure. As a result, the interim period has already witnessed widespread early retirements accompanied by large retirement packages. One example of the complexity of the process is the integration of three former armies – Umkhonto we Sizwe of the ANC, the Azanian People's Liberation Army of the PAC and the South African Defence Force – into the new South African National Defence Force.
- A list of 34 principles – the Constitutional Principles – that are entrenched in the interim constitution as the framework of the final constitution. It is the next topic to be discussed.

3. The Framework of Constitution-making

The 34 Constitutional Principles are the outcome of the negotiating process in the Negotiating Council and were intended to form the framework of the final constitution. They are fully entrenched in the interim constitution and cannot therefore be repealed or amended, irrespective of the majority.

The fact that they are binding on the final constitution, plus the fact that they had been negotiated by nominated representatives before any elections were held, partly accommodates the one-phase approach of the IFP and NP. The fact that the elected constitution-making institution (Constitutional Assembly) will be responsible for negotiating the final constitution, albeit restricted by the principles, partly accommodates the one-phase approach of the ANC and PAC.

The inclusion of the principles has most probably been influenced by the Namibian constitution-making process. As a result of the negotiations by the Western Contact Group regarding the implementation of Security Council resolution 435 (1978), the agreement reached between the interested parties in the Namibian conflict included a document with eight constitutional principles that had been drafted in 1982. They became regarded as an internationally sanctioned framework for a Namibian democratic election and constitution-making process. After the general election the Constituent Assembly adopted the principles as the framework for the drafting of the post-independence constitution (Van Wyk et al., 1991: 2, 8).

The eight Namibian constitutional principles were much less prescriptive than those in the South African constitution. The only exception is the principle that Namibia must be a unitary, sovereign and democratic state, compared with the South African principle that South Africa must be one sovereign state with a common South African citizenship and a democratic system of government. Nowhere has a specific form of state been mentioned.

In spite of the many similarities, many differences between the Namibian and South African principles exist. One major difference is that the Namibian principles were the result of a negotiating process in which the international community was one of the most important parties. In the South African situation, on the other hand, it has been the outcome of a negotiating process among internal parties, in which the international community has played only an observer role.

3.1 Status of the Principles

Almost all the sections of the interim constitution can be amended by a two-thirds majority in a joint sitting of Parliament. The Constitutional Principles are excluded, and fully entrenched. Therefore no majority will be sufficient to amend or repeal any of them. Accordingly, no government, even with more than a two-thirds majority, can override those principles. Hence, the constitution-making process is bound by decisions taken in the World Trade Centre.

In order to ensure that the principles are adhered to and included in the final constitution, the Constitutional Court has been established with the task of certifying that it is indeed the case, before the final constitution can be implemented. Another task of the court is to advise the CA (both houses of Parliament) or provincial legislatures in the process of constitution-making when they need advice regarding the constitutionality of an issue. Accordingly, its function is, *inter alia*, to offer advice regarding the implementation of the principles.

The nine provinces are expected by the interim constitution to negotiate their own, provincial constitutions. While the national constitution must incorporate all the principles, the provincial constitutions should not be in conflict with any of them. Once again, the Constitutional Court will be responsible for ensuring that the constitutions are constitutionally correct. The Freedom Alliance argued vehemently for the right of provinces to write their constitutions without any of those external constraints; in other words, to regard it as an original, exclusive provincial function. On 21 February 1994 the interim constitution was amended to remove the provision that the provincial constitutions must comply also with the national constitution. The only restraints remaining are their adherence to the principles, and the court's review function.

3.2 The Content of the Principles

The 34 Constitutional Principles can be categorized into five major topics, as follows.

(1) The transition period. Principle 32 states that the composition and functioning of the national executive must be entrenched up to April 1999. Moreover, Principle 33 states that no parliamentary election can take place before 1999, except if a motion of no confidence in the government has been adopted. It implies that elections can take place and a new GNU be formed, but it must occur in terms of the interim constitution, which means that the structure and functioning of Parliament and the GNU are entrenched for the period up to 1999.

(2) The status of the constitution. The constitution is considered to be the supreme law of the land, which implies acceptance of the principle of constitutional sovereignty. It is a radical break with the past, during which the principle of parliamentary sovereignty had been in force. Its implication is that the new constitution has established the principle of judicial review of legislative and executive/administrative actions and judicial interpretation of the constitution as the supreme authority. Principle 15 stipulates that amendments to the constitution shall require special procedures involving special majorities. Thus it will be a relatively rigid constitution.

(3) Fundamental rights. No South African constitution has ever included a bill of rights with judiciable human rights. Moreover, South Africa has been one of the few countries which was not a signatory of the UN's Universal Declaration of Human Rights. Chapter 3 of the interim constitution introduced such a bill of rights which includes first-, second- and third-generation rights. A number of the Constitutional Principles ensure that this new tradition must be entrenched. They refer to:

- universally accepted fundamental rights, freedoms and civil liberties that must be entrenched and justiciable;
- prohibition of discrimination and the protection of racial and gender equality and national unity;
- freedom of information to ensure open and accountable government and administration;
- diversity of languages and cultures that should be acknowledged, protected and promoted;

- recognition and protection of collective rights regarding organs of civil society on the basis of nondiscrimination and free association;
- the right of employees and employers to form and join employer organizations and trade unions and to bargain collectively, and the right to fair labour practices.

(4) Democratic principles. These include representative government embracing a multiparty system, regular elections, universal adult suffrage, a common voters' roll, proportional representation, participation by minority parties in the legislative process in a manner consistent with democracy and democratic representation at each level of government.

Those principles reflect a procedural approach toward democracy. The assumption is that if the formal procedures are applied in a fair manner, the system is per definition democratic. However, it has lost sight of the moral dimension of democracy, especially its social responsibility to ensure socio-economic justice, which is also absent in the South African constitutional principles, except for a few, fundamental rights in chapter 3. It is probably assumed that the moral dimension, which is fundamentally important in reversing apartheid, should be an objective of public policy (such as the Reconstruction and Development Programme (RDP)) and not constitutionally determined.

(5) The form of state and government. Principle 1 states that South Africa must be one sovereign state, with one common citizenship and a democratic system of government. On 21 February 1994 it was qualified by the adoption of Principle 34 which states that the general application of the right to self-determination does not exclude the right to self-determination of any community sharing a common cultural and language tradition. Moreover, a movement claiming such a right must prove substantial support in the community concerned. If a territorial entity has been constitutionally established before the final constitutional text is passed by the CA, the final constitution must entrench that territory's continuing existence. The purpose of Principle 34 is to create an opportunity for the proposals of a sovereign Zulu kingdom and a conservative, Afrikaner homeland (volkstaat) to be argued in the CA without any limitations instituted in terms of Principle 1.

Separation of powers between the legislature, executive and judiciary is entrenched, as well as the provision of appropriate checks and balances. In addition, the principle of formal legislative procedures at all tiers of government has been included. Those principles are aimed at ensuring that the power and authority of Parliament cannot be circumvented by executive actions, or that the executive can usurp the judicial functions. In the South

African context, it is important that executive prerogatives are limited and justiciable. The independence of the judiciary is also guaranteed.

The legal system has been addressed by a number of principles. First, equality of all before the law has been ensured, as well as an equitable legal process. Principle 7 states that the judiciary should be appropriately qualified, independent and impartial. An extremely important function of the judiciary in future will be to safeguard and enforce the constitution and all fundamental rights in line with the philosophy of constitutional sovereignty.

Probably the most contentious part of the principles relates to the ones dealing with inter-governmental relations. It is important to note that inter-governmental relations are ostensibly the single most important determining factor of the form of state. In the negotiating process the question whether the constitution provides for a unitary or federal state has become a highly politicized issue.

The principles dealing with this issue state that South Africa must be a united state, that the boundaries of the nine provinces will remain unchanged and that the (concurrent) powers and functions of the provinces will not be less than or inferior to those listed in Schedule 6 and contextualized in section 126 of the interim constitution (this Principle 18(2) is at the heart of the IFP's call for international mediation). It is also stated that the powers and functions of the national and provincial authorities must be defined in the final constitution (it is typical of several federal constitutions). Therefore it cannot be left to a future Parliament and government to define the powers and functions of the provinces as a matter of public policy. Special majorities will be required to amend those powers and functions, and the provinces concerned will have to be directly involved.

In view of the unitary-federal debate, Principle 19 is extremely significant, because it states that the powers and functions of the provincial and national tiers must include concurrent and exclusive powers, which almost certainly will result in a federal relationship. However, a crucial vacuum still exists regarding which powers will be exclusive in nature. Eight criteria have been identified which must guide the allocation of powers to the two tiers of authority. Summarized, they are financial viability, effective public management, the promotion of national unity, legitimate provincial autonomy and acknowledging cultural diversity.

Local government also received attention in the principles, albeit extremely vague in formulation. The interim constitution also provides little guidance regarding local government and it has been left to the Local Government Transition Act (1993) to stipulate the details. The final constitution, however, must be more specific and therefore the principles acknowledge that a framework of local government powers, functions and structures must be included.

A new dimension of the constitution is the inclusion of traditional leaders in specially created institutions, such as the provincial Houses of Traditional Leaders and the national Council of Traditional Leaders. The Constitutional Principles ensure that the institution, status and role of traditional leadership will be recognized and protected. Indigenous law will also be recognized in so far as it is not in conflict with the fundamental rights of the constitution. One of the issues contested by the IFP before the 1994 elections was the status of the Zulu monarch. As a result of the mediation by Professor Washington Okumu of Kenya, it had been included in the agreement of 19 April 1994 that brought the IFP into the elections. Accordingly, Principle 8 has been amended to include that 'provisions in a provincial constitution relating to the institution, role, authority and status of a traditional monarch shall be recognized and protected in the constitution'. It paved the way for the constitutional accommodation of the Zulu king in the constitution of KwaZulu-Natal.

A crucial component of the structuring of the state is its inter-governmental fiscal arrangements. The principles stipulate that the fiscal powers and functions of the national and provincial authorities will be defined in the final constitution and not by the government of the day. In the interim constitution provinces are excluded from access to any form of sales or income taxes, which remains the exclusive prerogative of the national authority. Currently, the relationship between the national and provincial authorities is determined by the Financial and Fiscal Commission. Other aspects of inter-governmental relations are discussed in the nonstatutory Inter-governmental Forum, where national ministers meet members of the provincial Executive Councils for developing conventions regarding their concurrent functions.

4. The Institutional Dimension of Constitution-making

The institutional dimension of the negotiating process is imperative insofar as it has caused the failure of Codesa, but on the other hand, it was also the mobilizing force in the short-lived Patriotic Front. Since the adoption of the Harare Declaration in 1989 by the Organization of African Unity, the Commonwealth, the Non-aligned Movement and, in an adapted form, by the United Nations, the notion of an elected constituent assembly as the main constitution-making institution has been the dominant view. In terms of the consensus that developed regarding the transitional process, the first phase would consist of nominated party representatives negotiating an interim constitution, while the final constitution would be negotiated and drafted by the elected Constitutional Assembly.

According to the interim constitution, the CA is constituted by a joint sitting of the National Assembly and Senate. Hence, for the first time the negotiating process received a statutory status and became more fully institutionalized. Based on the experiences at Kempton Park, and especially the problems experienced in Codesa, the negotiating and drafting process has been delegated to committees: the six, multiparty theme committees (30 members each), the Constitutional Committee (46 members) and the Management Committee (12 members). In addition a panel of seven constitutional experts has been established by the CA, together with a maximum of three technical experts per theme committee and the Constitutional Court which can also offer its advice on request. The theme committees cannot take binding decisions and therefore do not engage in real bargaining; they submit their reports to the Constitutional Committee which is the real driving force and negotiating forum.

A small group of technical experts assists the Management Committee to analyse and interpret the reports of the theme committees. They also prioritize the matters for discussion, though they do not take any decisions regarding those issues. They recommend to the Management Committee the order of priority in which issues need to be negotiated in order to facilitate the process. The Management Committee operates as a 'clearing house' for determining the programme of the Constitutional Committee as well as regulating and feeding the committee with issues for discussion. Hence it fulfils a crucial gatekeeping function.

The Constitutional Committee identifies key issues which would require debate and finalization by the CA. It also decides whether further instructions should be given to the theme committees or Management Committee. Finally, it can request the CA to provide further instructions for drafting in areas of agreement and for debate of contentious areas (Constitutional Committee, 1995: 3–4).

A major obstacle for the CA to overcome is the perception that the negotiating process has become detached from the population. It had also been a serious shortcoming in the Codesa process: the negotiators, even the populist South African Communist Party (SACP) and ANC, were accused of losing contact with their constituencies. As a result the CA decided to launch a Public Participation Programme to allow for participation by the public. Theme committees held area forums in many parts of the country which enabled the public to voice their views about aspects of the constitution-making process (*Constitutional Talk*, 1995: 5).

The approach followed by all the institutions of the CA is to identify areas of consensus and areas of disagreement. For instance, at the beginning of 1995 Deputy Minister Mohammed Valli Moosa (1995) referred to the areas of agreement and disagreement listed in the Constitutional Committee's first report. Disagreement existed over whether the head of government and head of state must be separated; whether proportional representation should be extended to the executive (a permanent government of national unity); whether the deputy president and president could be members of the same political party; whether the president should be directly or indirectly elected; and whether there should be a government through Parliament or a government by Parliament. Other contentious points identified by Theme Committee 1 in February 1995 were the nature and extent of the powers of the various levels of authority; whether Parliament will be bi- or unicameral in structure; Parliament's supremacy as a law-maker; the constitutional entrenchment of minority party participation in the legislative process; government by majority rule; the content and constitutional entrenchment of participatory democracy; and South Africa as a secular state (Theme Committee 1, 1995: 49). Areas of agreement included support for a parliamentary system instead of a cabinet system of government and that the executive must be accountable to Parliament.

A decision with a dire impact on the institutional arrangements of the constitution-making process has been the IFP's withdrawal from the CA in view of its inability to convince the ANC and NP of the need for international mediation. Though the two-stream negotiating approach of the Kempton Park phase could not be reimplemented, the IFP's absence effectively hamstrung the CA's proceedings for several months during mid-1995. It raises important questions: what effect would the absence of about 10 percent of the adult population in the form of the IFP have on the long-term legitimacy of the final constitution? Is it necessary for a general consensus to exist before a constitution can claim legitimacy? A simple response is no. But it depends largely on how sustainable that opposition is. If the final constitution is not plagued by systemic dysfunctionalities, such opposition is unlikely to be sustained, except if a consolidated, territorial base for opposition, such as KwaZulu-Natal exists. On the other hand, if the opposition members are dispersed throughout the country, their opposition is likely to disappear.

Another institutional component of the negotiating process is the Department of Provincial Affairs and Constitutional Development, headed by Roelf Meyer, chief NP negotiator at Kempton Park, and Mohammed Valli Moosa, one of the ANC negotiators. The chief bureaucrat of the Department is Neil Barnard, a former head of the National Intelligence Service under P. W. Botha and a major protagonist of the 'total strategy' against the communist 'total onslaught' spearheaded by the ANC and SACP. His intellectual background is an academic career at the conservative University of the Orange Free State in the field of strategic studies, especially Cold War strategy. Before the 1994 elections the Department was available to the NP as a support system in the negotiating process. Since 1994 that function has changed, and it is currently mainly involved in developing strategies for implementing the interim constitution, in particular the consolidation and implementation of provincial and local government. In this respect, a formation has been established (MINMEC: the Minister plus Members of the provincial Executive Councils) where Roelf Meyer meets regularly with the provincial MECs responsible for local government. At this level most of the problems regarding the transformation of local government are addressed. Transformation at local government level is particularly problematic, because it is the terrain where the public will experience the democratization and transition most directly. Unfortunately, the negotiators at Kempton Park paid scant attention to this issue and formulated a few general principles included in chapter 10 in the interim constitution. Instead, the structuring of the three-phase transition process was left to the Local Government Transition Act and local negotiating forums. A major omission on the part of the legislatures has been rural local authorities. As a result, it was left to the provinces to negotiate different types of rural authorities, *inter alia* district councils, transitional representative councils and transitional rural councils. Their purpose is also to accommodate traditional leaders (magoshi, amakhosi and others) as nominated members of the councils, who would, in combination with elected councillors, be responsible for rural areas.

An institutional dimension that is also influential in the constitution-making process is the intra-party decision-making structures: the ANC's National Working Committee and National Executive Committee (NEC), the IFP's National Council and the NP's Federal Council plus executive. The ANC's NEC in particular has played a prominent role. It convened a National Constitutional Conference in March/April 1995 as well as one in July 1995. Instances of differences of opinion among ANC members in the theme committees have been referred to the NEC for final decision. One issue in which the NEC plays a significant role is the future of the president and deputies. It is safe to say that the position of president in the interim constitution was tailor-made for Nelson Mandela, while his crown princes became executive deputy president (Thabo Mbeki) and chairperson of the CA (Cyril Ramaphosa). Thereby a succession struggle has been postponed. With Mandela not available after 1999 and the ANC probably the only party in government, a new dispensation is necessary.

In March/April the ANC favoured a deputy president along with a president (ANC National Constitutional Conference, 1995: 18–19). However, in July it suggested a prime minister and president, which would mean that Mbeki, who is widely tipped as a future president, would not be the head of government. The premier would in effect exercise day-to-day political control, which would complicate the question whether Mbeki or Ramaphosa would be in control of the situation. The NEC is expected to resolve the issue (*The Star*, 1995: 3).

In the case of the IFP, the institutional influence of its National Council as a legitimation instrument of the views of leaders such as Mangosuthu Buthelezi and the secretary general, Ziba Jiyane, is overshadowed by the role of individuals such as Mario Ambrosini. Ambrosini is an American lawyer who accompanied the American constitutionalist Albert Blaustein to South Africa as advisers for the IFP in the negotiating process at Kempton Park. Ambrosini remained behind and gained the confidence of Buthelezi as an adviser. As a result he has developed a status of extraordinary influence – mostly a hardline approach – in the IFP, though he is not elected to any position in the party.

Without an institutional analysis of the constitution-making process the genuine nature of the transition in South Africa cannot be understood. Another dimension that should also be included is the call for international mediation.

5. International Mediation

The second means of constitution-making in South Africa, after institutionalized negotiations in the CA, is international mediation. At the initial stage of the negotiating process in 1991 the PAC proposed international facilitation in order to reduce the advantageous position of the NP as government and introduce a nonpartisan officiating agency. However, Codesa and the Multiparty Negotiating Process decided against international involvement – international actors acted only as observers.

The IFP, on the other hand, has introduced a new perspective on international involvement. Since March 1994 it has promoted international mediation as a means of bridging its differences with the ANC in particular. It raises the first question: is mediation the most appropriate means to resolve the issue?

Mediation 'is a form of third-party intervention into disputes, directed at assisting parties to find their own mutually acceptable settlements' (Anstey, 1991: 249 and 1993: 1). The objective of mediation is not only to reach a settlement but also could be to seek sufficient movement for allowing negotiations to continue without further third-party assistance, or to remove specific obstacles to negotiating, or to reduce tension in the relationship, or to assist parties to define the issues at stake more clearly (Anstey, 1993: 2). In summary, it is clear that mediation is aimed at resolving a dispute. However, the exact role of a mediator is still debated. The two dominant views are, first, that the parties are mature negotiators who are capable of making their own decisions as to what constitutes an appropriate or just result, and therefore a mediator should not impose it on them. Hence, the mediator's task is not to create a temporary and artificial balance between power imbalances. The second view is that the primary purpose of mediation is to balance the power between the parties to ensure a 'fair' agreement (Boskey, 1994: 367–70). Subsequent discussions reveal that the IFP has ostensibly the latter view in mind.

International mediation is normally aimed at resolving a dispute regarding interpretations of an agreement or a particular document, regarding mutually exclusive positions in a negotiating process, or to remove a deadlock in negotiations or resolve a walk-out by one of the parties, or to resolve physical conflict. In the past few years the best examples of international mediation were Jimmy Carter's involvement in North Korea and Bosnia; the Norwegian foreign ministry's mediation in the Palestinian/ Israeli issue; Lord Owen and Lord Carrington in Bosnia; and the role of South Africa, Botswana and Zimbabwe in resolving the crisis in Lesotho. Accordingly, typical issues for mediation in the South African context could be: the way in which the concurrent powers of provinces (Schedule 6 in the constitution) must be interpreted; or to reconcile the differences of opinion regarding allocation of powers from the national to the provincial authorities since the establishment of the new provinces.

5.1 Origin of the Call for Mediation

At the end of 1993 the IFP submitted a Yellow Paper containing amendments to the interim constitution, which the NP tabled in Parliament. However, the ANC succeeded in delaying the process before the interim constitution was enacted. The first two months of 1994 saw negotiations between the ANC, NP and Freedom Alliance during which the NP withdrew its support for the Yellow Paper amendments. It reached a deadlock when on 21 February 1994 the NP and ANC supported amendments to the interim constitution without the IFP's concurrence.

During March and April 1994 the IFP and ANC were engaged in intensive negotiations regarding possible international mediation to end the deadlock and to secure the IFP's participation in the April 1994 general elections. On 10 April 1994 the IFP, ANC and also the NP agreed on an agenda (the Consolidated Terms of Reference) for international mediation. Seven international mediators, including Henry Kissinger and Lord Carrington, were identified. However, after their arrival Cyril Ramaphosa and Roelf Meyer objected to the 'purpose' of the mediation in particular. The ANC proposed two conditions for the mediation to commence, namely that the IFP must commit itself to accepting that no amendment of the interim constitution will be tabled before the election and that the outcome of international mediation would constitute a recommendation to the Constitutional Assembly. Second, the IFP must endorse and recognize the interim constitution and election date (26–7 April 1994). The IFP rejected both and thus the mediation failed to materialize.

One of the mediators, Professor Washington Okumu of Kenya, remained behind and brokered an agreement between the ANC, IFP and NP on 19 April 1994. The main elements of the Agreement for Reconciliation and Peace were:

- the IFP agreed to participate in the general election;
- the parties agreed to recognize and protect the institution of the Zulu king and the Kingdom of KwaZulu, for which purpose the interim constitution would be amended before the election;
- 'any outstanding issues in respect of the King of the Zulus and the 1993 Constitution as amended will be addressed by way of international mediation' (Agreement, 1994: 1–2).

Accordingly, the IFP recognized the interim constitution and committed itself to the election process and election date.

In January 1995 the Constitutional Committee of the Constitutional Assembly (CA) agreed that international mediation should be discussed in the context of the constitution-making process. It resolved that the issue ought to be dealt with by the leaders of the three signatories. Cabinet established the '3M (Roelf Meyer [NP], Mohammed Valli Moosa [ANC] and Sipho Mzimela [IFP]) Committee' to investigate the implementation of the Agreement. They reached a deadlock, because the NP and ANC did not consider the Consolidated Terms of Reference still binding on all the parties, in addition to the ANC's opinion that the Zulu kingdom no longer formed part of the terms of reference. Consequently, President Mandela delegated the issue to Deputy President Thabo Mbeki for facilitation.

On 6 March 1995 a special IFP General Conference resolved that the party could no longer participate in the CA and should suspend its involvement. However, the walk-out would only be effected a month thereafter if international mediation failed to commence. Since the end of March 1995 the IFP is no longer participating in the CA, while no progress has been made regarding international mediation (Buthelezi, 1994a: 1–3; IFP, 1995a: 1; IFP, 1995b: 2; IFP, 1995c: 3–7; *The Star*, 21 March 1995: 10).

5.2 The Issues at Stake

An evaluation of international mediation should not only focus on mediation itself but rather on the root issues which it reflects. The questions that it raises are:

(a) how should the final constitution be negotiated; what is the most appropriate mechanism?

(b) is constitution-making a *sui generis* process that requires a special form of decision-making other than a special majority?
(c) is international mediation the most appropriate mechanism to be applied under present circumstances?
(d) is the Agreement for Reconciliation and Peace still binding on the signatories?
(e) what are the matters to be mediated; is the Consolidated Terms of Reference an appropriate agenda for mediation?

5.3 Constitution-making Mechanisms

Arguably, at the heart of the differences regarding international mediation are divergent perspectives with regard to its purpose. Implicit in the IFP's argument is a two-pronged motivation.

First, it views it as a substitute for the CA negotiating process. For instance, in a submission to the 3M Committee it said:

> The IFP always opposed the notion of a Constitutional Assembly charged with the task of drafting a constitution for the country by virtue of majority rule. There are fundamental issues, such as those of federalism and pluralism, which cannot be decided by majority rule, no matter how large is the majority concerned. (IFP, 1995b: 6)

In the same submission it was also made clear that 'international mediation, and not the Constitutional Assembly, would offer the path to settle the issue of the form of state' (IFP, 1995b: 2). Another variation of this opinion is that the purpose of international mediation, in the IFP's opinion, is to provide inputs to the constitution-making process after the April 1994 elections. On the other hand, though the IFP rejects the legitimacy of the CA as the constitution-maker, it argues that the CA is responsible for determining the role of international mediation in the constitution-making process (IFP, 1995a: 2).

The IFP's approach is ostensibly a continuation of its approach during the multiparty negotiations at Kempton Park. It was highly successful as *de facto* leader of the Freedom Alliance in establishing a second, parallel negotiating process outside the Negotiating Council which enhanced its bargaining position vis-a-vis the ANC and NP and delivered tangible results. The main difference in the two situations, however, is that the CA is much more institutionalized than the Negotiating Council, with a statutory status and popular legitimacy based on the outcome of a general election. Accordingly, much less space has been left outside the CA for a second, parallel negotiating process. The demise of the extra-parliamentary Conservative Party (compared to the parliamentary Freedom Front) is largely indicative of this.

Implicit in the IFP's approach is an acknowledgement that, based on the principle of electoral support, it is too small and geographically concentrated for effective, round-table bargaining. Hence, a two-sided negotiating table, with the IFP on the one side, is most preferable, but given the fact that the CA's round table is highly unlikely to change, it could only be achieved under special conditions, such as international mediation.

Immediately it raises the issue of the relationship between the CA and other extra-systemic negotiations. Where will the final locus of decision-making be? International mediation could only be morally defensible if all seven political parties in the CA were involved, which in the end might be detrimental to the IFP. Suppose most of the other six parties take their places opposite the IFP, it would mean its effective marginalization in the sense that it would be the IFP against a multiparty caucus.

The second IFP motivation for mediation is ostensibly to entrench its powerbase in KwaZulu-Natal. The results of the 1994 general elections, albeit not very accurate, have confirmed that apart from areas on the East Rand and in the Eastern Transvaal (Mpumalanga), the IFP is a regional party confined to KwaZulu-Natal. Hence, it is logical for it to entrench its position there in the form of more powers granted to the provinces, and it has gone so far as to propose an asymmetrical federal state in favour of the province of KwaZulu-Natal. Because in its view it will not be able to secure it by means of the negotiating process in the CA, the alternative is international mediation. The Agreement has created the loophole that by invoking Constitutional Principle 18(2) it will secure more provincial powers in the final constitution without bargaining for them in the CA.

In contrast with the IFP, the ANC maintains a limited interpretation of international mediation. Thabo Mbeki is of the opinion that mediation refers to a dispute, and hence outstanding issues should be identified which are in dispute. He denies that any such issues have been identified (Mbeki, 1995: 3). The IFP rejected such an interpretation:

> International mediation does not depend on the development of a deadlock in the negotiation process in the Constitutional Assembly, and is not a tool to solve a deadlock. In fact, the Agreement for Peace and Reconciliation ... requires that international mediation is to commence even before the constitution-making process in the Constitutional Assembly was properly structured. (IFP, 1995b: 1)

Thus the call for international mediation symbolizes a lack of consensus regarding the mechanism for constitution-making. Moreover, the Agreement that enables international mediation is confined to the interim constitution and Zulu kingdom, while the IFP's main target is the CA, which is responsible for the final constitution.

5.4 Decision-making in the Negotiating Process

A question of universal relevance is: what must be the majority needed in writing a constitution – a simple majority, a two-thirds majority or general consensus? Related to this question is another: is constitution-making such a unique process that it cannot be governed by the normal, democratic, political rules of the game?

At Kempton Park the principle of sufficient consensus was used, but the IFP challenged its application in court. In contrast, the CA must take decisions by a two-thirds majority, but if an impasse is reached after three years of negotiations, the new constitution can be adopted by a simple majority. In either scenario, the Constitutional Court remains responsible for certifying the constitution's compliance with the Constitutional Principles.

The IFP opposes the CA, because of the majoritarian principle. 'Simply put, the IFP rejected the notion of an election to empower a Constitutional Assembly charged with the task of writing a new constitution by virtue of majority rule, claiming that some fundamental issues related to pluralism and federalism cannot be decided by majority rule' (IFP, 1995b: 1). In view of the fact that sufficient consensus as well as a two-thirds majority is unacceptable to the IFP, it is clear that no form of round-table, multiparty negotiations would be acceptable to it, because potentially it could be overruled by the others. Hence, a two-sided mediation process is the only option.

The IFP has succeeded in creating the impression that its insistence on international mediation is for the sake of federalism and pluralism. However, the majority of parties in the CA (the NP, Democratic Party, Freedom Front and African Christian Democratic Party) also propagate it, while only the ANC and PAC are not overtly federalist. The ANC and PAC together cannot muster a two-thirds majority in the CA, which means that federalist parties will also have to concur with the final constitution. That has given them effective bargaining power in the CA, irrespective of extremely small electoral support.

Another consideration is the fact that in South Africa only political parties are responsible for the constitution-making and all other social formations have been excluded since the start of talks in Codesa, which introduces implicitly into the negotiating process a set of rules associated with parties. Parties' power is mostly determined by an electoral process which invokes the democratic principle of majoritarianism, normally a simple majority, but for constitutional amendments a special majority is often required. Other principles could have been used if political parties were not to be the primary actors in the process, like the American founding fathers.

The dilemma of all constitution-making processes directed by political parties (which has been the dominant approach over the last few decades) is that parties have a temporary existence and their electoral support may change over time. How will it affect a constitution that is supposed to last for generations but which reflects the sentiments of particular parties at a specific point in time? Not even a general consensus among all the parties would alleviate this dilemma. Two options are available, though both are undesirable. The first is to assume that the constitution will have to be amended quite often and therefore not to create one that is too rigid. Second, it could be a lean constitution (like the American one) without much detail and confined to general principles, excluding aspects such as the restitution and restructuring of, *inter alia*, the economy, affirmative action, land issues and gender.

5.5 The Most Appropriate Mechanism

If, for a moment, the Agreement of 19 April 1994 is set aside, an important question is: which mechanism will be most appropriate in order to address the current differences of opinion and the IFP's objectives? The main issues raised by the Consolidated Terms of Reference are exclusive, original powers for the provinces (even on an asymmetrical basis), including the right to taxation and of writing their own constitutions without any review, and second, the Zulu monarchy and Kingdom of KwaZulu. They involve Constitutional Principles 18(2), regarding provincial powers, 34, regarding the right to self-determination, and 13(2), regarding the constitutional position of the Zulu king. The IFP reduces them to two concepts: federalism and pluralism.

Extension of provincial powers to include exclusive powers, which by means of Principle 18(2) will form part of the final constitution, does not involve a dispute regarding the interpretation of the present list of con- current powers. The IFP rather argues for an extension of the list (in other words, new issues are introduced), which is a typical agenda of a negotiating process and not mediation. The present situation has not been preceded by negotiations that are deadlocked or in dispute. Hence, the situation is suitable for facilitation but not mediation. In the Consolidated Terms of Reference it had been implied in the sense that the mediators were not meant to be adjudicators (i.e. arbitrators) 'but rather an agency dedicated to the facilitation of an agreement between the parties' (IFP and ANC, 1994: 1). Facilitation entails less pro-active involvement in the process, and is primarily aimed at establishing a neutral officiating agency which is respon- sible for directing the negotiating process. Mediators, on the other hand, normally have access to all the caucuses of the parties involved and try to convince them of the merits of an opposing view or of accepting a com- promise formulated by the mediator. The psychological impact of the relative bargaining powers of the parties normally has less of an effect on mediators than on the parties, and hence the IFP's reluctance to engage in negotiations, even if they were to be facilitated.

The second major issue is the Zulu king and kingdom. The issue is linked by the IFP to the first one in the following way:

> The issues relating to the Monarchy and the restoration and the securing of the Kingdom of KwaZulu are of particular importance to reconcile our differences about the national constitutional framework necessary to enable the Province of KwaZulu-Natal to adopt a constitution restoring and securing the Kingdom of KwaZulu. (Buthelezi, 1994b: 1)

The background to the issue is the refusal to allow the Zulu monarch to attend the plenaries of Codesa I and II in 1991 and 1992 and Buthelezi's belief that the monarch was an important instrument to bolster and consolidate the IFP constituency. With the impending demise of the KwaZulu homeland during the transition period, the pretence of Zulu autonomy or self-rule would be removed. Hence, its continuation was vested in the restoration of the Zulu monarchy and kingdom in terms of the 1834 boundaries, as an autonomous and sovereign kingdom. Between January and April 1994 serious negotiations were conducted between delegations of the king and NP government. It culminated in a deadlock at the Skukuza summit (IFP, 1995b: 4).

It had been agreed on 19 April 1994 that both the monarchy and kingdom would be entrenched in the Constitutional Principles (which was done subsequently) and be effected in the provincial constitution of KwaZulu-Natal. If any mediation regarding this issue needs to take place, it should involve the provincial legislature of KwaZulu-Natal in which the IFP is in the majority. Thus, mediation would imply that it is in dispute with itself. However, the monarchy will be indirectly affected by an extension of the powers of the provinces, which has already been discussed as a matter to be negotiated. Insofar as provincial powers are not involved, mediation at the national level regarding the Zulu monarchy seems to be inappropriate.

5.6 The Binding Nature of the Agreement

Section 4 of the Agreement for Reconciliation and Peace morally obliges the ANC and NP to participate in international mediation. However, in view of the inappropriate nature of mediation under present circumstances for successfully addressing the issues raised by the IFP, plus the vagueness of 'any outstanding issues', the Agreement was a serious error of judgement. For example, the status of the Consolidated Terms of Reference is nowhere clarified. Presumably, the Agreement was motivated by an overriding concern that the IFP should join the election process in 1994. However, if the conventional interpretation of law is applied, it could possibly be argued that due to its vagueness, that part of the Agreement cannot be enforced. But it does not reduce the moral obligation of the ANC and NP to honour their commitment or come to a mutual agreement with the IFP about an alternative.

In addition to the first problem, the fact that the ANC and IFP have divergent interpretations of the purpose of mediation (dispute resolution versus negotiations), and that it is not defined in the Agreement, also hinders its implementation.

Finally, it is clear that the Agreement refers only to outstanding matters regarding the interim constitution and Zulu monarchy. However, it is clear that the IFP's intention is to extend coverage of mediation as wide as possible with the view that the outcome needs to be incorporated in the final constitution. Accordingly, the dispute regarding interpretation of the Agreement is a classic case for mediation: mediation-about-mediation.

5.7 The Consolidated Terms of Reference

Though the ANC and NP do not reject the principle of international mediation, their main objection is that it is unclear what the disputed issues are. The IFP's response has been that it is bound by the Consolidated Terms of Reference, which are synonymous with 'any outstanding issues'. The problem is that the Agreement for Reconciliation and Peace does not refer to them explicitly and therefore it remains a matter open for interpretation.

The terms of reference referred to five topics. First is the constitutional status of the provinces, including their powers, their fiscal and financial autonomy and their power to determine their own provincial constitutions. The second topic relates to the constitution-making process: the Constitutional Court's role of review and certifying the Constitution's compliance with the Constitutional Principles, plus the procedure for constitutional amendments. The third topic is more practical in nature: the process of rationalization and empowerment of the new provincial administrations. The final two topics referred to citizenship and the qualifications of voters, and the Zulu monarchy and kingdom (IFP and ANC, 1994: 1–2).

There is one pertinent question regarding the Consolidated Terms of Reference which has not yet been answered or even asked: does the fact that between the conclusion of the Consolidated Terms of Reference and the election Professor Okumu mediated an agreement, which resulted in constitutional amendments, alter the binding and relevant nature of the Consolidated Terms of Reference? For example, the position of the Zulu monarch, except for possible broadening of his powers as a result of the extension of provincial powers, has been finalized. The extension of powers could be dealt with under the provincial powers. Except for the third topic, which is suitable for mediation, all the topics related to constitutional negotiations and hence are not really applicable for mediation. Accordingly, deciding on new terms of reference about issues in dispute, is the only viable alternative.

6. The Role of Violence

Since approximately 1983 KwaZulu-Natal has been the focal point of political violence, first between the IFP and United Democratic Front (UDF) and since 1990 between the IFP and the ANC. It has also spilled over to the East Rand. Immediately before the 1994 general elections violence reached a climax, but in the first eight months thereafter has declined sharply. A recurrent increase emerged in the beginning of 1995. The tendency of 1994 was apparently being repeated in 1995.

Several factors could have influenced it, among others the preparations for the local government elections on 1 November 1995, which revived the battles of 1994 for territory and support. The election period overlapped the Constitutional Assembly's timetable for finalizing the draft text of the final constitution in the middle of 1995. Seen together with the IFP's ostensible inability to enforce the Agreement for Peace and Reconciliation that had to be implemented before the draft text was finalized, an intensification of political tension was unavoidable.

Added to those issues are the IFP's insistence that the investigation into the massacre at the ANC's Shell House headquarters in 1994 must be completed, and President Mandela's role in the matter established; and the public 'humiliation' of Mangosuthu Buthelezi by the ANC. Finally, the national government's attempt to alienate the amakhosi (traditional leaders) from the IFP in the sense that the ANC wishes to implement legislation with the effect that the provincial Houses of Traditional Leaders will receive their remuneration from national government, and not from the provincial governments, is another aggravating factor.

Samuel P. Huntington (1968: 41, 45) formulated a hypothesis that it is not the absence of modernity but the efforts to achieve it, that produce political disorder and violence. According to him, the degree of instability is related to the rate of modernization. Democratization and institutionalization (in other words, constitution-making in the South African context) are forms of development. Hence, the implication of Huntington's view is that the political violence in South Africa could be a symptom of the transitional process, which is implicitly a positive indicator of development.

Such a view is primarily based on Seymour Martin Lipset's crises of legitimacy of the status quo in periods of radical change, but does not consider violence as a possible strategic means in a negotiating process. Though it is not argued that the IFP uses a masterplan which involves political violence, the party is the common denominator in most incidences of violence and therefore is associated with it. What contribution can it make in its negotiating stance? Threat of violence is known as an effective deterrent against political marginalization. The IFP's capacity for the use of violence is generally known and therefore threats in the form of brinkmanship in order to secure concessions in the negotiating process would constitute an alternative to electoral power.

Accordingly, it is predictable that after the local government elections the level of violence could decrease substantially, similar to the tendency after April 1994, and after the May 1996 deadline for the final constitution most of the present determining factors of the violence would be removed. The question remains whether brinkmanship will again result in a compromise before the situation becomes untenable.

7. Evaluation

The international community has praised the transitional process in South Africa as one of the major successes in the late twentieth century. However, South Africans are more reserved in their opinion.

The final stage of the negotiating process is perceived to be far less a truly negotiating process than the one in the Negotiating Council. It is far more formalized in committees while public involvement and debate through the media and other means have decreased since the April 1994 elections. In that regard the ANC's and PAC's objective, for the real negotiations to take place in the CA, has not materialized, and the interim constitution developed a semi-permanent symbolism. One example is the current national flag, which was initially presented as an interim arrangement, but which has assumed a permanent status.

An important aspect of the argument in this paper is that constitution-making is a crucial component of state-building in South Africa. However, it would be misleading to analyse state-building only in terms of constitution-making, because an equally important component of it is the Reconstruction and Development Programme. State-building in South Africa is about reversing apartheid, which permeated all aspects of the social fabric. Though the RDP is presented as a policy programme, its significance as a philosophy for development should be appreciated in terms of political development, including the formation of a new state.

As a developing country it is unlikely that the new constitution will remain unchanged for very long and, therefore, a conclusion that the transition has been finalized with the adoption of the final constitution would be incorrect. The more the ideological impact of the political parties on the negotiating process is replaced by pragmatic considerations, the more an equilibrium should be reached regarding constitutional stability. However, it should not be interpreted as necessarily reflective of a lack of legitimacy, except for the IFP's view, but rather symptomatic of an untidy transition conducted in a relatively short period with many aspects still unfinished.

NOTE

This chapter was written in July 1995 – about 11 months before the adoption of the constitution on 9 May 1996 – and therefore reflects the status of constitutional negotiations at the time. Eventually international mediation did not materialize, the IFP boycotted the CA for the entire period, while the last few weeks of the negotiations recalled many of the patterns developed at the World Trade Centre – especially the bilateral meetings between the ANC and NP about three outstanding clauses in the bill of rights (protection of private property, employers' right to lock out workers and the right to single-medium education). The day after the adoption of the constitution, the NP decided to withdraw from the GNU. Hence, in several respects the new constitutional dispensation has started sooner than expected.

REFERENCES

Agreement (1994) Memorandum of Agreement for Reconciliation and Peace between the Inkatha Freedom Party/KwaZulu Government and the African National Congress and the South African Government/National Party, 19 April, mimeo.
ANC (1995) Building a United Nation: Policy Proposals for the Final Constitution, 31 March–1 April, Johannesburg, mimeo.
Anstey, Mark (1991) Negotiating Conflict: Insights and Skills for Negotiators and Peacemakers. Kenwyn: Juta.
Anstey, Mark (1993) Practical Peace-making: a Mediator's Handbook. Kenwyn: Juta.
Boskey, James B. (1994) 'The Proper Role of the Mediator: Rational Assessment, Not Pressure', Negotiation Journal 10(4) (October): 367–72.
Buthelezi, Mangosuthu (1994a) Statement by the President of the Inkatha Freedom Party Mangosuthu Buthelezi, Chief Minister of KwaZulu and President of Inkatha Freedom Party, 19 April, mimeo.
Buthelezi, Mangosuthu (1994b) Letter of Mangosuthu Buthelezi to Cyril Ramaphosa, 9 December, mimeo.
Constitutional Committee (1995) Minutes of the thirteenth meeting of the Constitutional Committee, 27 February, mimeo.
Constitutional Talk: Official Newsletter of the Constitutional Assembly (1995) no. 1, 13–26 January.
Huntington, Samuel P. (1968) Political Order in Changing Societies. New Haven, CT and London: Yale University Press.
IFP (1995a) Submission to the Constitutional Committee on International Mediation, 23 January, mimeo.
IFP (1995b) The Status of International Mediation in Terms of the Agreement for Peace and

Reconciliation (submitted to the 3M Committee), mimeo.

IFP (1995c) International Mediation: an Essential Chronology, 31 March, mimeo.

IFP and ANC (1994) Consolidated Terms of Reference for International Mediation Agreed Upon by the IFP and the ANC, 10 April, mimeo.

Mbeki, Thabo (1995) Letter of Thabo Mbeki to Mangosuthu Buthelezi, 30 March, mimeo.

Meyer, Roelf (1995) 'Lessons from the Government of National Unity for a Future South Africa', unpublished speech delivered at the 'A New Executive for South Africa?' conference, University of Pretoria.

Moosa, M. Valli (1995) 'Requirements for an Executive in the Deeply Fragmented South African Society', unpublished speech delivered at the 'A New Executive for South Africa?' conference, University of Pretoria.

Nyang'oro, Julius E. (1993) 'Reform Politics and the Democratisation Process in Africa', mimeo, AAPS 20th Congress, Dar-es-Salaam.

Theme Committee 1 (1995) Amended Report from Theme Committee 1, 15 February, mimeo.

Van Wyk, David, Marinus Wiechers and Romaine Hill (eds) (1991) *Namibia: Constitutional and International Law Issues*. Pretoria: VerLoren van Themaat Centre for Public Law Studies, University of South Africa.

4. THE PRESIDENT AND THE EXECUTIVE

Robert Schrire

The history of a state and its people rarely has a dramatic beginning or an end. Despite the continuities of the past however, South Africa has a unique opportunity to reinvent itself and the outcome of the current negotiations for a new constitutional and political framework is clearly a watershed which will introduce a new set of dynamics that will shape future epochs.

Despite this opportunity, the constitution-making is not taking place in a vacuum but is being shaped by the legacy of the past which weighs heavily upon future opportunities and prospects. The minds of South Africans have been shaped, often in decisive ways, by the various interpretations of the recent past. The very real change which an African National Congress (ANC)-dominated government represents cannot by itself sweep away the continuities of the past, including white domination of the public service and the race-based inequities in the distribution of wealth, income and human resources and the dynamics of ethnicity and communal conflicts (Schrire, 1992: 1).

The Legacy

The history of South Africa's polity is dominated by the use of political power to attain and maintain socio-economic ends. A white minority inherited political power in 1910 and during the next eight decades used this

I would like to express my appreciation to my colleagues Hermann Giliomee and David Welsh for their valuable comments and criticisms.

power to entrench itself politically and to advance its economic, cultural and social interests. In few states of the world has the idea of the political kingdom had as much significance as in South Africa.

For whites then, political power held the key to all other public values. Over time, the white electorate manifested an ever greater willingness to grant its political representatives a 'blank cheque' to secure its interests. Fewer and fewer questions were asked about the often brutal means which were used and as long as political leaders promised to protect 'white interests' few questions were raised about ultimate ends. The political system developed a remarkably high degree of stability: between 1948 and 1990 not a single change of government took place and of the five men who had occupied the positions of prime minister/president, one died in office of natural causes, one was assassinated, and three eventually retired as a result of age or ill-health.

For black South Africans the lessons of political power were equally clear, if somewhat different. Political power was the mechanism of their subjugation and exploitation. If white control was the medium of their enslavement, black control over the political kingdom was the means for their liberation. The struggle for dominance of the political system, and especially its powerful executive, had begun.

Most observers interpreted this power struggle as zero-sum: either the whites would dominate or the blacks would take control. Increasingly, the white political elite, strongly supported by its electorate, sought to neutralize the black challenge by creating a powerful and increasingly authoritarian executive state. The Westminster legacy made this process technically easy: parliamentary sovereignty and the fusion of executive/legislative authority, a first-past-the-post electoral system and weak provincial powers made the centralization of power in the executive possible.

If this legacy of Westminster made the accumulation of unrestricted executive power feasible, the dynamics of South African politics made this trend all but inevitable. The successful mobilization of Afrikaner ethnicity led in time to a *de facto* one-party state in which electoral competition became increasingly marginalized. Indeed non-Afrikaner whites responded to growing pressures for fundamental change from black South Africans and the international community by increasingly supporting the government and ruling party. Lengthy incumbency of strong leaders such as Verwoerd, Vorster and Botha in the context of perceived threats to the status quo contributed to the dominance of the executive over the legislature, and National Party (NP) leaders over their caucus.

However, this executive power could not be used to ensure the permanent paramountcy of white interests. The strategy of crushing domestic opposition with an iron fist and threatening the smaller states in the region if they failed to cooperate with South Africa was at least partly successful.

The reform component of the overall strategy was less successful in creating legitimacy for the socio-political system. The tricameral parliamentary arrangement had only limited success in co-opting Coloureds and Asians and increased the militancy of blacks and anti-system Coloureds and Asians. Similarly, the important reforms in policy towards trade union rights, economic liberalization and educational reforms failed to bring about either accelerated economic growth or industrial peace.

The strategy of top-down authoritarian reform, adopted by the Botha regime between 1978 and 1989, thus failed, in large part because of a combination of black resistance, world pressures and the consequent economic weaknesses of the state and the economy. However, while it was widely anticipated that the struggle for control over the state would only be resolved after a protracted and costly conflict, the rise of a reformist leadership in the National Party stunned the country and the world by reaching a negotiated settlement with its most important challenger, the ANC. Few have noted the irony that it was only possible for the NP to abdicate from power through a policy of stealth because of the status and dominant influence of the executive with its enormous powers and lack of public accountability!

Indeed the only power bloc capable of derailing F. W. de Klerk's reform strategy was his own party caucus. However, such was the hold that successive NP leaders exercised over their own party that providing the cabinet remained united, almost any policy changes could be sold to the party at large. The reform policy became irresistible once a whites-only referendum had been won decisively, in large part because of the effective use F. W. de Klerk and his colleagues made of their executive powers including control over the public media and superior organizational and financial resources.

Executive Power and Political Interests

Political parties and elites advocate rules and systems which favour their perceived interests. As long as whites were politically dominant, they supported the centralization of power in the executive because they sought to place maximum power in the hands of their leaders to contain the black demand for political rights. Thus the NP, as the repository of white interests, followed a policy of centralization of power from its early days in power in the late 1940s to the beginning of its abdication from supreme power in 1989 (Boulle, 1994: 17–23).

The dynamics which flowed from this context favoured the uninterrupted growth of executive power. The executive became increasingly powerful, and autonomous, relative to both Parliament and its own parliamentary caucus. Executive power was used ruthlessly to undermine independent sources of political power such as the judiciary and provincial authorities. A complex web of legislation was introduced to limit the power of groups in society such as the media, business and trade unions from challenging executive authority. Over time increased controls were placed over almost all aspects of black life including access to resources, political rights and freedom of choice and association. Although the South African executive more closely resembled the British system in constitutional structure, during the 1980s it came to resemble more closely the French model in terms of the exercise of power and political behaviour under the presidency of P. W. Botha. Parliament became increasingly subordinate to the cabinet and within the executive itself, power and authority became increasingly exercised by the president and his associates. Both Parliament and the formal cabinet suffered a serious decline in power and influence.

This was the political legacy inherited by F. W. de Klerk in 1989. However, unlike his predecessor, he recognized both the urgent need to make fundamental changes to the constitutional order and the advantages of a more collegial method of governing. The 'imperial presidency' began to be dismantled and the cabinet and political leaders began to play a more influential role in decision-making within the NP. As the process of reform gathered momentum, political groupings outside of the constitutional framework began to play an increasingly important role in governing, and new transitional structures were developed to co-govern the country and ensure that in the forthcoming elections incumbency could not be used to influence the outcome.

Once the NP had begun to come to terms with the full implications of democratic reform, from about 1990, its constitutional position changed dramatically. Faced with the looming realities that it would be a minority force in a nonracial democracy, it discovered somewhat belatedly the virtues of decentralization and the constitutional state.

Its thinkers and leaders began increasingly to advocate 'power-sharing' defined as a system which ensured that all major political factions with substantial support would form part of both the legislature and the executive. The NP somewhat optimistically proposed that the national cabinet should be based upon an enforced or statutory coalition between the largest parties represented in the legislature, even if one party had a solid majority of legislative supporters there. This would thus entail an overrepresentation of minority parties and an underrepresentation of a possible majority group.

In addition, executive power would be limited. The then existing powerful presidency would be replaced by a more constrained and diffused executive structure. It would operate on the principle of consensus within the governing elite. One institutional possibility that embodied this principle was the Swiss model, where the executive by convention is collegial, with a rotating presidency. Swiss political institutions that operate on the principle of 'amicable agreement' rather than majority rule have been an important element in fostering the stability of a democratic polity in spite of potentially disruptive linguistic and religious cleavages. The system was much admired by F. W. de Klerk and his advisers. Another possibility would have been to elect the president from the lower house and a premier from the upper house with the condition that both offices could not be filled by candidates from the same political party.

Two additional controls over central executive power were proposed by the NP: first, was the insistence on a rigid constitution containing such checks and balances as a bill of rights covering key interests such as property rights, cultural interests and civil liberties enforceable by the supreme court, based possibly upon the German Constitutional Court model. Judicial review and the principle of constitutional sovereignty would thus be a central characteristic of the legislative process.

Second, the system proposed by the NP during the negotiations in the early 1990s would have been founded squarely upon federal principles. Power would be devolved to regional and local government authorities and this would be enshrined in the constitution. The boundaries of these geographical units, their powers and their ability to raise their own financial resources and extract resources would be entrenched.

Thus the thrust of the NP proposals during the pre-election negotiations was towards more limited government. It is no coincidence that the original creators of the executive state were now the strongest advocates of its dissolution; or that the party which had achieved power on the basis of ethnic exclusivity was now the strongest advocate of power-sharing and multiracial coalition government. Power was to be separated, shared and controlled.

The ANC, by contrast, initially favoured a more highly centralized system with a powerful executive subject only to modest constitutional limitations (ANC, 1992).

Black South Africans, for so long excluded from the political kingdom, increasingly sought from 1960 to participate in the polity on the same basis as whites, and demanded full equality within the then existing state structures. Indeed, ANC leader Nelson Mandela as recently as 1990 seemed to equate 'normal' democracy with majoritarian Westminster-style government. It was perfectly reasonable for blacks, as the victims of the South African state, to demand their turn as the new beneficiaries of political power. Thus after 1960, when black politics was largely prevented from operating legally in South Africa, political groupings such as the African National Congress, then in exile, and later the United Democratic Front, did not devote much attention to constitutional issues but demanded full participation in a unitary Westminster-type polity.

In addition, such a system would have served their interests as they had every reason to be confident that they would enjoy a massive parliamentary majority after a one-person-one-vote election. The interests of the ANC thus clearly lay in a system of government which favoured majority rather than minority interests, and the exercise of power rather than its limits.

Between 1990 and 1992 ANC thinking tended to favour a traditional western-style majoritarian democratic model. It supported a South Africa which included the homelands and was centralized in structure, though with 'strong and effective' local and regional government. Although these local authorities would have important functions to perform, they would remain subordinate to the central government and would exercise only delegated powers. The state, in other words, would be unitary, though with some weak federal characteristics such as an upper house composed of provincial representatives.

The ANC proposed that Parliament be elected on the basis of universal adult franchise and proportional representation. A National Assembly would serve as the lower house and would be elected on a straightforward proportional representation basis. The ANC maintained that a system of proportional representation would meet the legitimate interests of ethnic and other minorities. It would be charged with the task of drawing up legislation. The upper house, to be called the Senate, would be elected on a basis which gave smaller regions overrepresentation. It would be of lesser importance than the National Assembly, but would have the power to delay the adoption of legislation and would also act as guardian of the constitution. The implicit model of these legislative proposals appeared to be a hybrid of the British Westminster system and the US Senate, with the innovation of proportional representation.

The proposals were, perhaps deliberately, somewhat vague about the nature of a future executive authority. The ANC initially supported the presidential form of government with a prime minister and cabinet, perhaps inspired by the French model. After considerable internal deliberations, the ANC opted to have the president elected by Parliament. It also advocated a justiciable bill of rights, an independent judiciary and an ombudsman.

The Inkatha Freedom Party (IFP) was the strongest and most consistent advocate of a federal system in which the provinces, not the central government, would be the key players in policy-making and implementation. Unlike the other parties, it advocated that residual powers should lie with the provinces and that the role of the central government, other than in the areas of defence and foreign policy, should be relatively limited. In general, a dispute over policy and authority should be resolved in favour of provincial authorities in the absence of constitutional strictures to the contrary. Indeed, in many ways the IFP proposals contained confederal rather than federal elements – a trend which has accelerated since the 1994 elections.

Negotiations and Compromises, 1990–94

The details of the lengthy negotiations which produced broad support for the interim constitution have been analysed elsewhere (Louw, 1996; van Tonder, 1996). Suffice it to note here that the final agreements represented considerable compromises from both the ANC and the NP, the two major players.

The ANC, although it rejected in principle the concept of statutory power-sharing or special rights for political minorities, agreed to the so-called 'sunset' clauses in terms of which the ANC agreed to a coalition government irrespective of the size of the majority of the winning party. It also agreed to somewhat greater, if unspecified, powers for the regional governments than it had originally advocated. Other important concessions included the protection of property rights and a complex set of compromises which related to issues of past injustices. One of the most important changes in ANC policy was its acceptance of proportional representation as an appropriate electoral system for a divided South Africa.

Most of the key concessions however, were made by the NP. Under the impact of the negotiations and the dynamic forces thereby created which included unprecedented levels of mass action and political violence and massacres, the NP retreated from its original positions. It accepted the sunset clauses, thereby also accepting that from 1999 the final constitution may be based upon a majoritarian executive. Federalism was also a casualty of the give-and-take of the negotiations and the interim constitution contains only a vague echo of the NP's original commitment to a federal system. The final major concession was the NP's acceptance of a two-thirds majority for the passage of the final constitution by the National Assembly after initially holding out for a 75 percent ratification majority. If the National Assembly is unable to agree on a constitution with a two-thirds majority, a referendum must be held to break the deadlock and only a 60 percent majority vote is then required for final passage of the new constitution.

The Interim Constitution

Between 1994 and 1999, when the next general elections are scheduled to be held, South Africa will be governed under the interim constitution negotiated by the ANC and the NP with the participation, and support, of most of the smaller parties, with the notable exception of the IFP.

From the perspective of the executive, the key elements of the interim constitution may be summarized as follows:

(1) The Constitution is the supreme law of the Republic and binds all legislative, executive and judicial organs of government.

(2) Citizens will enjoy such freedoms as association, speech and expression and the right to privacy.

(3) Parliament consists of a National Assembly and Senate and legislative authority is vested in this body.

(4) Parliament has the full power to control, regulate and dispose of its internal affairs as well as to pass legislation.

(5) The National Assembly and Senate sitting jointly will constitute the Constitutional Assembly which has the task of drafting and adopting a new (final) constitution.

(6) The President shall be the Head of State.

(7) The President is elected by the National Assembly at its first sitting from amongst its members. The President, upon election, ceases to be a member of the National Assembly and is elected for a five year term.

(8) The President has the following powers:
   (a) to assent to, sign and promulgate Bills duly passed by Parliament;
   (b) in the event of a procedural shortcoming in the legislative process, to refer a Bill passed by Parliament back for further consideration by Parliament;
   (c) to convene meetings of the Cabinet;
   (d) to refer disputes of a constitutional nature between parties represented in Parliament or between organs of state at any level of government to the Constitutional Court;
   (f) to appoint, accredit, receive and recognize ambassadors;
   (g) to appoint commissions of enquiry;
   (h) to make such appointments as may be necessary under powers conferred upon him or her by this Constitution or any other law;
   (i) to negotiate and sign international agreements;
   (j) to proclaim referenda and plebiscites;
   (k) to pardon or reprieve offenders;
   (l) in the development and execution of the policies of the national government;
   (m) in all matters relating to the management of the Cabinet business;
   (n) in the assignment and allocation of functions to an Executive Deputy President.

(9) The President shall exercise and perform all powers and functions assigned to him or her by this Constitution or any other law, except those specified in subsections and where otherwise expressly or by implication provided in this Constitution, in consultation with the Cabinet: Provided that the Cabinet may delegate its consultation function with reference to any particular power or function of the President, to any Minister or Ministers.
   (a) The President shall be the Commander-in-Chief of the National Defence Force.
   (b) The President may:
      (i) with the approval of Parliament, declare a state of national defence;
      (ii) employ the National Defence Force.

(10) Every party holding at least 80 seats in the National Assembly shall be entitled to designate an Executive Deputy President from among the members of the Na-

tional Assembly.

Should no party or only one party hold 80 or more seats in the National Assembly, the party holding the largest number of seats and the party holding the second largest number of seats shall each be entitled to designate one Executive Deputy President.

(11) The Deputy Presidents will perform the functions requested of them by the President.

(12) The President or an Executive Deputy President shall cease to hold office on a resolution adopted at a joint sitting of the National Assembly and the Senate by a majority of at least two-thirds of the total number of members of the Houses and impeaching the President or such Executive Deputy President on the ground of a serious violation of this Constitution or the other laws of the Republic, or of misconduct or inability rendering him or her unfit to exercise and perform his or her powers and functions.

(13) The Cabinet shall consist of the President, the Executive Deputy Presidents and not more than 27 Ministers appointed by the President in accordance with this section.

A party holding at least 20 seats in the National Assembly and which has decided to participate in the government of national unity, shall be entitled to be allocated one or more of the Cabinet portfolios in proportion to the number of seats held by it in the National Assembly relative to the number of seats held by the other participating parties.

(14) Cabinet portfolios shall be allocated to the respective participating parties in accordance with the following formula:

A quota of seats per portfolio shall be determined by dividing the total number of seats in the National Assembly held jointly by the participating parties by the number of portfolios plus one.

(15) The President shall after consultation with the Executive Deputy Presidents and the leaders of the participating parties:

(a) determine the specific portfolios to be allocated to the respective participating parties in accordance with the number of portfolios allotted to them;

(b) terminate any appointment:

(i) if he or she is requested to do so by the leader of the party of which the Minister in question is a member; or

(ii) if it becomes necessary for the purposes of this Constitution or in the interest of good government.

This shall be implemented in the spirit underlying the concept of a government of national unity, and the President and the other functionaries concerned shall in the implementation of that subsection endeavour to achieve consensus at all times: Provided that if consensus cannot be achieved on:

(a) the exercise of a power the President's decision shall prevail;

(b) in the case of a person who is not a member of the President's party, the decision of the leader of the party of which such person is a member shall prevail; and

(c) in the case of a person who is a member of the President's party, the President's decision shall prevail.

(16) (1) Meetings of the Cabinet shall be presided over by the President, or, if the President so instructs, by an Executive Deputy President: provided that the Executive Deputy Presidents shall preside over meetings of the Cabinet in turn unless the exigencies of government and the spirit underlying the concept of a government of national unity otherwise dictate.

(2) The Cabinet shall function in a manner which gives consideration to the consensus-seeking spirit underlying the concept of a government of national unity as well as the need for effective government.

(3) Where an Executive Deputy President presides over a meeting of the Cabinet otherwise than in the capacity of Acting President, a decision in the Cabinet or any matter shall be submitted to the President before its implementation and shall upon its ratification by the President be deemed to be a decision taken in consultation with the Cabinet.

(17) A Minister shall be accountable individually both to the President and to Parliament for the administration of the portfolio entrusted to him or her, and all members of the Cabinet shall correspondingly be accountable collectively for the performance of the functions of the national government and for its policies.

(18) The Constitutional Court shall have jurisdiction in the Republic as the court of final instance over all matters relating to the interpretation, protection and enforcement of the provisions of this Constitution, including:

(a) any alleged violation or threatened violation of any fundamental right;

(b) any dispute over the constitutionality of any executive or administrative act;

(c) any inquiry into the constitutionality of any law, including an Act of Parliament, irrespective of whether such law was passed or made before or after the commencement of this Constitution;

(d) any dispute over the constitutionality of any Bill before Parliament or a provincial legislature;

(e) any dispute of a constitutional nature between organs of state at any level of government;

(f) the determination of questions whether any matter falls within its jurisdiction; and

(g) the determination of any other matters as may be entrusted to it by this Constitution or any other law.

(19) The nine provinces of the country will have competence with Parliament to make laws for the province in the following areas:

agriculture, casinos, racing, gambling and wagering, cultural affairs, education at all levels, excluding university and technikon education, environment, health services, housing, language policy, local government, nature conservation, excluding national parks, national botanical gardens and marine resources, police, subject to certain limitations, provincial public media, public transport, regional planning and development, road traffic regulation, roads, tourism, trade and industrial promotion, traditional authorities, urban and rural development and welfare services.

(20) A province shall be entitled to an equitable share of revenue collected nationally to enable it to provide services and to exercise and perform its powers and functions (*Government Gazette*, vol. 343, chapter 6, sections 75–95).

These constitutional clauses provide the framework within which politics takes place. Of equal importance, however, is the dynamics of personalities, interests and conflicts. The exercise of power usually reflects the interplay between the formal rules of the game and the informal dynamics which can never be statutorily constrained.

Three factors have dominated these dynamics since the elections of April 1994. The larger-than-life personality of 77-year-old President Nelson Mandela has cast a huge shadow over all other political players. His personal commitment to reconciliation and 'nation-building' has dominated the political debate and has, if only temporarily, glossed over many potential cleavages. Second, the rather unusual agreement to form a statutorily based government of national unity for a five-year period irrespective of the electoral performances of the contending parties has modified the normally combative strategies which opposition parties adopt to further their electoral interests and lowered the stakes of the founding elections.

A third factor which has shaped political behaviour has been the powerful influences stemming from the global community. In part because of the economic weakness of the South African economy as a result of decades of misrule, most political decision-makers recognize the importance of attracting foreign investment and of retaining domestic business confidence. They have thus hesitated to take bold interventionist initiatives which would cause immediate and widespread panic in the national and international business community. Although the ANC favours fundamental economic changes, it recognizes that stock prices would plummet and the overall level of business confidence would hit rock bottom if the government acted in a manner which hurt business interests. As described by Grover (1989:3):

> ... policies strongly opposed by business if adopted by government would ensure that businesses, fearing market instability and suspicious of inflationary pressures, would dramatically restrict investment and employment, giving rise to higher unemployment and economic stagnation. In short, a presidential initiative of this type would trigger a reaction known as 'capital strike'. Shattered business confidence would result in a swift rebuke to the president with results manifesting themselves in the form of punishment inflicted on the economy, and hence, on peoples' economic well-being.

This scenario was used to explain the consequences for the United States should a president seek to take bold but unpopular economic decision such as major tax increases. The 'automatic punishing recoil' of the market would surely be many times greater in the South African context!

It is thus difficult to discern which trends, if any, will continue in the post-Mandela era when a new generation of political elites begins to operate under a 'permanent' constitution in which the ANC almost inevitably will control the executive. Where will power be located? What role if any will the legislature play in the formulation of policy and the supervision of policy implementation? What kinds of relationships will develop between the ruling party and its extra-parliamentary members?

It is highly unlikely that a future executive will continue to function in the same way as the present transitionary executive after the next elections are held in 1999. One characteristic of the present system has been the relative weakness of the executive relative to other parliamentary players and extra-parliamentary interests. In addition the ANC, although clearly the dominant influence in the executive, has not been as influential as might have been expected given its massive electoral mandate.

In part because of his age and lame-duck status as a one-term only president, Nelson Mandela has not sought to accumulate significant personal powers and has been content to act as a chairman of the board. Although he has been an important national symbol and has been largely active in dramatizing issues of personal concern, he has been prepared to allow the day-to-day running of government to be conducted by others. Thus no powerful office of the president has been created nor have his personal staff accumulated the kind of political influence prevalent during the Vorster and Botha administrations.

The government of national unity has also served to limit presidential and executive power. Despite the ANC's electoral landslide, important and powerful leaders such as the NP's F. W. de Klerk, who is also a deputy president, and the IFP's Mangosuthu Buthelezi are members of the cabinet. They enjoy an influence out of all proportion to their electoral support, in part because they represent powerful factions within society with the proven capacity to destabilize the state if estranged from the government, and partly because of the fear that uncontained political conflict would have very serious economic consequences. Mandela and his close associates believe that the breakdown in the government of national unity would cause a flight of capital from the economy and destroy the prospects for new foreign investments.

As a result of these and other factors, the first ANC-dominated executive has been characterized by caution rather than boldness, restraint rather than a willingness to use its latent power. As a result, the ANC caucus, and especially the chairmen of several of the important parliamentary committees such as justice, have asserted their independence and have refused to act as mere rubber stamps for executive decisions. Perhaps in reaction to the authoritarianism of the past, the ANC has elevated the concept of public consultation and transparency to a holy principle. As a consequence, a plethora of commissions and committees have been incorporated into the now cumbersome decision-making process.

Although South Africa continues to experience high levels of conflict and violence, especially in KwaZulu-Natal, the government of national unity has functioned with surprising amity. Even non-ANC leaders such as the IFP's Buthelezi, who have fiercely resisted central government initiatives when wearing their 'provincial' hats, have cooperated within the cabinet as reasonably loyal members of the team. As a result, many potentially decisive issues such as land reform, affirmative action and the truth and reconciliation commission have all received, with greater or lesser reservations, broad cabinet approval.

Although negotiations over the final constitution are continuing, it is already possible to discern the outlines of the ultimate agreements. The final constitution must be compatible with the 34 principles agreed to by the major parties prior to the 1994 elections. At the most general level, most of the major parties support the following principles:

- an indirectly elected president who combines the roles of both head of state and head of government;
- a separation of powers;
- a system of checks and balances;
- an executive which is responsible to the legislature;
- an independent judiciary including a constitutional court;
- a justiciable bill of rights.

Of course, several not insignificant differences remain. Perhaps of greatest significance is the NP's continued support for statutory power-sharing (coalition government), a principle rejected by the ANC and the other major participants.

Equally significant are differences over the powers of the president. The ANC, perhaps surprisingly, favours a two-term limit on the office of the president, whereas the NP does not favour any limits on incumbency. While all of the other major parties favour a presidency which combines the functions of head of state and government, the IFP favours a weak ceremonial presidency with a prime minister as head of government.

At the level of detail, important differences also remain. The broad principles outlined above, where considerable consensus exists, do not automatically translate into agreement on the 'details' which are frequently of decisive importance. For example, 'separation of powers' and 'checks and balances' can be interpreted in many different ways and the institutional mechanisms created to give effect to them could vary significantly. Thus the detailed constitutional provisions could create either a strong or a weak executive. The ANC fear is of an executive so limited in authority that it is unable to make the fundamental changes to the apartheid legacy of race-based socio-economic inequalities that it believes are necessary. The fear of smaller parties such as the IFP and the NP is of course the opposite: that the executive will have too much authority to bring about dramatic changes which have the potential to harm the interests of themselves and their constitutencies.

It should be noted that the main areas of conflict between the parties represented in the National Assembly do not revolve around issues of presidential prerogatives but are centred around the relationship between central and provincial governments. With the possible exception of the IFP, all the other parties participating in Parliament are prepared to participate in the centrist ANC-drafted proposals if they are accepted, although both the Democratic and National Parties advocate a more decentralized system with stronger federal features. Only the IFP appears resolutely opposed to a constitution which falls short of granting the provinces comprehensive federal powers and it is not clear how the IFP will react to a centralist system if it is accepted by the Constitutional Assembly.

Conclusions

It is increasingly recognized that the executive is the engine of the political system of the modern state. As one of the recent submissions to the Constitutional Assembly stated:

> ... the executive is by far the most powerful and prominent branch of government. With the vast bureaucracy at its disposal, the executive is the only branch that has the expertise, information and infrastructure effectively to cope with the demands made on modern governments. The executive is furthermore better equipped to act on short notice and to plan ahead. For these and other reasons, governmental initiative has long since shifted to the executive and, to a considerable degree, the function of the legislature has been reduced to little more than the legitimation of executive initiatives. (National Party submissions to Theme Committee 2, 28 March 1995)

The demands on executive authority, not only in South Africa but throughout the democratic world, are almost insuperable. In cabinet systems, such as South Africa's, the executive elite is expected simultaneously to retain parliamentary support, ensure that the broad public continues to support the government, devise public policies and supervise and evaluate their implementation.

No small team can adequately perform these functions. The challenge to South Africa's executive is compounded by such factors as:

- the increased global interdependence and the consequent decline in state power;
- the intractable socio-economic problems inherited from the past including rapid population growth, high levels of unemployment and unsustainable racially based inequalities in the distribution of income, wealth, and human skills;
- high levels of mass politicization, which reflect the legacy of the 'struggle', and consequent high mass expectations;
- powerful and effective interest groups such as organized business and labour with the capacity to damage society if their interests are affected;
- an asymmetry in power between an ANC-dominated political system and a largely hostile civil society power structure including business, agriculture, the media and the professions;
- an unknown power map in which the limits of executive power relative to

the judiciary and the regional political powers have not yet been tested.

In many ways the interim executive in South Africa represents a 'pause in history'. It has been characterized by a unique government of national unity and a collegial leadership style. It has, as yet, not reflected some of the near universal trends in the exercise of executive power such as the centralization of power and authority in the office of the president/prime minister, the institutionalization of executive power, the decline of Parliament and the creation of informal systems of influence based upon the patronage of the leader.

It seems almost inevitable that these trends will also develop in the South Africa of the future. Indeed, they existed in all the pre-Mandela cabinets and have roots deep within society. The 'personal' presidency of Nelson Mandela is unlikely to survive its incumbent and a majority of South Africa's political elite seems to have chosen the strong state rather than the model of emasculated government.

Indeed, if the thrusts of the ANC constitutional proposals are ultimately accepted, South Africa will continue to have a system based more upon Westminster than upon a separation of powers. Despite the importance of the Bill of Rights and Constitutional Court, the constitution will give the executive the foundation to accumulate considerable powers – the rejection of a genuine separation of executive–legislature power makes this all but inevitable. Allied to the increasingly centralist direction of ANC thinking, in part a reaction to the increasingly confederalist demands of Buthelezi and his ethnic constituency, the prospects for genuine federalism, not entirely extinguished in the interim constitution, appear increasingly bleak. Centralization of power in the hands of central government and within the executive itself appears to be the most likely outcome.

However, all executive systems reflect a mixture of invention and evolution. The exercise of power is never a linear extrapolation from the rules. Traditions develop which often change power relations in significant ways and this too may happen in South Africa. Peter Hennessy (1986: 2) has traced the evolution of the doctrine of collective cabinet responsibility in Great Britain as follows:

> The King did nearly all business with the Ministers in the room called his closet. He normally saw them one by one. A Minister had no strict right to discuss anything in the closet but the business of his own department; but a senior Minister – especially if he were Leader of the House of Commons or had pretensions to consider himself as Prime Minister – could range more freely . . . The business of the closet does not appear, at first sight, to have afforded the Ministers much opportunity for collective action. But they knew how to counteract the tendency to separate and confine them. On any question of general political importance, they would agree beforehand what to say, and then go into the closet, one by one; and repeat the identical story.

Similar informal dynamics will develop in South Africa.

The direction in which constitutional decisions are moving seems likely to produce a set of rules which favour the accumulation of executive authority. However, as the above case illustrates, the interplay between these rules, political elites and powerful interests could produce a power distribution which is either significantly more or less centrist than constitutional intentions.

The future challenge then will be how to balance the need for authority with the danger to liberty which power always entails. South Africa had the good fortune to have Nelson Mandela as its first democratic leader. But no society can base its future on the assumption of wise and altruistic leadership. However, the greatest shadow hanging over the fragile South African democracy does not originate from constitutional decisions or the nature of the executive. The greatest threat lies in the probable decisions of the citizenry to vote in preponderant numbers for one party (the ANC) under present and foreseeable circumstances. And no constitutional engineering can guarantee a democracy in the face of such electoral behaviour.

REFERENCES

ANC (1992) 'ANC Policy Guidelines for a Democratic South Africa', proceedings of the National Conference, May.

ANC (1995) 'Building a United Nation: Policy Proposals for the Final Constitution', 31 March– 1 April Johannesburg, mimeo.

ANC, DP, IFP and NP (1995) Submission to Theme Committee 2, March.

Boulle, L. (1994) 'The Head of Government and the Constitution', in R. A. Schrire (ed.) Leadership in the Apartheid State. Cape Town: Oxford University Press.

Burke, J. P. (1992) The Institutional Presidency. Baltimore: Johns Hopkins University Press.

Cunliffe, M. (1987) The Presidency. Boston: Houghton Mifflin.

de Villiers, B. (ed.) (1994) Birth of a Constitution. Kenwyn: Juta.

Grover, W. F. (1989) The President as Prisoner. Albany: State University of New York Press.

Hennessy, P. (1986) The Cabinet. Oxford: Basil Blackwell.

Koenig, L. W. (1981) The Chief Executive. New York: Harcourt Brace Jovanovich.

Louw, A. (1996) 'South Africa's Constitutional Development', in M. Faure and J.-E. Lane (eds) South Africa: Designing New Political Institutions. London, Thousand Oaks, CA and New Delhi: Sage.

Schrire, R. A. (1992) Wealth or Poverty? Critical Choices for South Africa. Cape Town: Oxford University Press.

Schrire, R. A. (ed.) (1994) Leadership in the Apartheid State. Cape Town: Oxford University Press.

van Tonder, J. (1996) 'The Salient Features of the Interim Constitution', in M. Faure and J.-E. Lane (eds) South Africa: Designing New Political Institutions. London, Thousand Oaks, CA and New Delhi: Sage.

5. THE CONSTITUTIONAL COURT

Kierin O'Malley

Introduction

Chapter 7 of the interim constitution (Act 200 of 1993) deals with the judicial authority and the administration of justice and *inter alia* provides for the creation of a supposedly independent Constitutional Court which is mandated to ensure that the new South Africa shall be a constitutional state, i.e. a state in which the constitution shall be the supreme law of the republic. As the guardian of the new constitutional order in South Africa, the Constitutional Court is widely touted as the ultimate protector of the new democracy and of minority interests and fundamental rights.

In addition to the Constitutional Court, the interim constitution also provides for the establishment of a number of other commissions which are mandated as guardians of different aspects of the new constitutional dispensation. They include a Human Rights Commission, a Commission on Gender Equality and the office of the Public Protector or ombudsman.

The Constitutional Court provided for in the interim constitution is given extensive powers of judicial review. It will be a politically very influential body. This court is a new constitutional phenomenon in a country which has a Westministerian tradition of parliamentary sovereignty and it is important to have a closer look at this aspect of the new, interim constitutional dispensation.

Given the judicial activism that the Court has already exhibited in the first year of its existence, an activism best illustrated in the Court's controversial ruling that the death penalty is an unconstitutional form of punishment in the new South Africa in spite of the fact that the interim constitution is totally silent on the question, the Constitutional Court could well become an excessively politicized body. South African law, and specifically its constitutional law, and the courts generally will become increasingly politicized and the crucial distinction between law and politics weakened. In fact, in its proposals for the final constitution the African National Congress (ANC) envisages and advocates a Constitutional Court which will be a 'contentious and politically central mechanism' (ANC, 1995: 38).

The result could be that the doctrine of the separation of powers, which Constitutional Principle VI of Schedule 4 requires the final constitution to comply with, will be weakened. Appointed, unaccountable judges will effectively become legislators in crucial areas of public policy. In the words of the American Robert Bork, 'a judge has begun to rule where a legislator should' (1990: 1).

A final constitution needs to be adopted by 10 May 1996, although the interim constitution is unclear as to whether the final constitution will come into effect then or in 1999 when the next general election will be held in terms of a constitutional stipulation. Principle 4 of the Constitutional Principles, with which the final constitution must comply, and which the Constitutional Court will oversee, also stipulates that the final constitution 'shall be the supreme law of the land'. There is no principle which requires that the final constitution make provision for a Constitutional Court. All the political parties represented in Parliament, including the ANC, have however expressed support for the idea that a Constitutional Court be provided for in the final constitution. One party, the strongly federal Inkatha Freedom Party (IFP), in fact supports the creation of separate judiciaries, including separate constitutional courts in each of the provinces. There is though little support for this view and the IFP has itself withdrawn from the Constitutional Assembly which is currently drafting the final constitution because of the refusal of the ANC and the National Party (NP) to implement the pre-election agreement to conduct international mediation on outstanding constitutional issues.

Models of Constitutional Courts: Decentralized Versus Centralized

Two constitutional court models or varieties of judicial review can be distinguished: decentralized and centralized. The decentralized model grants the power of judicial review to a wide range, if not all, of the courts within a given legal system; while the centralized model limits the power of judicial review to a single court or judicial organ (Cappelletti, 1992: 262).

The (North) American judicial system is the classic example of the decentralized model. All the courts of the American legal system, both federal (including the Supreme Court) and state courts, are granted the power of constitutional or judicial review. There is thus not a distinct constitutional court, i.e. a court which has sole and exclusive jurisdiction on matters constitutional, although with the passage of time, the American Supreme Court has progressively become a *de facto* constitutional court.

The decentralized or American model of constitutional courts is found in a number of the former British colonies, including Canada, Australia and India. The decentralized model of constitutional courts/judicial review is generally associated with the so-called common-law countries, i.e. those in the Anglo-American constitutional tradition, and not with the civil-law countries with their constitutional roots in continental Europe and the Napoleonic code.

The centralized model of constitutional courts, where only one judicial entity enjoys jurisdiction over constitutional matters, is exemplified in the German constitution of 1949 (now amended but unchanged as regards its constitutional court provisions) and the Italian constitution of 1949. The centralized model of constitutional courts has its origins in Europe and is essentially a European institution. Apart from the aforementioned states, the centralized model is also found in Austria, Spain and Portugal, and was also the model in Yugoslavia and Czechoslovakia prior to their dissolution. It is nonetheless the case that, worldwide, separate constitutional courts are the exception rather than the rule. In its 1989 report on Group and Human Rights the South African (SA) Law Commission stated, for example, that of the 125 constitutions that it had looked at, only 24 provided for a separate constitutional court, i.e. a centralized constitutional court.

The South African interim constitution makes provision for the creation of a separate central or national Constitutional Court with extensive powers of judicial review. The initial proposal of the SA Law Commission that the Appellate Division be divided into two chambers and that one of the chambers serve as a Constitutional Court was jettisoned during the negotiations at Kempton Park. Section 98 of the interim constitution stipulates that this court shall function as a 'court of final instance over all matters relating to the interpretation, protection and enforcement of the provisions of this constitution'. This includes *inter alia* the power to inquire 'into the constitutionality of any law, including an Act of parliament irrespective of whether such law was passed or made before or after the commencement of this constitution' and to adjudicate 'any dispute over the constitutionality of any Bill before parliament or a provincial legislature' (see section 98 [2]). In terms of section 98 (3) the Constitutional Court is granted exclusive jurisdiction over an important set of issues.

The constitutional court model chosen in the interim constitution, while of the centralized variety, is not, for example, as centralized as the German model of judicial review. While the central Constitutional Court provided for in the interim constitution has exclusive jurisdiction over, for example, bills and acts of the central Parliament, section 101 does grant local and provincial divisions of the Supreme Court concurrent jurisdiction in respect of certain constitutional matters (see below). Their power of judicial review however is limited. Given the essentially centralist/unitary, non-federal nature of the interim constitution, the exclusive jurisdiction of the Constitutional Court on bills and acts of the central Parliament is of crucial significance. In addition, section 101(5) of the interim constitution stipulates that the Appellate Division 'shall have no jurisdiction to adjudicate any matter within the jurisdiction of the Constitutional Court'. The lower courts, i.e. magistrates' courts, have no powers of constitutional review at all, and can only refer matters concerning constitutional issues to divisions of the Supreme Court.

The adoption of an essentially centralized model of judicial review in terms of the interim constitution is not really surprising, although interesting given the fact that South Africa is essentially a common-law country and that countries that form part of the Anglo-American legal tradition have invariably opted for the decentralized model of judicial review. The South African interim constitution is thus a hybrid as far as this is concerned.

When at the end of the 1980s it became clearer that a new constitutional order was going to have to be established and debates surrounding a bill of rights and judicial review began, the dominant opinion in South Africa was clearly in favour of the decentralized model. The majority of those who submitted opinions on the matter to the SA Law Commission in the second half of the 1980s were in favour of the decentralized model, i.e. that the ordinary courts of the land should enjoy the power of judicial review (van der Westhuizen, 1991: 3). The Law Commission's 1989 Interim Report on Group and Human Rights had favoured the extant supreme courts as guardians of the constitutional order and had raised a number of objections to the creation of a separate Constitutional Court. These included considerations of the possible politicization of such a court, cost implications and the difficulties surrounding the appointment of a legitimate Constitutional Court given the diverse and divided nature of the country's population structure.

From the early 1990s it became increasingly apparent, however, that the idea of a separate Constitutional Court was enjoying growing support, both in academic and political circles. The ANC released a draft bill of rights in November 1990 which *inter alia* made specific provision for the establishment of a Constitutional Court (van Wyk, 1991: 106). Leading ANC thinkers, however, also repeatedly emphasized that the mechanisms for enforcing the provisions of the envisaged bill of rights be 'broadly based' and 'not restricted to a small class of judges defending the interests of a small part of the population' (Sachs, 1991: 35). A growing number of academic articles and research supportive of the idea of a separate Constitutional Court also appeared in the early 1990s (see, for example, Asmal, 1991; Kruger, 1991; Motala, 1991; Saayman, 1993; van der Westhuizen, 1991 and Wiechers, 1991).

It was thus not surprising that the SA Law Commission's 1991 Report on Constitutional Models indicated a shift in thinking towards the idea of a separate Constitutional Court. The Law Commission did not, however, advocate the creation of a totally separate Constitutional Court, but rather that the Appellate Division be divided into two chambers one of which would serve as a Constitutional Court (par 22.224). In terms of the report, any South African court, including magistrates' courts, would enjoy the power of judicial review. There would nonetheless be a final Constitutional 'Court' (specifically a chamber of the Appellate Division) of appeal. This proposal of the Law Commission was broadly based on what the Commission described as a 'mixed' model of judicial review used *inter alia* in Portugal.

The proposal from the SA Law Commission received a generally critical response from the organized legal profession, especially from the bar (see *The Consultus*, April 1992; Kruger, 1993) and given the ANC's clear preference for an essentially centralized model of judicial review and the organization's growing dominance during the 1993 Kempton Park negotiations, the largely centralist Constitutional Court provisions in Chapter 7 are scarcely surprising.

Powers and Functions of Constitutional Courts

The specific powers and functions of constitutional courts vary with the scope of judicial review in different countries, but their essential role is to (a) protect fundamental individual and/or group rights (usually embodied in a bill of rights) and (b) protect the constitutional foundations of a state.

In a number of countries – France and Portugal, for example – the constitutional courts exercise what is called preventative jurisdiction as far as human rights protection is concerned. Bills passed by their parliaments do not become law until tested against bill of rights provisions by these courts and found satisfactory. Constitutional courts also protect human rights by exercising judicial review over executive and other administrative actions.

Constitutional courts protect the constitutional foundations of states in various ways. These include defining and maintaining the separation of powers between executive, judicial and legislative branches of government and the division of powers between the various levels of government in a federation or decentralized unitary state. Constitutional courts also protect the constitutional integrity of the state (for example, in Germany) by banning political parties, resolving disputes between various federal organs and between the federation and the constituent states.

The powers allocated to the Constitutional Court in terms of the interim constitution are wide-ranging. They include dealing with all alleged or threatened violations of the so-called fundamental rights set out in Chapter 3. These 'rights' are extensive and their vague and loose formulation leave them open to varying interpretations. In terms of section 98(2) the Constitutional Court will also enjoy *inter alia* exclusive jurisdiction in disputes concerning the constitutionality of (a) executive and administrative conduct at all levels of government; (b) all laws, provincial and national, and including laws passed prior to the commencement date of the constitution; and (c) disputes 'between organs of state at any level of government'.

The powers of the Constitutional Court are further extended by provisions which stipulate that the Court has jurisdiction to decide whether any matter falls within its jurisdiction and that bills, not laws, of both the central and provincial legislatures fall within its potential jurisdiction. The interim constitution also empowers the national Parliament by an ordinary law to extend the jurisdiction of the Constitutional Court. In addition to this, the first Constitutional Court is mandated to decide whether the final constitution conforms with the constitutional principles set out in Schedule 4 of the interim constitution. Given the excessively vague formulation of the 34 Constitutional Principles listed in Schedule 6, the task of testing the draft final constitution against these principles is certainly going to be a taxing and contentious one. Whatever the Constitutional Court decides, it will be seen as having made a political decision.

Section 101 of the interim constitution deals with the Supreme Court and does grant provincial and local divisions of the Supreme Court jurisdiction in respect of certain constitutional matters. These include Chapter 3 infringements and disputes over the constitutionality of laws other than acts of Parliament and between second and third tiers and organs of government. The central Constitutional Court is however the court of final instance, i.e. appeal, in all these matters. The ANC's latest proposals for the final constitution are that the Constitutional Court remain the highest court of appeal for constitutional matters, but that 'most courts should be given the power to deal with constitutional matters' (ANC, 1995: 39). A decentralized model of judicial review more in keeping with the country's common-law background is thus likely to be embodied in the final constitution.

Composition and Mode of Appointment

Constitutional Court judges (whether of *de jure* constitutional courts such as the German or *de facto* constitutional courts such as the American) are internationally either appointed for life – as in the USA – or for relatively long terms – as in the Federal Republic of Germany. In the case of the latter, appointments are usually staggered to achieve a degree of continuity. Most countries, in an attempt to ensure a degree of independence and impartiality from the judicial structures empowered with the power of judicial review, also place the power of appointment in the hands of a number of different organs of state. Both the lower and upper houses of the German federal Parliament, for example, are involved in each electing half of the judges of the Constitutional Court. Heightened majorities, in the German case 66 percent, are required for election. In Italy one-third of the Constitutional Court judges are appointed by the president, the Parliament and the judiciary itself. All three branches of government also have a say in the appointment of judges in Israel (Corder 1992a: 221). The American method of appointment – namely, presidential with confirmation by the Senate – is well known. In France the members of the Constitutional Court are appointed by the president with the approval of Parliament. Common to all these different modes of appointment is the fact that the power of appointment is not left exclusively in the hands of any one branch of government, and in particular not in the hands of the executive.

The South African interim constitution provides for a Constitutional Court of 11 judges (10 plus the president of the Constitutional Court). All the judges of the Constitutional Court (including the president of the court) are elected for a non-renewable period of 7 years. The ANC's proposals for the final constitution are that this period be extended to a non-renewable 10-year term (ANC, 1995: 40). It is perhaps unfortunate that the first set of appointments to the court were not for varying lengths of time so as to stagger future appointments and maintain a degree of continuity. Given the interim nature of this constitution, this criticism should not, however, be exaggerated. The ANC proposes that in the final constitution half of the judges be replaced every 6 years (ANC, 1995: 40).

A more serious criticism concerns the procedure spelt out in the interim constitution for appointing the 11 judges of the Constitutional Court. This was one of the last issues dealt with at the Kempton Park/World Trade Centre talks which produced the interim constitution at the end of 1993. Prior to the 'compromise' proposal concerning the appointment procedure of the Constitutional Court judges (see below for a description of it) embodied in the interim constitution, an agreement had been reached between the ANC and the NP – who together decided all the crucial questions during the process of drafting the interim constitution – that the state president acting on the advice of the power-sharing cabinet would appoint all the members to the Constitutional Court.

The NP had agreed to this procedure on the assumption that the central cabinet would be constitutionally prescribed to take all decisions on a consensual basis or at least a 66 percent majority vote. When this assumption of the NP failed to materialize (the precise wording eventually agreed upon of the crucially important section 89[2] of the interim constitution being: 'the cabinet shall function in a manner which gives consideration to the consensus-seeking spirit underlying the concept of a government of national unity as well as the need for an effective government'), the negotiations dispute over the Constitutional Court arose. The NP belatedly realized that it was going to have to renegotiate the appointment procedure of the Constitutional Court judges, but it was the legally trained member of the small, liberal Democratic Party and its chief constitutional negotiator, Tony Leon, who really fought the issue and persuaded his then party leader Zac de Beer to threaten to refuse to approve the draft interim constitution unless the appointment procedure was changed. Leon argued that if the Constitutional Court judges were simply to be presidential appointees, the judges would be political lackeys and that the idea of a constitutional state and of a government of law not of men would be grievously harmed (*Sunday Telegraph*, 21 November 1993).

In terms of the 'compromise' proposal now embodied in the interim constitution, the president of the Constitutional Court and the other 10 judges are all appointed by the President of the RSA (section 99[1]). The former are 'appointed by the President in consultation with the Cabinet and after consultation with the Chief Justice' (section 97[2]). It has been argued that this requires the cabinet to concur with the President's appointment, but this is incorrect. Section 233(3) of the interim constitution does equate the phrase 'in consultation with' with concurrence, but adds the crucial rider that 'if such other functionary is a body of persons it shall express its concurrence with its own decision-making procedure'. This is the case with the cabinet, which then makes section 89(2) applicable. The president of the Constitutional Court is thus effectively an appointment of the President and the majority party represented in the cabinet to whom the President is accountable. The Chief Justice, who has to be consulted regarding the appointment of the president of the Constitutional Court, is himself also effectively a presidential nominee (section 97[1]).

Concerning the other 10 judges of the Constitutional Court, four are appointed by the President from the ranks of sitting judges 'in consultation with the cabinet and the Chief Justice' (section 99[3]). These four are also effectively appointments by the President and the majority party in cabinet. The other six judges need not be sitting judges and are appointed 'by the President in consultation with the cabinet and after consultation with the president of the Constitutional Court (section 99 [4]). These six have to be chosen from a list compiled by a Judicial Services Commission, a new body created by the interim constitution, and consisting of lawyers, legal academics and representatives from the political parties represented in the national Parliament.

In performing its functions vis-a-vis the Constitutional Court, the Judicial Services Commission consists of 17 members. These 17 members are:

- the Chief Justice
- the president of the Constitutional Court
- one Judge-President designated by the Judges-President [the Judges-President are judges of the Supreme Court who are elected by their fellow judges within a specific provincial or local division of the Supreme Court to act as Judge-President of the Court]
- the National Minister of Justice or his or her nominee
- two practising advocates designated by the advocates' profession
- two practising attorneys designated by the attorneys' profession
- one professor of law designated by the deans of all law faculties
- four senators designated *en bloc* by the Senate by a majority of at least 66 percent of all its members, and
- four persons, two of whom shall be practising attorneys or advocates, who shall be designated by the President in consultation with the Cabinet.

(section 105)

The NP portrayed the agreed-upon appointment procedure of Constitutional Court judges as ensuring the independence of the Constitutional Court, which would be above politics and the ultimate guardian of the rights of all and especially of minorities. While there were many who viewed this compromise over the appointment of the Constitutional Court judges as ensuring an independent and apolitical Constitutional Court, there were others who were less sure (O'Malley, 1994: 80). They argued that the Judicial Services Commission was so structured that the majority party in the national legislature would also effectively control it. Heightened or special majorities are not required for decisions by the Judicial Services Commission (section 105[4]).

The Constitutional Court in Practice

The appointment of the 11-member Constitutional Court was finalized by the middle of October 1994. Arthur Chaskolson, a lawyer with clear ANC sympathies – he had been the ANC's chief legal and constitutional adviser during the Kempton Park/World Trade Centre talks – was appointed president of the Constitutional Court by President Mandela shortly after the April 1994 elections. Apart from his well-known political affiliations with the ANC, Chaskolson's prominent role in the drafting of the interim constitution means that he now has the task of interpreting this very same document.

The 11-member Court consists of nine men (six of whom are white) and two women (one of whom is white). Women's groups in South Africa were generally critical of the appointments, maintaining that a greater number of women ought to have been appointed (*Weekly Mail & Guardian*, 14–20 October 1994). The members of the Court are its president, Chaskolson, and Justices Ackermann, Didcott, Goldstone, Kriegler, Langa, Madala, Mahomed, Mokgoro, O'Regan and Sachs. The Judicial Services Commission held public hearings at which 24 candidates were interviewed to identify 10 to place on a list to be submitted to the president, Nelson Mandela. From this list Mandela chose justices Didcott, Kriegler, Langa, Makgòro, O'Regan and Sachs in accordance with section 99(4) of the constitution. Two of the justices (Sachs and O'Regan) are known supporters of the ANC, the remainder best being described as 'progressive' or ANC sympathetic. Mandela excluded from the list the independent and leading liberal South African legal academic John Dugard as well as the only candidate known to have some sympathy for the Inkatha Freedom Party (IFP), vice-chancellor and rector of the University of Zululand, Charles Dlamini.

The four justices appointed by Mandela from among current judges of the Supreme Court were Ackermann, Goldstone, Madala and Mahomed. None of them are known to have views contrary to the 'progressive' ideology of the ANC. No sitting judges with known conservative views or with views known to be in conflict with those that form part of broad ANC policy views were appointed, let alone considered by the Judicial Services Commission.

The composition of the Constitutional Court is thus heavily biased in favour of the majority party in the Government of National Unity, the ANC. Apart from the president of the Court, justices O'Regan and Sachs have been (and possibly remain) members of the ANC. Those with known ANC sympathies include Ackermann, Goldstone (who headed the Goldstone Commission into allegations of third-force violence during the transition) and Mahomed. Justice Didcott has his roots in the left-liberal tradition in South Africa and is known for his 'progressive' views on human rights and his outspoken opposition to the death penalty. Little is known of Madala, Langa or Mokgoro, who were virtually unheard of before their appointment.

Neither of the two smaller parties, the NP or the IFP, which enjoy representation in the tri-party Government of National Unity have any 'representation' in the Court. The National Executive, and specifically the

President, ultimately controlled and determined the composition and hence the likely ideological direction of the Court. This has been borne out by various Court decisions, including decisions declaring the death penalty and corporal punishment unconstitutional and a decision empowering the Court to avoid a strict, literal interpretation of the interim constitution.

Within South Africa, criticism of the Constitutional Court being politically biased in favour of the ANC is increasingly heard. The dangers are exacerbated by the strongly judicial activist role the Court clearly envisages for itself and which it has already undertaken in part. In its relatively short life the Court has already shown a clear willingness to make constitutional law and determine public policy when the constitution is in fact silent on an issue.

A number of political parties, including the NP, responded to the Court's ruling on the death penalty by calling for a referendum to be held to highlight the illegitimacy of the Court's decision given the overwhelming support for the death penalty among South Africans. The Court is thus already encountering criticism of being anti-democratic and of 11 non-elected and non-accountable justices enforcing their morality on the entire population. A showdown between the Constitutional Court and the popularly elected political branches of government has not yet occurred, but will occur if the Court continues to see its task not simply as that of a referee within the constitutional system but as a, if not the, central player in the policy-making process. Constitutionalism has been threatened in countries as diverse as the United States and India when the judiciary, and specifically constitutional courts, have opposed the social and economic understandings of constitutions by political branches (Jiyane, 1992: 15).

Conclusion

The interim constitution provides for a mixed form of judicial review with the separate Constitutional Court at the apex supported by the non-Appellate Divisions of the Supreme Court which are granted less extensive powers of judicial review. It is unclear what the advantage of a separate Constitutional Court is if the power of judicial review, albeit a limited form, is also granted to certain ordinary divisions of the Supreme Court. The choice of an essentially centralized model of judicial review is also contrary to both the country's common-law status and the idea of parliamentary sovereignty, but has been deemed necessary by South Africa's elite to mark a clean break with the old 'apartheid-order'. A decentralized model of judicial review however appears likely to emerge in the final constitution.

The method of appointing Constitutional Court judges is problematic in that one branch of government – the executive and specifically the majority party and its leader, the President – effectively dominates this process. That such a procedure was embodied in the interim constitution is largely attributable to what has accurately been described as the 'lamentable' lack of attention paid to the method of judicial appointment (Corder, 1992a: 207).

The Constitutional Court is thus unlikely to enjoy the independence that it needs to be an effective guarantor of the legitimacy of the constitution. The choice of an essentially centralized model of judicial review in itself means the politicization of judicial review; the determining influence of the majority party in government in appointing the Constitutional Court judges will only intensify this politicization. A highly politicized and controversial Constitutional Court can thus be expected, especially given the fact that inadequate measures exist to ensure that the Court will enjoy legitimacy in the eyes of all segments of South Africa's deeply divided ethnic society. In the words of van der Westhuizen, 'the composition of such a bench will at least have to be perceived to be representative of all the people of this country, for the sake of its legitimacy' (1991: 7). This legitimacy simply does not currently exist.

The Constitutional Court is unlikely to prove as politically independent a constitutional entity as many would like it to be. This means that an increasingly politicized appointment and confirmation process can be expected. This will certainly happen if the majority party, the ANC, begins to use the Constitutional Court to make politically unpopular decisions which run contrary to the views of a majority of South Africans. The appointment procedure of the Constitutional Court judges gives the majority party within the Government of National Unity a virtually unchecked say in the appointment of the judges. This is borne out by the fact that an overwhelming majority of the 11 justices on the Court have strong links with the ANC. There is in fact not one judge on the Court who is known to be broadly sympathetic to any of the other political parties in the country.

A further danger is that the entire legal system and the law will become discredited and delegitimized by an excessively politicized Constitutional Court. Robert Bork's prescient warnings of the political seduction of the law and the harm that this does to the legitimacy of the law appear to have fallen on deaf ears in South Africa, in spite of warnings from a few outspoken legal academics (see Corder, 1992b).

In a recent contribution to the debate about the Constitutional Court in South Africa, Sartori agrees with the observation that the Court is effectively an ANC court and suggests that the only way to deal with the problem is for the constitution to stipulate that minority parties be entitled to appoint a majority of the members of the court (*Business Day*, 2 August 1995). In its latest submissions to the Constitutional Assembly, the NP appears to have heeded Sartori's advice. The party proposes that Constitutional Court judges be elected by Parliament on a multiparty basis (*Natal Witness*, 4 October 1995).

Sartori perceptively views the Government of National Unity as the facade for ANC rule that it is, and convincingly argues that the current Constitutional Court dispensation is unsatisfactory and inadequately protective of minority interests.

To constitutionally prescribe minority-party domination of the Constitutional Court is however itself problematic. Regular standoffs between an elected majority-party government and a minority-party controlled Constitutional Court would occur. The Court will also still be clearly functioning as a political body. What is necessary for the continuation of democratic and constitutional rule in South Africa is for the courts, and especially the Constitutional Court, to remain above politics. Minority interests are best protected by a carefully crafted and detailed constitution which *inter alia* establishes an appointment procedure to the Constitutional Court, which is itself carefully crafted to ensure that no one party or interest group enjoys near exclusive 'representation' on the Court. This can be done without constitutionally mandating that minority parties appoint a majority of the justices: for example, by constitutionally stipulating that minority parties enjoy a veto over all appointments to the Constitutional Court.

Consociational theory is surprisingly silent on how courts, and specifically constitutional courts, in multiethnic societies should best be structured to restrain centrifugal ethnic forces. While much has been written on methods of ensuring proportionality and balance in the executive and legislative structures of ethnically deeply divided states, little attention has been paid to courts of law. While at first glance somewhat surprising, this apparent lacuna may in fact reflect the realization that if courts and the law are to enjoy legitimacy, they cannot afford to be seen to be subject to the horsetrading and expediency that is so characteristic of politics. In the words of Robert Bork:

> The democratic integrity of law, however, depends entirely upon the degree to which its processes are legitimate. A judge who announces a decision must be able to demonstrate that he began from recognized legal principles and reasoned in an intellectually coherent and politically neutral way to his result. Those who would politicize the law offer the public, and the judiciary, the temptation of results without regard to democratic legitimacy. (1990: 2)

The constitutional law of the new South Africa is unfortunately currently being politicized by the Constitutional Court itself. The appointment procedure leaves much to be desired and a more politically balanced (neutral) process is needed for the final constitution. The legitimacy of the Constitutional Court and its decisions will otherwise be weakened. Sartori's well-intentioned suggestion is however not the route to follow. The route is for checks and balances to be built into the appointment procedure and for the crucial distinction between politics and law to be recognized by the justices.

REFERENCES

ANC (1995) 'Building a United Nation. Policy Proposals for the Final Constitution', 31 March–1 April, Johannesburg, mimeo.

Asmal, K. (1991) 'Constitutional Courts', *Comparative and International Law Journal of South Africa* 24 (3).

Bork, R. (1990) *The Tempting of America: The Political Seduction of the Law*. London: Sinclair-Stevenson.

Cappeletti, M. (1992) 'Judicial Review of the Constitutionality of State Action', *Tydskrif vir die Suid-Afrikaanse Reg* no. 2.

Corder, H. (1992a) 'The Appointment of Judges: Some Comparative Ideas', *Stellenbosch Law Review* 2.

Corder, H. (1992b) 'Lessons from North America. Beware the "Legalization of Politics" and the "Political Seduction of the Law" ', *South African Law Journal* 109(2).

Jiyane, Z. (1992) 'Reconciling Judicial Review with Democracy in South Africa', paper presented at an IPSA on 'Problems of Democratisation in Africa', Abuja, Nigeria, 20–24 September.

Kruger, J. (1991) 'Die Regbank in 'n nuwe Suid-Afrika', *Stellenbosch Law Review* 2(3).

Kruger, T. J. (1993) 'A Constitutional Court for South Africa?', *Consultus* 6(1).

Motala, Z. (1991) 'Independence of the Judiciary, Prospects and Limitations of Judicial Review in Terms of the United States Model in a New South African Order: Towards an Alternative Judicial Structure', *Comparative and International Law Journal of South Africa* 24(3).

O'Malley, K. (1994) 'The Constitutional Court', paper delivered at Workshop on the South African Interim Constitution organized by the Department of Political Sciences, University of South Africa.

Saayman, L. (1993) *'n Afsonderlike Onafhanklike Konstitusionele Hof: 'n Lewensvatbare Opsie vir Suid-Afrika?* Pretoria: UNISA.

Sachs, A. (1991) 'Towards a Bill of Rights for a Democratic South Africa', *Journal of African Law* 35(1) and (2).

van der Westhuizen, J. (1991) 'The Protection of Human Rights and a Constitutional Court for South Africa', *De Jure* 24(1).

Van Wyk, D. (1991) 'Die ANC se Konsephandves van Menseregte', *Tydskrif vir Hedendaagse Romeins-Hollandse Reg* 54(1).

Wiechers, M. (1992) 'Regional Government in the New South Africa: The Role of the Courts'. *Tydskrif vir Hedendaagse Romeins-Hollandse Reg* 54(4).

6. THE ELECTORAL SYSTEM

Murray Faure

The Past

The history of electoral systems in South Africa and of the concomitant political debate that it invoked can be divided into a number of distinct phases. The following offers a few highlights in this regard.

During the 19th century elementary electoral systems developed in the Cape Colony, the colony of Natal, the constitutional arrangements of the Voortrekkers and later in the Boer Republics of the Orange Free State and Transvaal. These systems became more sophisticated as colonies became more autonomous, and as a matter of fact toward the end of the 19th century Lord Bryce described the Orange Free State as a model republic of 19th-century democracy. Except for the Cape Colony, organized political parties had little influence on the functioning of these electoral systems (du Plessis, 1979: 49–80; Nieuwoudt, 1966: 71–80 and 1979: 23–48).

With the unification of South Africa in 1910 the electoral systems of the pre-existing British colonies were supplanted by a single-member geographical constituency system that functioned on the basis of relative majorities. The principles of this system, which was used for the election of members of Parliament and the various Provincial Councils, remained essentially unaltered for more than 80 years. The system was retained when the country became a republic in 1961 (Pienaar, 1979: 81–102) and in 1983 when South Africa's bicameral Parliament made way for the so-called three-chamber Parliament. With minor adaptations the same system was also used in the so-called self-governing territories and the 'independent' homelands created by the policies of the National Party government.

In a political sense, the main features of this system were that it denied on racial grounds the franchise to the largest portion of the population, and that it severely distorted the relative strength of political parties in Parliament. While blacks and Coloureds initially retained the franchise which they had in the former colonies of Natal and the Cape, it was effectively removed in 1936 and 1955 respectively. The franchise extended to Coloureds and Indians in the three-chamber Parliament of 1983 was nothing more than tokenism since it still precluded these population groups from electing representatives to that parliamentary chamber which had sovereign legislative authority in the land. The classic illustration of disproportionality in South African electoral history is the 1948 election where the National Party/Afrikaner Verbond drew 42 percent of the vote and won 79 seats, as against the United/Labour Parties which drew 52 percent of the vote, but which won only 71 seats. Scholars have shown that for the period 1961–81 the National Party (NP), on average, drew more than 50 percent of the vote, but held approximately 75 percent of the seats in Parliament. The disproportional ratio is quite dramatic (Butler, 1983: 53; Mackie and Rose, 1974).

During the period 1983–90 the three-chamber Parliament as a distorted application of, among others, Lijphart's ideas on consociational democracy (proportionality, elite cooperation, mutual veto, etc.) did not live up to expectations and increasingly lost legitimacy among its own supporters. Against the background of escalating instability in the country, the National Party government conceded that the Westminster electoral system (winner-takes-all or first-past-the-post system) was not the most appropriate electoral system for a deeply divided plural society like South Africa. The appeal of (especially Lijphart's) consociational ideas persisted and was hotly debated in government and academic circles as a possible way of salvaging the deepening political crisis in the country. This debate ranged from an emphasis on the definition of groups vis-a-vis other groups (horizontal representation) to the way in which groups themselves should be represented from within (vertical representation) to the desirability of consociationalism *per se* (Basson, 1984; Faure, 1987: 3–23 and 1988: 143–69; Lijphart, 1985; Thompson, 1986: 12).

The period 1990–94 is the most crucial period in South Africa's entire political and constitutional history, and with regard to electoral matters it signified a rapid growth in consensus among major political actors about the desirability of proportional representation (PR). This period covers President de Klerk's famous address to Parliament on 2 February 1990, Nelson Mandela's release from prison, the negotiations of Codesa I and II and the debates in the Technical Committee on Constitutional Issues and its interface with the Multiparty Negotiation Council. During this period several proposals for electoral reform were made as parties and scholars stated (or restated) their views on the issue of electoral change. The events that led to the adoption of a new constitution and electoral system cannot be discussed in detail here, but listing some of them will provide an understanding of the context from which a new system was forged. The main events were:

1990: A report was submitted by the President's Council's Committee on Constitutional Affairs which expressed itself favourably on the advantages that PR could offer the country (President's Council, 1990). Contact was also established between government and the Electoral Reform Society in the UK and the Society offered to provide expert assistance on electoral reform. In Cape Town the African National Congress (ANC) held a workshop on electoral reform. The majority of participants expressed a preference for PR in a new dispensation (UWC/CDS, 1990).

1991: The Human Sciences Research Council's (HSRC) Centre for Constitutional Analysis assessed that PR was the most desirable system for South Africa (de Villiers, 1991). The Democratic Party's Congress also expressed itself in favour of a PR system where 300 of the 400 members of the National Assembly would be elected from 100 three-member constituencies, while the remaining 100 would be elected from national lists, the threshold being 3 percent (Besprekingsdokument, 1991: 1–3). The NP produced a policy document entitled 'Constitutional Rule in a Participatory Democracy', which, among others, recommended a PR system for the First House of Parliament and a ballot that provided for candidate preference (National Party, 1991: 11). This change in electoral policy by the NP has been described by Johnson as 'a deathbed conversion to PR as the only way to moderate the tide of African nationalism' (1993: 21).

1992: The ANC Policy Guidelines for a Democratic South Africa were adopted at the National Conference of 28–31 May. It provided for a system of PR whereby a two-chamber Parliament would be elected – the National Assembly from a common voters' roll and the Senate, which would be representative of regions and directly elected. This document also provided for a single ballot that would elect both Houses of Parliament (ANC, 1992: 3–4). A second report was also submitted by the Committee on Constitutional Affairs of the President's Council. The document, entitled 'Report on a Proportional Polling System for South Africa in a New Constitutional Dispensation', recommended a 400-member lower house, 300 of whom would be elected by multimember constituencies – the regions – on a party list basis. One hundred seats would be used as 'compensatory' seats to guarantee proportionality and, to this end, the Hagenbach-Bischoff method of allocation would be used (President's Council, 1992: 85–6). Codesa II also entertained the idea of a 400-member Parliament elected on a strict PR basis, with half of the members being elected on a regional basis, and the other half on the basis of national lists. In 1992 the government also announced its timetable that would lead up to the country's first free and open election in April 1994.

1993: During this year a number of academics explored the merits and demerits of PR as a measure of electoral reform, notably Frost (1993), Johnson (1993), Reynolds (1993) and Sisk (1993). The year also saw the recommencement of the multiparty negotiation process on 1 April. This process took up almost seven months of negotiations. The process entailed the consideration of countless drafts, memoranda of advice on electoral matters to the various parties, secret bilaterals, referrals to technical committees and numerous resubmissions before the interim constitution was adopted with sufficient consensus at the plenary session of the Negotiation Council on 17 November. Parliament ratified the interim constitution on 22 December 1993, together with related legislation, such as the Electoral Act, effectively making it the new supreme law of the land after 27 April 1994 (Faure, 1994: 114).

1994: The period up to the election on 27 April entailed further negotiations between the major political actors. These were aimed at ensuring an all-inclusive and legitimate election in which all parties participated, and at changing the vote to grant each voter two ballots – one for the central legislature and one for the provincial legislatures. The interim constitution itself is divided into a number of chapters that deal with specific aspects, such as Parliament, the National Executive, etc. A number of important schedules supplement the interim constitution. The electoral system is referred to by various chapters of the interim constitution, and specifically Schedule 2 and the Electoral Act outline its details. Schedule 2 should be read together with the interim constitution, the Electoral Act and the Regulation of Gatherings Act in order to form an overall picture of the present electoral system and the arrangements that pertained to the electoral process (Faure, 1994: 114).

The Present

The explanation of the present electoral system below is based on provisions in the Electoral Act, the interim constitution and, especially, Schedule 2 of the interim constitution.

Basic Elements

The present system provides for a Parliament of 490 members as well as nine provincial legislatures. The National Assembly of Parliament has 400 members while the Senate consists of 90 indirectly elected members. Two hundred members of the National Assembly are elected by using provincial party lists with a fixed number of representatives from each province, namely:

Western Cape	21 seats
Eastern Cape	28 seats
Northern Cape	4 seats
Natal	40 seats
Orange Free State	15 seats
North West	15 seats
Northern Transvaal	20 seats
Eastern Transvaal	14 seats
Gauteng	43 seats

The remaining 200 members of the National Assembly are elected on a national basis using national party lists. The Senate is composed of 10 members from each of the nine provinces. Parties that are represented in a provincial legislature nominate the 10 senators for that province on the basis of each party's relative strength in the legislature. Members of provincial legislatures are elected on the basis of provincial party lists, while a fixed number of seats is laid down for the size of the nine legislatures, namely:

Western Cape	42 seats
Eastern Cape	56 seats
Northern Cape	30 seats
Natal	81 seats
Orange Free State	30 seats
North West	30 seats
Northern Transvaal	40 seats
Eastern Transvaal	30 seats
Gauteng	86 seats

Features

The system has the following features (Faure, 1994: 120–21):

The ballot. Franchise is granted to citizens who are 18 years or older. Each voter has two ballots: one for party preference at the national level and one for party preference at the provincial level. No provision is made for candidate preference, and the only differentiation that is possible is to vote for different parties at the two levels. The ballot used for the national level, therefore, cannot differentiate between party preference for provincial representation in the National Assembly and party preference on a national basis. The ballot used for party preference at provincial level, of course, also affects the composition of the Senate in an indirect manner.

Party lists. Closed ordered party lists are used at both the national and provincial levels. The voter is bound to the order of candidates as decided by the parties.

Seat allocation. Proportional allocation of seats takes place at both the central and provincial levels. The Droop quota is used at both levels. First, the allocation of seats that each party has won at the level of provincial representation in the National Assembly is conducted, after which the allocation of seats that each party has won at the national level is undertaken. The latter procedure uses the size of the whole legislature, i.e. 400, which implies that the 200 seats already allocated in the first step must be deducted from the allocation obtained by using the Droop quota based on 400 seats. Seats not filled with an initial allocation are filled by taking the party that has the highest surplus in the initial allocation.

In a certain sense, the representation of the provinces in the central legislature makes them extremely large multimember constituencies, while the allocation at national level, similar to procedures in Israel and the Netherlands, uses the whole country as one very large multimember constituency. Smaller parties with regional support are not disadvantaged by the method of allocation, while smaller parties with a countrywide level of support can also benefit from the national allocation procedure.

The threshold. The minimum vote required to win a seat (expressed in percentage) is extremely low. The threshold differs for the provincial and national lists, and those of the provincial legislatures are about half the size of those for the provincial allocation for the National Assembly. In the case of the Gauteng province, the threshold for the National Assembly is approximately 2.27 percent, while the threshold for the provincial legislature is approximately 1.14 percent. The threshold for the Northern Cape province in the National Assembly is in the region of 25 percent, while that for the provincial legislature is about 3.33 percent. For both the National Assembly and the provincial legislatures the respective thresholds of the various provinces differ, unless they have the same number of seats. Approximately 1/400th of the vote cast for the national party lists of the National Assembly (i.e. about 0.25 percent) constitutes the threshold, but the number of seats already allocated provincially is subtracted from the seats won in this way, effectively making this threshold about 0.50 percent. The threshold for the National Assembly as a whole is 0.24938 percent.

The Election of April 1994

In the election of 27 April 1994 the electoral system yielded the results shown in Table 1 (*Constitutional Talk*, 1995: 4; *DP Newsletter*, 1994; Pienaar, 1994; and *Sunday Times*, 8 May 1994: 7):

Table 1 indicates that an estimated 22.7 million voters had the opportunity to participate in the country's first-ever open and free election. The table also reflects the measure of proportionality with regard to regional representation at both the regional and national levels. A significant measure of overrepresentation obtains for sparsely populated provinces, such as

Table 1. Estimated Voters and Seat Allocation per Province

Province	Voters (000s)	Seats Provisional Assembly	Seats National Assembly	Seats Senate
Western Cape	2406	42	21	10
Eastern Cape	3177	56	28	10
Northern Cape	439	30	4	10
KwaZulu-Natal	4585	81	40	10
Orange Free State	1637	30	15	10
North West	1730	30	15	10
Northern Transvaal	2287	40	20	10
Eastern Transvaal	1586	30	14	10
Gauteng	4862	86	43	10
TOTAL	22,709	425	200	90

Table 2. Election Results – National Assembly and Senate

Party	Votes (000s)	Percentage	Seats National Assembly	Seats Senate
ANC	12,237.6	62.6	252	60
NP	3983.7	20.4	82	17
IFP	2058.3	10.5	43	5
FF	424.6	2.2	9	5
DP	338.4	1.7	7	3
PAC	243.5	1.3	5	–
ACDP	88.1	0.5	2	–
Remaining 12	169.3	0.7	–	–
Spoilt papers	147.8	0.7	–	–
TOTAL	19,681.4	100.0	400	90

Note. Totals not exact due to rounding.

the Northern Cape, with regard to regional legislatures where the minimum size of provincial legislatures is laid down at 30 members. This is also the case for representation in the Senate, but unlike the proportionality found elsewhere in the system with regard to seat distribution, the equal representation of provinces in the Senate supposedly reflects a feature that is typical of federal arrangements.

Table 2 shows that the three largest parties netted more than 90 percent of the votes cast for the National Assembly. The ANC is by far the largest party with almost 63 percent support at the national level, and a two-thirds majority in the Senate.

Table 3. National versus Provincial Votes

Party	National Totals	Provincial Totals	Difference
ANC	12,237,655	12,137,307	-100,348
NP	3,983,690	3,492,467	-491,223
IFP	2,058,294	2,047,083	-11,211
FF	424,555	639,643	+215,088
DP	338,426	538,655	+200,229

An interesting point that is reflected by Table 3 is the measure of differentiation in the ballot for the national and the provincial levels. The larger parties drew more votes at the central level, while the smaller parties drew significantly more votes at the regional level.

Table 4 indicates the provincial strength of parties. The ANC has the majority support in all the provinces except for the Western Cape and

Table 4. First Four Parties Per Province

Province	Parties and Ballot Percentages			
	1	2	3	4
Western Cape	NP (53.2)	ANC (33.0)	DP (6.6)	FF (2.1)
Eastern Cape	ANC (84.8)	NP (9.8)	DP (2.1)	PAC (2.0)
Northern Cape	ANC (49.7)	NP (40.5)	FF (6.0)	DP (1.9)
KwaZulu-Natal	IFP (50.3)	ANC (32.2)	NP (11.2)	DP (2.2)
Orange Free State	ANC (76.6)	NP (12.6)	FF (6.0)	PAC (1.8)
North West	ANC (83.3)	NP (8.8)	FF (4.6)	PAC (1.7)
Northern Transvaal	ANC (91.6)	NP (3.3)	FF (2.1)	PAC (1.3)
Eastern Transvaal	ANC (80.7)	NP (9.0)	FF (5.7)	PAC (1.6)
Gauteng	ANC (57.6)	NP (23.8)	FF (6.2)	DP (5.3)

KwaZulu-Natal where the NP and the Inkatha Freedom Party (IFP) have the most support, respectively.

Assessment

South Africa's short experience with the system suggests the following weak and strong points (Faure, 1994: 121–24).

Overinflated legislatures. A striking feature of the electoral system is the large number of legislators who populate the legislatures. The different legislatures themselves do not present the problem, but the contingent of law-makers in some of them do. A total of no less than 915 legislators, 490 on the central level and 425 on the provincial level, is clearly unnecessary. The argument that a federal state inevitably requires some duplication in authorities is well known, but not appropriate in the South African context. The South African state is not a classical federation, and neither is it a decentralized unitary state. The collective number of legislators could be reduced considerably. This would not 'depersonalize' the already impersonal seat/voter ratio of about 1 to 50,000 for the National Assembly in any significant way, but it would make the system considerably cheaper. There is, finally, also little evidence to suggest that large legislatures necessarily make better laws than smaller ones.

Lack of voter accountability. A serious concern is the effect of the party list system on voter accountability. While there can be little doubt that proportional representation in conjunction with the party list system guarantees an acceptable degree of proportionality, the present system with closed ordered party lists is bound to erode the accountability of representatives to the electorate. Candidates no doubt seek listing by the party bosses as a first priority, and there is really no way for the voter to discriminate between a party and its candidates. It is entirely a party matter who makes the list and who remains there. Voters will not necessarily forfeit their choice for a party because certain unacceptable candidates are listed – hence the fact that small parties ride the back of larger ones without the voters being in a position to prevent it. The consequences of party lists and a ballot to be used for party preference only are indeed a serious erosion of voter accountability and a strengthening of party bureaucratic tendencies.

Problems pertaining to the ballot: comprehending the vote, meaningful choice for the voter and the interests of provinces. Reasons why the April 1994 election yielded such a high poll percentage are well understood by observers of South African politics. What is not so readily realized is the fact that the ballot that was used was extremely complicated. Initially, a single ballot was to be used, but shortly before the election a decision was taken in favour of a double ballot. This was an improvement, but the calculation of the effect that two ballots have on four different categories of government requires a high level of reasoning from the 'average' voter if he or she is to make an informed decision (one ballot is used for the national and provincial components of the National Assembly, and the second for the province, and indirectly, the province's representation in Senate). If added to this is the fact that all parties did not participate at both levels in all the various provinces, as well as relatively low literacy levels, the complexity pertaining to the ballot becomes apparent. If national issues furthermore dominate an election (as was the case in April 1994), the interests of provinces could be jeopardized since voters prioritize in a different way compared to elections where only regional representatives are elected.

The ballot as used in the last election remains problematical with regard to comprehensibility, meaningful choice for the voter (the question of having candidate preference in some form) and the interests of regions. The matter justifies urgent reconsideration.

High proportionality, representativeness and legitimacy. The most obvious advantage that the present electoral system has is its high proportionality. Proportional representation in conjunction with the party list system may be short on voter accountability, but such systems, especially when allocation is also done at the national level, are known to provide a high degree of representativeness. This is important if any new political dispensation hopes to develop the legitimacy of its institutions. While the party list system is bound to be conducive to centralist and bureaucratic tendencies in the party system, the present electoral system concurrently (and possibly also as a result of such tendencies) contains the dynamic and opportunities for smaller parties to actively seek and acquire representation. This was not readily possible under the previous winner-takes-all system, but it is built into the method of seat allocation in the new system, and it is further facilitated by some low thresholds in the system. This is an advantage for any heterogeneous society, as long as it does not develop excessive levels of fragmentation. Smaller parties finding representation could also be conducive to the forming of coalitions, and as long as this does not polarize the system around extremities, but rather strengthens the middle ground, the system might turn out to be more successful on this score than most observers expect. Yet there can be no denying the fact that proportional representation holds the paradox of promise and risk for a divided society like South Africa.

The Future

The Constitutional Assembly (and especially Theme Committee 2 of the Assembly) is presently engaged in the process of drafting South Africa's so-called 'final constitution'. The process of drafting the constitution cannot be explored here, except to mention that it is aimed at being a consultative and all-inclusive process in which opinions from all levels of society are solicited. In this process, the Constitutional Assembly must adhere to the constitutional principles contained in the interim constitution which are intended to govern the writing of the new constitution. Of these, the most important one is Principle 8 which requires that there shall be representative government, and in general proportional representation. This principle is generally construed as not necessarily a requirement for a system of proportional representation, but a requirement that the representation that a new electoral system will put in place be proportional in nature.

With this in mind, the challenge for the future is, of course, how the present system can be changed in such a manner that it will not only retain its high proportionality, but that it will also incorporate a streamlined legislature and a measure of voter accountability as well as meaningful choice for the voter. Accomplishing such an objective is of course no simple exercise since improving one dimension of an electoral system is almost always at the expense of others. In this respect, it is significant to note that the ANC recently pronounced itself in favour of elections 'based on proportional and constituency representation', and that its 'position on the total number of representatives in the National Assembly is ... under consideration' (ANC, 1995: 17).

A defensible way in which this objective can be accomplished is by effecting the following changes to the present electoral system.

Reducing the Size of Legislatures

The present system could be streamlined by reducing the size of some of the provincial legislatures, and especially that of the National Assembly. In the National Assembly the 200 members elected from national party lists should be retained, while the 200 members elected from provincial party lists could be abolished. In their place, provision could be made for the election of another 100 members elected from single-member geographical constituencies using relative majorities. These constituencies could be distributed nationally over the provinces on a proportional basis using the same criteria which presently allocates seats to the provinces in the National Assembly. A seat distribution of more or less the following would result, representing a fair outcome in terms of population distribution:

Western Cape	10 seats
Eastern Cape	14 seats
Northern Cape	3 seats
Natal	20 seats
Orange Free State	8 seats
North West	7 seats
Northern Transvaal	10 seats
Eastern Transvaal	7 seats
Gauteng	21 seats

The financial saving resulting from such a change could amount to a few hundred million rands over a five-year period. Apart from the obvious savings which will result from a 25 percent reduction in size, the introduction of a dimension of geographical representation will effectively reduce other shortcomings of the system as well.

Introducing Voter Accountability

While not a feature of the present system, the need for some measure of geographical representation and concomitant voter accountability has already been expressed by several political parties. In the absence of preferential voting for candidates and geographical representation under the present system, the introduction of 100 members elected on the basis of geographical constituencies will provide for a measure of voter accountability. Symbolically, it could also convey this sentiment to the 200 members elected from national party lists. This awareness will be heightened by using *by-elections* in the case of vacancies for these 100 seats, and by also introducing the constitutional measure of the *recall*, a set of procedures whereby a member can be recalled by his or her constituency if satisfactory performance is lacking and representation of constituency interests is not taken care of.

Consideration could also be given to the possibility of using the voters' ballot for national party lists (see below) to indicate some form of candidate preference, i.e. affording voters the opportunity of indicating desirable/ undesirable candidates. This will have a wholesome effect and will enable parties to ascertain which candidates are popular with the electorate. If this is decided on, it will imply that *closed ordered* party lists will have to make way for lists that are *flexible*.

Members elected from constituencies should be allowed to vote on the basis of individual conscience in the legislature. The *recall* coupled with the use of *by-elections* provides for sufficient measures to renew a constituency mandate to a candidate.

Comprehending the Ballot, Meaningful Choice for the Voter and the Interests of Regions

The introduction of 100 geographical constituencies will require that voters be granted a double ballot: one for the preferred party chosen from the competing national party lists, and one for the candidate of a political party which contests the election in the voter's constituency. The former ballot is a vote for a preferred party at national level, while the latter is a vote for a candidate (and a party) at the local constituency level. The constituency vote will introduce a personal dimension to elections which will not only require parties to put up their very best candidates at this level, but will also strengthen accountability in terms of election promises and constituency-related issues. The implication of such a double ballot is easier to grasp than that of the present system and it would go a long way to facilitate voter education programmes. There should naturally be a common voters' roll, but voters should register in the constituency where they intend to vote. If, on the day of the election, a voter is not in his or her constituency, he or she should be allowed to vote for the national party lists only. Elections for provincial legislatures should be held at a different time, like those for local government.

Retaining Fairness, Representativeness (Proportionality) and the Legitimacy of Institutions

Fairness, proportionality and the legitimacy of legislative institutions can be retained in spite of the fact that single-member constituencies 'waste' votes and normally lead to an overrepresentation of large parties. Such a reconciliation can be accomplished along the following lines:

- Votes cast in each constituency for a particular candidate (not those for national party lists) are used to determine the outcome for a particular constituency. The 100 candidates elected in this manner are then assigned their seats in the National Assembly. This regional constituency allocation is conducted *before* the allocation of seats in terms of votes cast for national party lists is undertaken.
- Only votes cast for national party lists (not those for candidates in constituencies) are used to determine the allocation of the remaining 200 seats to the National Assembly. This is undertaken in exactly the same manner as the present system allows for. This allocation is undertaken *after* the assigning of constituency seats. The Droop quota is used, and there should be no legal threshold (like Germany's 5 percent, for example) which will make it difficult for small parties to obtain representation. Only the natural mathematical threshold brought about by the 200 seats should obtain, allowing for a quota of approximately 100,000 votes per

seat with an electorate of 20 million.

$$\frac{\text{Votes}}{\text{Seats} + 1} + 1 = \text{Quota, i.e.} \ \frac{20,000,000}{(200) + 1} + 1 = 99,503.4875$$

Once the number of seats that each party has won on this basis is determined, the relative strength (number of seats) of each party vis-a-vis the 200 seats is extrapolated to 300 seats by multiplying the number of seats of each party by 3 and dividing the result by 2. From this result the number of seats that a party has won on the constituency basis is deducted, the effect being that constituency seats receive precedence in the allocation while the remaining seats for each party's share are filled from the national party lists. In this way almost complete proportionality for the legislature as a whole is obtained.

• An almost identical result will be obtained if the Droop quota is used with a seat number of 300 and the multiplication by 3 and the division by 2 are left out of the calculation.

Such an electoral system will retain the strong points of the present system and largely eliminate its weak points. It will have the following features. It will no doubt yield high proportionality, making it fair, representative and legitimate. The National Assembly that it will create will be more stream-lined and considerably cheaper than the present transitional body. Cost savings alone could go a long way to eliminate misery in different spheres of society. Small parties will acquire representation, especially in terms of the national party lists. The threshold of the proposed new system will be less than 1 percent, which means that small parties, i.e. parties with approx-imately 100,00 supporters among voters on a national level, will be assured of representation. Voter accountability and a personal dimension in repre-sentation will be introduced by also using geographical constituencies and the recall. The new system's double ballot will be easier to understand than that of the present system, thus facilitating voter education and reasoned choice on the part of the voter. Provinces will still be represented in the legislature on a proportional basis, both with regard to constituencies and national party lists. Issues in and problems of individual constituencies or areas will receive more attention than the present system allows for. Independent candidates will be able to make themselves available for election, which is not possible under the present system.

Conclusion

South Africa's electoral arrangements represent an important dimension of the country's constitutional transformation. As an instrument of reform its implications should not be underestimated. However, in and by itself, it is only a subsidiary component of a much larger set of rules and procedures that are presently being defined and which will shape the nature of politics in South African society. What will guarantee the success or failure of this new democracy is not the rules and procedures themselves, but the political will to make them work for the purposes for which they were designed.

REFERENCES

ANC (1992) 'ANC Policy Guidelines for a Democratic South Africa', Proceedings of the National Conference, May (subsequently adopted at National Conference, 28–31 May 1993).

ANC (1995) 'Building a United Nation. Policy Proposals for the Final Constitution', 31 March– 1 April, Johannesburg.

Basson, D. A. (1984) *Kiesstelsels van proporsionele verteenwoordiging* (Report POL 6). Pretoria: HSRC.

Bogdanor, V. and D. E. Butler (eds) (1983) *Democracy and Elections: Electoral Systems and Their Political Consequences*. Cambridge: Cambridge University Press.

Butler, D. E. (1983) 'Variants of the Westminster Model', in V. Bogdanor and D. E. Butler (eds) *Democracy and Elections: Electoral Systems and Their Political Consequences*. Cambridge: Cambridge University Press.

Constitutional Talk (1995) Official newsletter of the constitutional assembly, 17 March–6 April, no. 5.

de Villiers, B. (1991) *An Electoral System for the New South Africa*. Pretoria: HSRC Centre for Constitutional Analysis, year 2, no. 2.

de Villiers, B. (ed.) (1994) *Birth of a Constitution*. Kenwyn: Juta.

Demokratiese Party (1991) *Besprekingsdokument oor 'n nuwe kiesstelsel vir Suid-Afrika*.

DP Newsletter (1994) 'April '94 Election: a Brief Analysis', July. Pretoria.

du Plessis, A. (1979) 'Die Britse tydperk (1795–1803; 1806–1910)', in C. F. Nieuwoudt, G. C. Olivier and M. Hough (eds) *Die politieke stelsel van Suid-Afrika*, pp. 49–80. Pretoria: Human & Rousseau.

Electoral Act 1993. Pretoria: Government Printer.

Faure, A. M. (1987) 'Demokratiese kiesstelsels: ontwikkeling, tipes, toepassings', *Politeia* 6(1): 3–23.

Faure, A. M. (1988) 'Kiesstelsels in die demokrasie', in A. M. Faure, D. J. Kriek, G. S. Labuschagne, A. du P. Louw and J. Venter (eds) *Suid-Afrika en die demokrasie*, pp. 143–69. Pinetown: Owen Burgess.

Faure, A. M. (1994) 'The Electoral System', in B. de Villiers (ed.) *Birth of a Constitution*, pp. 101–24. Kenwyn: Juta.

Frost, M. (1993) 'Choosing an electoral system', *Die Suid-Afrikaan* no. 43, February/March.

Interim Constitution of the Republic of South Africa, 1993.

Johnson, R. W. (1993) 'PR at Work: a Case Study', *Die Suid-Afrikaan* no. 43, February/ March.

Lijphart, A. (1985) 'Electoral Systems, Party Systems, and Conflict Management in Segmented Societies', paper prepared for presentation at the International Conference on Intergroup Relations of the Human Sciences Research Council, Pretoria, 10–11 September.

Mackie, T. T. and R. Rose (1974, 1976, 1982) *International Almanac of Electoral History* 1st and 2nd edns. London.

National Party (1991) *Constitutional Rule in a Participatory Democracy* (the National Party's framework for a new democratic South Africa), National Party.

Nieuwoudt, C. F. (1966) 'Die konstitusies van die Vrystaat- en die Transvaalse Republieke', in F. A. van Jaarsveld and G. D. Scholtz (eds) *Die Republiek van Suid-Afrika: Agtergrond, ontstaan en toekoms*, pp. 71–90. Johannesburg: Voortrekkerpers.

Nieuwoudt, C. F. (1979) 'Die staatsreëlings van die Voortrekkers en die Boere', in C. F. Nieuwoudt, G. C. Olivier and M. Hough (eds) *Die politieke stelsel van Suid-Afrika*, pp. 23–48. Pretoria: Human & Rousseau.

Pienaar, P. J. (1979) 'Staatkundige ontwikkeling van Uniewording tot Republiekwording', in C. F. Nieuwoudt, G. C. Olivier and M. Hough (eds) *Die politieke stelsel van Suid-Afrika*, pp. 81–102. Pretoria: Human & Rousseau.

Pienaar, P. A. (1994) 'Results of the April 1994 Election', unpublished manuscript, Department of Geography, University of South Africa.

President's Council (1990) *Report of the Committee for Constitutional Affairs on Decision-making and Conflict Resolution Mechanisms and Techniques in Constitutional Systems*. Cape Town: Government Printer.

President's Council (1992) *Report of the Committee for Constitutional Affairs on a Proportional Polling System for South Africa in a New Constitutional Dispensation*. Cape Town: Government Printer.

Reynolds, A. (1993) *Voting for a New South Africa*. Cape Town: Maskew Miller Longman.

Schedule 2 of the Interim Constitution of the Republic of South Africa, 1993.

Sisk, T. D. (1993) 'Choosing an Electoral System: South Africa Seeks New Ground Rules', *Journal of Democracy*: 4(1): 79–91.

Thompson, G. (1986) 'Change Without Bloodshed', *The Star* 12 February:12.

UWC/CDS (1990) *Workshop: Electoral Systems: a Discussion Document*. Cape Town.

7. SOUTH AFRICA'S PARTY SYSTEM

Susan Botha

1. Introduction

The South African party system displays regularities, irregularities and peculiarities. Criteria used in the study of party systems in western Europe were not always in the past suitable for the South African political context. This was to a large extent the result of legislation that on the one hand controlled the vote in general and on the other controlled the place, legality and membership of a political party. Thus the nature of the party system in South Africa was to a large extent predetermined by legislation as an external factor.

Most of the negative legislation affecting the party system had been repealed shortly before and after the dawn of the new South Africa. The present party system represents a transitional phase in which the political forces that normally operate within a party system have been freed from unnecessary external intervention. This in itself poses a problem in an analysis of the present party system for it will still be some time before the full impact of the normalization process on the party system will be realized.

This discussion on the South African party system briefly deals with the past, present and future of the party system in terms of a number of indicators. Political parties are not considered to be unitary actors in the South African party system (see Robertson, 1976). It is not possible, however, to pay attention to all aspects of the party system.

2. The South African Party System Prior to April 1994

The party system in South Africa was in the past multifaceted and at least three different types of 'party systems' could be identified: a *dominant party-system* that organized and represented the white electorate for parliamentary purposes and that had established its hegemony over the other 'party systems'; a number of *party subsystems* that catered exclusively and legally, but within an arena prescribed by the dominant party-system, for the 'quasi-enfranchised'; and a *quasi-party system* that catered for the majority of the unenfranchised separately and parallel to the dominant party-system. These various 'party systems' interacted with one another and this interplay had a major influence on the development of the present party system and also on developments of and within the political system as a whole.

Though the party system as a whole has its roots in political forces prior to the 1910 union of the two British colonies (Cape and Natal) and the two Boer Republics (Transvaal and the Orange Free State), the establishment of the Union of South Africa represented a major historic event in the development of the party system.

The decision not to extend the franchise to the unenfranchised non-whites (blacks, Coloureds and Indians) effectively barred the majority of the population from participation in elections. The unenfranchised non-whites turned to political organizations that are usually referred to as extra-parliamentary organizations. The best-known example is undoubtedly the African National Congress (ANC) which was founded in 1912, two years after Union. The disillusionment among non-whites with government policy that followed Union was a major contributing factor in the founding, not only of the ANC, but also of other organizations that channelled the political voice of the unenfranchised and those few enfranchised non-whites (i.e. a handful that had qualified vote) who were later disenfranchised. The organizations of the unenfranchised were excluded from participation in parliamentary politics by the dominant party-system and some of them were even banned. These organizations led to the development of a quasi-party system that functioned parallel to the dominant party-system. Initially, the aforementioned organizations campaigned for inclusion in the latter system, but later on aimed at replacing it with their own system and thus became anti-system.

The apartheid ideology of the National Party (founded in 1914) government was based on the idea that each group should have its own political structures. Therefore a number of political structures were created through which the unenfranchised were, in the opinion of the National Party, 'enfranchised' (thus they are called 'quasi-enfranchised'). The most important political structures for the quasi-enfranchised were a number of

councils, usually with elected and nominated members with advisory powers only, notably: the Natives Representative Council (1936), the Coloured
Persons' Representative Council (1968) and the South African Indian
Council (1964). These councils were later replaced by political structures
with more powers. The systematic creation of black homelands (sometimes
referred to as Bantustans) with varying degrees of self-rule and independence (commencing with the Black Authorities Act of 1951) is important in
this regard. Transkei was the first to become 'independent' (1976). It was
followed by Bophuthatswana (1977), Venda (1979) and Ciskei (1981)
(Thompson and Prior, 1982: 92). Other homelands with self-governing
structures were: Gazankulu, KaNgwane, KwaNdebele, KwaZulu, Lebowa
and Qwaqwa. The Community Councils (1977) made provision for representation of urban blacks at local level. The 1983 constitution made provision for more formal representation of the Coloureds and Indians (on a
separate voters' roll) in separate houses of Parliament, namely the House of
Representatives and the House of Delegates respectively. Parliament's
House of Assembly, representing whites, dominated the functions of Parliament however. These political structures led to the development of a
number of political parties and subsequently gave birth to a number of party
subsystems.

Voter Participation

Voter participation in the past in South Africa should be analysed within its
proper political context. Provision has to be made for the unenfranchised
who would, under normal circumstances, have been ordinary voters. Table
1 provides an indication of voter participation in elections by the white
voters.

Table 1. Percentage of White Voters who Participated in Elections

Year	1915	1920	1921	1924	1929	1933	1938	1943	1948	1953
%	75.9	68.7	72.2	79.4	80.8	63.9	81.6	78.4	80.4	88.0

Year	1958	1961	1966	1970	1974	1977	1981	1987	1989
%	89.6	77.6	75.9	74.3	70.2	64.7	65.0	67.7	69.5

Sources: Compiled from data obtained in Faure et al., 1988; *Rand Daily Mail*, 2 December
1977; SAIRR, 1987/88, 1989/90; Schoeman, 1977; *The Friend*, 2 May 1981; Van Vuuren et al.,
1987; Weide and Weide.

There was a certain amount of fluctuation in voter participation from one
election to another. Overall, voter participation in the dominant party-
system (i.e. among whites) was relatively high but with indications of a
decline in the later years of the old system.

Statistics on voter participation in the party subsystems are controversial due to a low level of voter registration. The number of registered voters for the House of Representatives doubled, e.g. from the 1984 election to the 1989 election (and is partly responsible for the statistical drop in voter participation) (Table 2).

Table 2. Voter Participation for the House of Representatives and the House of Delegates (%)

	1984	1989
House of Representatives	30.94	20.1
House of Delegates	20.29	23.3

Sources: Compiled from data obtained from SAIRR, 1989/90: 547–54; Van Vuuren et al., 1987.

Voter participation by the Indians and Coloureds in elections for their respective houses in Parliament was low. Voter participation was in fact lower than the actual figures suggest, for voter participation was calculated in terms of registered voters. As already mentioned, few potential voters registered for elections.

Statistics on voter participation in the homelands are equally controversial. A large number of theoretically potential voters resided outside the homelands and did not participate in elections either for practical or political reasons. Furthermore, voter participation was affected by the fact that in each of the homelands there was usually only one effective political party.

A low level of voter participation therefore characterized the party subsystems. This was largely due to the lack of legitimacy that the political structures experienced in the subsystems. These political structures were regarded as milestones in the history of apartheid, with the result that those who participated in elections for them were often victimized by their own people. The role of intimidation in these elections should therefore not be underestimated. The low voter turnout in the party subsystems should however not be interpreted as non-participation in the European sense, for a 'boycott vote' is also an important form of political expression.

'Voters' in the quasi-party system either could not participate in elections or chose to boycott elections in which they could participate. In the quasi-party system 'voter participation' of the unenfranchised found an outlet in strikes, worker stay-aways, boycotts and demonstrations. A high level of participation in these actions was often obtained, in particular in metropolitan areas. On the election day (for the tricameral Parliament) in 1987,

96 percent of workers in the Port Elizabeth/Uitenhage area observed a call for a stay-away. On the other hand only 2 percent of Coloureds in the Cape Town area observed the call (Van Vuuren et al., 1987: 129).

The extent to which the plurality election system influenced voter participation is largely theoretical. Voters who supported a political party that had no candidate in a particular constituency normally did not participate in that election. Voter participation was often negatively affected when a particular political party dominated a particular constituency. The fact that seats were not always contested was also a factor. This was true of both the dominant party-system and the party subsystems. In the 1933 election (whites) only 72 out of 150 seats were contested (Schoeman, 1977).

Number of Political Parties

Determining the number of political parties and the fractionalization of the party system were the areas where western criteria were least applicable. Neither was the standard definition of a political party in terms of its participation in elections suitable, for there were a number of organizations that resembled political parties yet were barred from participation in elections. Provision had to be made for organizations that did not participate in elections due to the fact that they were prevented from doing so by legislation. Thus neither Sartori's rules of counting (1976; 1994) nor Rae's (1971) fractionalization index was in the past suitable within the South African context.

There were a number of organizations that channelled the 'vote' of the unenfranchised since 1910. Not all could however be regarded as political parties out in the cold. On the basis of their political agendas and the fact that they were striving for political power the African National Congress (ANC, 1912), Pan Africanist Congress (PAC, broke away from the ANC in 1959), South African Communist Party (SACP, 1921), Azanian People's Organization (AZAPO, 1978) and the Congress of South African Trade Unions (COSATU, 1985) could for analytical purposes be regarded as political parties and are for the purpose of this discussion regarded as quasi-parties. The strength of these quasi-parties in terms of support was in the past difficult to determine. Due to the fact that these organizations were often banned (ANC in 1960, PAC in 1960 and SACP in 1950), opinion polls were not reliable.

The structures in the subsystems led to the creation of a number of political parties that were officially registered as political parties and that did participate in elections of the subsystems. However, few of these political parties were of real significance. Likewise, not all of the registered political parties that could participate in elections held in the dominant party-system among the white electorate were of real importance, e.g. the

Ecology Party (established 1989) and a number of right-wing parties have never participated in elections.

If the real number of political parties were to be considered, the party system as a whole could be regarded as a multiparty system. In order to determine the impact the large number of political and quasi-parties had on the party system, the degree of competition that was present within the system and the ideological distance between the various political and quasi-parties have to be borne in mind.

Competition

The party system as a whole lacked competition in the past. The dominant party-system maintained its hegemony over the party subsystems and the quasi-party system through proscription and prescription.

There was, however, a high degree of competition prevalent in the dominant party-system for the greatest part of the period 1910–53. The pattern of competition was initially characterized by multiparty competition, usually with four important players, resulting in the need for coalitions. During the period 1933–43 there was an absence of competition due to the fact that prior to the 1933 election the two most important parties, the National Party and the South African Party, decided to form an election coalition. Together they won 136 out of 150 seats. They later merged as the United South African National Party (UP) and subsequently again dominated the 1938 election. The republican faction within the old National Party broke away and reestablished a purified National Party that only became a factor when it won the election in 1948 with a majority of seats, albeit with a minority of votes. A brief period of two-party competition between the 'new' National Party (NP) and the UP followed. After the 1958 election and until the 1994 election, the NP completely dominated the political scene in South Africa. From 1958 until the 1994 election the dominant party-system was a predominant-party system. The plurality election system contributed to the establishment of the NP as a predominant party for it was usually overrepresented in Parliament.

In each of the party subsystems there was also one party that dominated the political scene, with the result that these subsystems could also be regarded as predominant-party systems. Competition was further diminished due to the fact that homeland legislatures consisted of both elected and designated members with only Bophuthatswana, Gazankulu and KaNgwane having had a majority of elected members (SAIIR 1989/90: 475). In addition, opposition parties were often banned and 'military regimes' took over in Ciskei, Transkei and Venda.

Likewise, the quasi-party system again was overwhelmingly dominated by the ANC–SACP alliance.

Ideological Distance

Each of the 'party systems' was characterized by a lack of competition. Consequently, the ideological distance between the various political parties in each 'party system' is not that important, but becomes more important when the system as a whole is considered. Furthermore, the classic left–right division between the extremes of communism and conservatism was not always applicable.

Each 'party system' had its own ideological differences. Race was important in party ideology in the dominant party-system but it was subordinate to the republican ideal. Until the resolution of the republican ideal in 1961, there were, on the one hand, the Afrikaner nationalist and anti-imperialist republicans and, on the other hand, the pro-British imperialists and monarchists. Thereafter the ideological division was mainly between the pro-apartheid ideology and the liberal pro-integration ideology. Both sets of ideological differences reflected a basic divide between the Afrikaners' quest for self-determination vis-a-vis the possibility of political subordination. These ideological differences were troublesome in the history of South Africa but they did not result in the breakdown of the system. Thus the multiparty period of the dominant party-system portrayed, in Sartori's terms, a moderate pluralism that probably contributed to the development of a brief period of two-partyism in the dominant party-system. A capitalism–socialism divide, which was subordinate to the idea of self-determination, provides some clues to the present, for the NP ideology reflected strong socialist, though anti-communist, tendencies (see Kleynhans, 1987).

The party subsystems were again characterized by differences in opinion regarding their role in the apartheid system vis-a-vis their role in the liberation struggle. Ideological differences regarding the economy also existed but, with the exception of Inkatha Yenkululeko Yesizwe (Inkatha, reestablished 1975), were less pronounced. Inkatha opposed sanctions and was in favour of a market economy.

In the quasi-party system the most important differences centred around the place and role of whites after liberation. The ANC favoured non-racialism, while organizations like AZAPO had a pro-black standing and the PAC adopted an anti-settler (i.e. an anti-white) position. Ideological differences regarding the economy centred around various models of socialism and communism.

When the party system as a whole is considered, it is clear that race was an important factor. Though political parties were often classified on a left–right scale, this in reality reflected the various parties' position on racialism. Thus towards the end of the old system the left (AZAPO, PAC) was pro-black, the ANC and Democratic Party (and its predecessors) occupied the middle with its non-racial standing, the right was occupied by the pro-white parties with the NP as the most moderate followed by the less moderate Conservative Party (CP) and the Herstigte Nasionale Party (HNP). Both the left and the right, as well as the ANC showed socialist tendencies. The left and right also reflected conservative tendencies in their ideas on the preservation of a traditional past, i.e. Africanism (blacks) versus Afrikaner nationalism (whites).

Characteristics of Political Parties

It would appear as if political parties in the past were structured in terms of race and ethnicity. Party membership was, however, also influenced by the fact that only the white electorate was enfranchised, thus most political parties in the dominant party-system did not see the need to recruit members from the unenfranchised. The South African Communist Party was, at the time of its establishment, the only political party that recruited members from both the enfranchised and unenfranchised and which had a multiracial membership and executive. The Progressive Party (a predecessor of the Democratic Party) and the short-lived Liberal Party recruited limited members from other race groups. The Prohibition of Political Interference Act (Act no. 51 of 1968), adopted by Parliament, prohibited membership of 'mixed' political parties. Thus membership of a particular political party was limited to one race group only. The apparent racial and ethnic nature of political parties should therefore be scrutinized within its proper social and political context.

In the case of the dominant party-system the National Party was mainly, but not exclusively, supported by the Afrikaners, while the Democratic Party (DP, 1989) and its predecessors were mainly, but not exclusively, supported by the English-speaking whites. It was estimated that in the 1987 election 49.3 percent of English-speaking whites supported the National Party and that a further 5.9 percent supported the Conservative Party (Van Vuuren, 1987: 190). The NP was supported by 61.1 percent of Afrikaners.

Each party subsystem catered by law for a particular race group and among blacks usually for a particular ethnic group. In the 'independent' homelands there was no official prohibition of political parties having 'mixed' membership. Organizations in the quasi-party system focused mainly on the interests of the disenfranchised. The ANC and the SACP had 'mixed' membership in terms of race and ethnicity. In spite of its pro-black standing, the PAC also recruited members from the Coloured and Indian communities and even had, on occasion, a white member. Thus race was of less importance in the quasi-party system and even in some of the party subsystems than it was in the dominant party-system.

Only the NP and Inkatha had the membership and integrated organizational structure of a mass party. The fact that most of the important quasi-parties were banned played a role in their membership and organizational structure.

The party system was characterized by the absence of religious parties, but the Dutch Reformed Church (the dominant church among Afrikaners) was occasionally referred to as the 'National Party in prayer'. Politics within the NP was said to have been dominated by the Afrikaner Broederbond (a secret organized brotherhood founded in 1918). Membership of the Afrikaner Broederbond was restricted to Afrikaner Calvinists – active members of the Dutch Reformed Church and its two sister churches. Though the NP could not really be regarded as a truly religious party, church and party overlapped. Calvinistic religious principles therefore played an important role in the National Party (Bloomberg, 1990; Wilkens and Strydom, 1980).

There was also a lack of single-issue parties and those that were founded, like the Ecology Party, were either irrelevant or had only limited success. The only class-based party of real importance was the SACP.

Voter Volatility

Voter volatility was in the past seriously affected by legislation and in particular legislation that prevented political parties from recruiting members from other race groups. Voter volatility is thus mainly of importance in the dominant party-system. The changing support of the most important parties in this system is an indication that voter alignment was not fixed.

Table 3. Percentage of Votes Obtained by the National Party in Elections

Year	1915	1920	1921	1924	1929	1933	1938	1943	1948	1953
%	29.9	35.2	37.5	34.9	40.6	31.3	29.6	35.8	37.2	49.1
Year	1958	1961	1966	1970	1974	1977	1981	1987	1989	
%	55.2	46.2	57.8	54.6	55.1	65.0	57.7	52.5	48.0	

Sources: Compiled from data obtained in SAIRR, 1987/1988, 1988/89, 1989/90: 550; Schoeman, 1977; *Sunday Tribune*, 2 May 1981; Van Vuuren et al., 1987; Weide and Weide.

Table 3 provides an indication that there was a degree of voter volatility present in the dominant party-system. It could, however, be argued that Afrikaners mainly supported the National Party.

Change and Stability

The older political parties and quasi-parties were characterized by the fact that they did not only represent interests. They were also able to adapt to changing circumstances and demands (not only of the electorate but of the political system as a whole). The party system was able to channel, and when necessary, to contain the political forces operating in the political system.

This 'adapt-or-die' principle was an important factor in the transition to the new South Africa. Political parties were in fact vehicles of change. For this purpose important adjustments were often made to party ideology. This sometimes resulted in misinterpretations of election results. Thus what was often interpreted as a voter swing to the right, away from the NP, was in fact the product of voter fall-out due to the NP's ideological swing to the left.

The party system in the past was characterized by the fact that it was multifaceted and that its artificial nature was to a large extent the product of government intervention.

3. The South African Party System After April 1994

The previous era came to an end as a result of a number of changes that preceded the April 1994 election. The most important of these changes was the abolition of apartheid and everything it entailed, e.g. the repeal in 1985 of the Prohibition of Political Interference Act (Act no. 51 of 1968). Furthermore, there was the unbanning of the quasi-parties and their leaders; the extension of the franchise to all South Africans of 18 years and older; the interim constitution; and the adoption of a system of proportional representation. These changes would have an important impact on the party system. The various 'party systems' were now integrated. It was also now possible to use standard criteria in an analysis of the party system.

Political parties could now recruit members from all ethnic and race groups and could participate in an election that was open to all. Political parties like the NP, DP and Inkatha (now the Inkatha Freedom Party [IFP]) now recruited members from all race groups (the ANC already had a nonracial membership). It could therefore be expected that the party system would be affected by all these changes.

Studying the effect of the 1994 election on the party system is however not without problems. There were allegations of serious shortcomings in the election which could have influenced the outcome of the election. For purposes of this discussion it is accepted that the outcome was a true reflection of how the people voted in the election.

Voter Participation

For the non-whites the 1994 election was an *uhuru* (liberation) election. To most of them it was not only a symbol of their liberation but also of their acceptance as first-class citizens and of the end to their second-class status of

Table 4. Estimated Composition and Turnout of the Electorate in Terms of
Race

Race	Number of Voters (Millions)	% of Electorate	Number that Voted (Millions)	% that Voted
Blacks	16.6	73	14.4	86.7
Whites	3.4	15	2.9	85.3
Coloureds	2.0	9	1.8	90.0
Indians	0.7	3	0.6	85.7
TOTAL	22.7	100	19.7	86.0

Source: Compiled from data published in Reynolds, 1994: chapter 11.

the past. It was therefore anticipated that they would turn out in large
numbers on election day even though the election was boycotted by
AZAPO (on the left) and very nearly so by the IFP.

For whites it was the first time that they had to participate in a nonracial
election that would negatively affect their dominant position of the past. It
is therefore not that surprising that the election was boycotted by organizations on the right, e.g. the Conservative Party, the Herstigte Nasionale Party
and other smaller parties.

The independent electoral commission had estimated the number of
eligible voters at 22.7 million (Reynolds, 1994). Table 4 provides detail on
the estimated composition of the electorate.

Voter participation was therefore high among all race groups. Voter
participation was also consistently high in all the provinces (Table 5).

The number of spoilt ballots was low and also consistently low for all the
provinces. This could be an indication that voters had a responsible attitude
towards participation in the election.

Table 5. Voter Participation in the Provinces

Province	% that Voted	% of Ballots Spoilt
Northern Transvaal	84	0.7
Eastern Transvaal	85	0.9
Gauteng (PWV)	86	0.6
North West	89	1.2
Orange Free State	83	0.8
KwaZulu-Natal	80	1.0
Eastern Cape	92	0.5
Northern Cape	92	0.8
Western Cape	87	0.5
National	86	1.0

Source: Compiled from data obtained in Reynolds, 1994: chapter 11.

Number of Political Parties

The players in the party system changed dramatically. Not only was there an increase in political parties that participated in elections for Parliament, but there was also a significant number of newcomers to the political scene, while a number of old ones disappeared. Not all these political parties (old or new) were successful. The relevance of a substantial number of political parties to the party system should be questioned.

The ANC and PAC are two former quasi-parties that are now registered as political parties. The ANC formed a pre-election alliance with the Congress of South African Trade Unions (COSATU) and the SACP. Most of the former political parties in the subsystems either disappeared from the scene or were absorbed by the larger parties and particularly by the ANC. The IFP is the only former subsystem party that became a factor on the national level and provincial level. The Dikankwetla Party of QwaQwa is the only other former subsystem party that managed to win a substantial number of votes on the provincial level, but no seats. Of the former all-white parties, only the NP and the DP participated in the election. The Freedom Front (FF) and the African Christian Democratic Party (ACDP) were the only newcomers that won seats both on the national and on the provincial level. The Minority Front (MF) was the only other newcomer that was able to win a seat on the provincial level (KwaZulu-Natal). There were 12 other newcomers that participated on the national level in the election but together secured less than 1 percent of the vote.

Table 6 provides a summary of the strength in terms of seats of the various parties that were able to win seats.

The ANC and the NP were the only parties that won seats in all nine provincial legislatures.

Any conclusions on the relevance of these political parties, including those that failed to win any seats, would be premature. Only the ANC and NP have a long history of political mobilization of the masses on a national scale. The majority of new political parties were founded shortly before election day and had leaders who were unknown to the public. The acceptance of a system of proportional representation probably contributed to an increase in the number of political parties.

Competition

On the national level the ANC polled 62.65 percent of the votes, three times that of its nearest rival, the NP, with 20.39 percent, and close to six times that of the IFP (second runner-up) with 10.54 percent (Reynolds, 1994: 183). Even though the constitution makes provision for a consociational executive, the presence of the other political parties in the cabinet can be afforded

Table 6. Strength of Political Parties in Terms of Seats Won

	ANC	NP	IFP	FF	DP	PAC	ACDP	MF
National Parliament	252	82	43	9	7	5	2	–
Northern Transvaal	38	1	–	1	–	–	–	–
Eastern Transvaal	25	3	–	2	–	–	–	–
Gauteng	50	21	3	5	5	1	1	–
North West	26	3	–	1	–	–	–	–
Free State	24	4	–	2	–	–	–	–
KwaZulu–Natal	26	9	41	–	2	1	1	1
Eastern Cape	48	6	–	–	1	1	–	–
Northern Cape	15	12	–	2	1	–	–	–
Western Cape	14	23	–	1	3	–	1	–

Source: Compiled from data obtained in Reynolds, 1994.

by the ANC. It is only in two provinces (Western Cape and KwaZulu-Natal) that the ANC is not the ruling party. In Northern Cape it is the ruling party, but it lacks a majority in the provincial legislature. The fact that federalism is not well developed in South Africa increases the possibility that central government (thus the ANC) may dominate the provinces.

All things considered, the present party system shows characteristics of a predominant-party system but there are also warning signs of the ANC being a hegemonic party in Sartori's terms (1976: 230–38).

Ideological Distance

Little has changed in the ideological distance of the various political parties except for the fact that the NP has officially denounced its apartheid ideology.

Race is still a factor among the left (black – AZAPO and PAC) and the right (white – FF, CP and HNP). The middle ground is occupied by the nonracial ANC, NP, IFP, DP and ACDP.

The ANC is in alliance with COSATU and the SACP, but manages to present a reformed socialist face to the world. When the occasion demands, it is still able to fall back on more conventional communist rhetoric. Though often forced to adopt a more capitalist standing, the ANC's basic thinking about social issues is still influenced by socialist principles.

Though the ideological distance between the extremes is great, the relative strength of these political parties appears to be weak at present and therefore will not have a major effect on the party system.

Characteristics of Political Parties

Except for the left and the right, political parties appear to be less structured in terms of race than in the past.

Though an estimated 94 percent of the ANC's votes came from blacks (i.e. 80 percent of the black vote), it was estimated that it secured 27.8 percent of the Coloured vote, 25 percent of the Indian vote and 1.7 percent of the white vote (Reynolds, 1994).

An estimated 49 percent of the NP's votes came from whites (65 percent of the white vote). In spite of its apartheid stigma, the National Party managed to secure 66.7 percent of the Coloured vote, 3.5 percent of the black vote and 50 percent of the Indian vote (calculated from Reynolds, 1994: chapter 11).

The party system is now characterized by the presence of political parties that represent particular interests but most of these have failed in the political market. Luso-South African Party campaigned for the interests of the Portuguese in South Africa, and the Minority Front for the minorities (but its support came mainly from the Indians). It is also the first time that true religious parties entered the political arena. The ACDP represents Christian principles. At the provincial level in the Western Cape two parties represented Muslim interests, namely the African Muslim Party and the Islamic Party. Had the latter two entered into an election alliance, it would have secured one seat in the provincial legislature (Reynolds, 1994: 200). The newly formed Green Party of South Africa participated in the Western Cape, but was unable to win a seat in the provincial legislature. There were also two parties that represented the interests of women only, but they also failed in the political market.

The organizational structure of the political parties at grassroots level could improve. The list system of proportional representation adopted in the constitution does not require a well-developed organizational structure at grassroots level. Political parties have also not yet succeeded in establishing a well-integrated organizational structure among their new recruits, partly due to the fact that there is no immediate need to do so.

The political parties that were able to adapt to the changing needs of the time survived the election, namely the ANC, NP, IFP and to a certain extent the Freedom Front (FF) which canvassed, at rather short notice, the vote on the right.

The PAC underestimated the needs of non-whites within a fast-changing and modernizing society in a global village. The PAC is *inter alia* opposed to the idea of private ownership of land, as in the apartheid era where non-whites were denied the right to own land. Non-whites were however exposed to the advantages of land ownership. The PAC learnt the hard way that the future cannot be lived in the past.

The DP has failed to shed its upper-class and elitist image. There has been little growth over the past number of years in potential members. There are also few non-whites who fit the DP's image. An increase in wealth could however provide additional potential members.

4. The South African Party System in the Future

The main question is whether the party system will follow the trends in Europe or whether it will follow in the footsteps of party systems in Africa. One could only speculate about the possibilities. In Europe there is a decline in voter participation and an increase in voter volatility, while in Africa, the rule often is one-party systems or military regimes.

The possibility exists that a decline in voter participation could strengthen the role of the dominant party. Thus for South Africa to develop into a proper multiparty system would require continued high levels of voter participation and voter volatility and an increase in the number of effective political parties. This would necessitate improved organizational structures of political parties at grassroots level.

There has been speculation about the possible breakup of the ANC-SACP-COSATU alliance. A breakup could level the playing field of the various political parties but is unlikely to have a major impact on the party system. Should the ANC fail to obtain a majority, the possibility of a coalition with the SACP and COSATU still exists. A substantial number of ANC officials are also members of the SACP.

The possibility exists that the present party system could in future develop into a multiparty system. If it does, the chances are that it will develop into polarized pluralism. The ideological differences would in all probability still exist and the 1994 election has shown that there is still an important ideological mentality, especially among the political parties on the left and the right. Alternatively, it could develop into a one-party system with all its negative implications.

5. Conclusion

South Africa's party system was in the past multifaceted. This was a consequence of legislation that determined the place and role of voters and political parties. Consequently, in an analysis of the party system, provision has to be made for the abnormal political context in which voters and political parties operated.

At present the party system is undergoing a process of normalization. The political forces are now finding their proper place and role in the political system, but it will still take some time to determine in what direction these forces will change the South African party system.

REFERENCES

Bloomberg, C. (1990) *Christian-Nationalism and the Rise of the Afrikaner Broederbond in South Africa, 1918–1948*, ed. Saul Dubow. London: Macmillan.

Daalder, H. and P. Mair (eds) (1983) *Western European Party Systems*. London: Sage.

Faure, A. M., D. J. Kriek, G. S. Labuschagne, A. du P. Louw and A. J. Venter (eds) (1988) *Suid-Afrika en die Demokrasie*. Pinetown: Owen Burgess.

Joyce, P. (1989) *The South African Family Encyclopaedia*. Cape Town: Struik.

Kleynhans, W. A. (1987) *South African General Election Manifestos 1910–1981*. Pretoria: University of South Africa.

Lane, J. E. and S. O. Ersson (1994) *Politics and Society in Western Europe*. London: Sage.

Lijphart, A. (1994) *Electoral Systems and Party Systems: A Study of Twenty-seven Democracies, 1945–1990*. New York: Oxford University Press.

Mair, P. and G. Smith (eds) (1990) *Understanding Party System Change in Western Europe*. London: Frank Cass.

Rae, D. (1971) *The Political Consequences of Electoral Laws*, 2nd edn. New Haven, CT: Yale University Press.

Reynolds A. (ed.) (1994) *Election '94 South Africa: The Campaigns, Results and Future Prospects*. Claremont, RSA: David Philip.

Robertson, D. (1976) *A Theory of Party Competition*. London: John Wiley.

Sartori, G. (1976) *Parties and Party Systems: A Framework for Analysis*. Cambridge: Cambridge University Press.

Sartori, G. (1994) *Comparative Constitutional Engineering: An Inquiry into Structures, Incentives and Outcomes*. London: Macmillan.

Schoeman, B. M. (1977) *Parlementere Verkiesings in Suid-Afrika 1910–1976*. Pretoria: Aktuele Publikasies.

South African Institute of Race Relations (SAIRR) (1988) *Race Relations Survey 1987/88*. Johannesburg: SAIRR.

South African Institute of Race Relations (1989) *Race Relations Survey 1988/89*. Johannesburg: SAIRR.

South African Institute of Race Relations (1990) *Race Relations Survey 1989/90*. Johannesburg: SAIRR.

South African Institute of Race Relations (1992) *Race Relations Survey 1991/92*. Johannesburg: SAIRR.

South African Institute of Race Relations (1993) *Race Relations Survey 1992/93*. Johannesburg: SAIRR.

Thompson, L. and A. Prior (1982) *South African Politics*. New Haven, CT: Yale University Press.

Van Vuuren, D. J., J. Latakgomo, H. C. Marais and L. Schlemmer (eds) (1987) *South African Election 1987*. Pinetown: Owen Burgess.

Weide, R. and S. Weide (undated) *Die Volledige Verkiesingsuitslae van Suid-Afrika 1910–1986*. Pretoria: Weide & Kie.

Wilkens, I. and H. Strydom (1980) *The Super-Afrikaners*. Johannesburg: Jonathan Ball.

8. SOUTH AFRICA'S CHANGING EXTERNAL RELATIONS

Marie Muller

Introduction

The external or foreign relations of any country may be conceptualized as the product of the interaction between its foreign policy and the foreign policies of the other members of the community of states. Foreign policy can be said to be caused by the perceptions and values of the decision-makers (Carlsnaes, 1986: 108). These perceptions and values are, in turn, caused by the organizational setting and objective conditions in which they are formed (Carlsnaes, 1993). Given the same decision-makers and the slow pace of change to which both the organizational setting and objective conditions are normally subject, foreign policies are therefore in a sense not very suscepti-ble to rapid change. This argument could also explain the relative continuity often characterizing the foreign relations of a particular state. The sudden and radical changes are really the exception rather than the rule, which in itself renders a case of sudden and radical change interesting, both histor-ically and theoretically.

Given a new set (or a partially new set) of decision-makers and sudden and sharp changes in many aspects of both the organizational setting and objective conditions, foreign policy is, according to the above conceptualiza-tion, bound to be influenced substantially. This also describes the South African case over the past number of years. Assuming that it is hardly likely that the international system will in the foreseeable future again undergo comparable fundamental change, it would seem, however, as though South African international relations could soon stabilize more or less. It has to be assumed that the African National Congress (ANC) will continue to dominate the new regime. There are, however, a number of areas where important changes can still be anticipated, mainly due to the fact that the new regime has in all likelihood not yet fully translated all its intentions and inclinations into policies and has certainly not implemented all its policies. Perhaps more interesting even is the fact that it seems to be as yet undecided about some of these – relations with the two Chinas is an excellent case in point. The country is still finding its new identity and others within the community of states have not yet fully adapted to the new South Africa either. For these and other reasons, South African foreign relations are changing, not changed.

Change in South African Foreign Relations

South African foreign relations used to be shaped by one overriding theme: its internal policy of apartheid.[1] From the South African side this implied that in foreign affairs everything was judged according to how it would affect the country's ability to defend itself against opposition to its domestic policy. From the international side any positive contribution South Africa could make in the international arena was usually disregarded in favour of attempting to convince or force the government of the day to change its ways. The South African situation was often described as a special case of colonialism and universally condemned as an institutionalized form of racism. The dominance of this one theme meant that other salient themes in post-Second World War international affairs, such as the North–South debate, human rights, migration and refugees, nuclear nonproliferation, disarmament and arms control, and the environment, were overshadowed to the extent that they virtually 'disappeared' from South African foreign relations. The only exception was the East–West divide or the Cold War,

---

1. It is perhaps worth noting, at this point, a few salient aspects of South Africa's participation in world politics. The Union of South Africa was formed in 1910, with no real concomitant change in the constitutional status of the constituting four British territories, Natal, the Cape Colony, the Orange Free State and the Transvaal (the latter two were formerly independent Boer republics, before they were annexed by the British in 1900 [Ballinger, 1969; Marais, 1991]). As a result of the Balfour Declaration of 1926, the Union of South Africa became an independent state and formally a participant in world politics. In 1948 the Nationalist Party came to power and pursued domestic policies which contrasted sharply with the *direction* in which international public opinion was moving in reaction to the racist excesses of Nazi Germany during the Second World War. As international politics changed more and more after the Second World War, the schism between South Africa's internal policies and the ways in which they were implemented, and international thought on race and self-determination, gradually increased, making it progressively more and more difficult for South Africa to effectively participate in international affairs.

which featured in a complex interaction with considerations of decolonization and racism, as these were captured in the policy of apartheid and
perceptions thereof. Despite the old South African government's best
efforts to convince the West that Cold War considerations should overshadow any dislike of its 'misunderstood' domestic policy (which was made
out not to be racist and, with regard to the independent homelands, an
alternative form of decolonization), and despite some rather resilient historical and economically based ties, South Africa was gradually isolated from
most of the world. The legitimacy of the South African government per se
was in contention and by 1989 South Africa was one of the most isolated
states recorded in modern times (Geldenhuys, 1990: 665–9). At the same
time, however, and for the same reasons, South Africa was increasingly
being penetrated and made subject to intervention by various other states
(Geldenhuys, 1989).

Due mainly to historic and ideological reasons, variations in South
Africa's relations with the outside world occurred largely along geographic
lines. As a consequence South African foreign relations were often viewed
by practitioners and observers, and consequently dealt with in scholarly
work, through a geographically defined lens. As the Department of Foreign
Affairs developed from 1945 onwards, it inclined more and more to being
organized along geographic lines (Muller, 1989) and much scientific research and many scholarly publications on the topic of South African
foreign policy and international relations used the same ordering principle.
South African policies towards southern Africa, Africa, western Europe,
North America, Latin America, the Middle East, the rest of Asia, central
and eastern Europe, Australia and New Zealand were discussed and contrasted. South African relations with each of these geographical regions
were analysed within the framework of how the relations were (negatively)
affected by the domestic policy of apartheid. Very seldom did one find much
in the way of a more diversified thematic treatment of South African foreign
policy or relations. The great issues of international politics after decolonization were simply overshadowed by the effect of South Africa's internal
policies. The most pervading change in South African foreign policy and
thinking on South African international relations has occurred in this
respect.

It no longer makes the same sense to think primarily in terms of geographic divisions. This is illustrated by the fact that as the South African
Department of Foreign Affairs is being reorganized, the pendulum seems to
be swinging in the direction of a more issue-based ordering principle
(Muller, 1996 [forthcoming]). Debates and research occur along the lines of
the great international political issues and, to a large extent, scholars have
become impatient with a geographic delimitation when dealing with South
African foreign relations and policy. For the first time since the Second

World War South Africa has really joined the various dialogues making up the substance of international politics. The international pariah of old, who had a voice only to defend its domestic policies and to try to gain or regain the support or tolerance of the non-communist world for these, has re-emerged into the international community with a voice on most of the great issues. It would be useful, therefore, to deal with the changes in South African foreign relations since 1990 in terms of two ordering principles: first, and as a fitting conclusion to the old era, change in South African foreign relations is traced along geographical lines; and, second, changes with regard to the great issues of contemporary international politics are traced. The former is an actor-oriented approach to analysing South African foreign relations, and the latter an issue-oriented approach.

An Actor-oriented Approach

Each of the regions listed is of course more than a mere geographic grouping. In the past in particular, each region represented a grouping of individual states with which South African relations had some character-istics in common. Thus South Africa's relations with individual countries in southern Africa, Africa, western Europe, North America, Latin America, the Middle East, the rest of Asia, central and eastern Europe, Australia and New Zealand, could be more or less typified, without completely disallow-ing for exceptions and anomalies. This is a useful shorthand when foreign relations have to be sketched in very broad outline. The sequence in which the various regions was listed is not purely coincidental either, as the analysis below makes clear. Reference was made before to the fact that by 1989 South Africa had been thoroughly isolated, penetrated *and* made subject to intervention.[2] These forms of engagement and disengagement between states may be usefully employed in further characterizing South African foreign relations.

If the list of actors is to be complete, one should add international institutions. This is not to imply that international institutions have reached a status equal to that of states as actors in international politics, but rather

---

2. Geldenhuys (1989: 272–3) defines these terms as follows: *isolation* is a form of disengage-ment and entails curtailing or severing existing ties and not establishing any new links; *penetration* entails maintaining a 'presence', whether diplomatic, economic, military or socio-cultural, and is generally desired, accepted or acquiesced in; *intervention* is a form of coercive and thus unwelcome foreign involvement, directed at the government in the first instance. A fourth phenomenon eventually also became relevant to the South African situation: *mediation* is an attempt by a foreign party (or parties) to assist the government and its domestic or external opponents to resolve their conflicts through negotiations.

that a country's position in such institutions or, put differently, its multi-lateral relations in the context of international organizations, gives a view of its external relations which cannot be obtained through analyses of various bilateral relationships only. In fact, due to the very important role that multilateral diplomacy played in forcing change in South Africa, the change regarding South Africa's position in most of these forums represents a very sharp break with the past (Hamill and Spence, 1993/94: 110). This involves both global and regional institutions.

Bilateral relations. By 1990 South Africa's relationship with its immediate neighbours in *southern Africa* could be broadly characterized as one of both dependence (of the subregion on South Africa) and conflict, either open or clandestine. A power configuration had developed which placed South Africa's neighbours largely at its mercy, both economically and militarily. This implied that, although they pleaded for and supported the isolation of South Africa through sanctions and disinvestment, they themselves could not hope to contribute. The states of southern Africa opposed South Africa's internal policies and wanted to see an end to them. However, in a sense they were kept hostage due to their poor power position relative to South Africa (Grundy, 1973). They did, of course, occupy the moral high ground and in many instances commanded the greatest influence in inter-national politics (Kriek, 1992). They had obtained not only diplomatic, but also material support from one or more outside powers, which in some cases included actual military support. South Africa resisted, using both overt and covert moves (Jaster, 1988) and became embroiled in a conventional war in Angola. If anything, in its relations with southern Africa, South Africa was the one to practise penetration and intervention, and even, on occasion, isolation (Grundy, 1973; Jaster, 1988).

   Two factors effected an immediate change in South African relations with its neighbours in southern Africa: the political changes which occurred within the communist bloc and more specifically the Soviet Union around 1989, and subsequently and partially as a consequence of the former, the start of negotiations between the South African government and its do-mestic political opponents (Benjamin and Gregory, 1992). The first tangible symptom of a changed situation was the peaceful settlement of the Namibian dispute and the granting of independence to this territory (21 March 1990), over which South Africa had been in conflict, in one form or another, since the end of the Second World War (Pitswane, 1992; Sar-akinsky, 1992). South Africa no longer felt threatened by 'World Commu-nism'. This hailed an immediate improvement in relations with southern Africa and contributed meaningfully to the negotiation process in South Africa itself (Sarakinsky, 1992: 137–8). Improved relations in southern Africa eventually led, after the April 1994 elections, to an extension of

South Africa's formal diplomatic relations with its neighbours,[3] and manifested in South Africa becoming a member of important regional economic
groupings such as the Southern African Development Community
(SADC), to which reference is made below. The culmination of internal
political change also implied the reincorporation into South Africa of the
so-called 'independent' homelands, Bophuthatswana, Ciskei, Transkei and
Venda, which had never been recognized by the international community
(Cilliers, 1993/94; Donaldson et al., 1992).

All of the above changes may be regarded as positive developments for
the region. However, this does not imply that South Africa's relations with
southern Africa are now entirely unproblematic. Apart from some continuities in relations, which will be referred to below and which could prove
to be problematic, there are also some negative changes to be noted. These
relate mainly to the very fact that political dividing lines have been removed, that borders have become much more porous, and that as a
consequence, various new 'security' problems have come to the fore. The
following may be cited as problems which arose or were amplified under the
new set of circumstances, and may further develop into serious sources of
tension and conflict in the region: the handling of refugees and the influx of
large numbers of illegal migrants; cross-border vehicle theft and cattle
rustling; arms and drug smuggling; contraband and the violation of customs
regulations; environmental degradation and the availability of water; the
spread of human, animal and plant diseases, including AIDS; and ethnic
conflict (Mills, 1995; Muller, 1993; Solomon, 1993; Van Aardt, 1994, 1996
[forthcoming]). The new South African government does, however, bear a
great burden of gratitude towards the southern African region for support
to the liberation struggle. The southern African states have great expectations as to what the new South Africa can and will do for the region. For the
moment at least, official relations between South Africa and its neighbours
are very cordial and *not* characterized by any 'unhealthy' forms of isolation,
penetration or intervention.

South Africa never really had substantial direct and open relations with
Africa beyond southern Africa, until the internal political changes of
1990–94. The old South African government tried to project itself as the
natural link between the West and Africa and often stressed that it desired
'leadership through service' in its relations with Africa. Great emphasis was
placed on functional areas, such as science and technology. However, most

---

3. South Africa had previously maintained formal diplomatic relations only with Malawi
and the four independent homelands. In neighbouring countries such as Lesotho, Mozambique, Swaziland and Zimbabwe, South Africa had trade missions, which actually performed some diplomatic functions as well (Muller, 1989: 262–4). The nondiplomatic status of
these ties served to underline the presence of a political conflict situation.

African states would have nothing of formal or open relations with South Africa as long as the latter's internal policies persisted (Grundy, 1973; Jaster, 1988; Nolutshungu, 1975). This did not mean that considerable trade did not take place between South Africa and the continent, that covert cooperation in some areas did not happen, or that South Africa did not have a few rather short-lived successes on the continent (Barber and Barratt, 1990: 146–50).[4] However, the comprehensive normalization of South African relations with the African continent would only come once it was clear that apartheid would disappear. Africa had succeeded in isolating South Africa from the continent fairly effectively and in exerting considerable pressure on the West, in particular, to force South Africa to change.

The speed of the change in relations was in the end remarkable, as many African countries did not wait for a new government before upgrading formal relations. By the end of 1993 South Africa had already established permanent missions in a number of African countries beyond Southern Africa (*Department of Foreign Affairs List*, October 1993). Trade with Africa increased immediately and dramatically, as did tourism, scientific and technological links (Esterhuysen et al., 1994: 64–75). It was clear that expectations were high as to what the 'integration' of South Africa into the life of the continent would mean.

'However welcome a democratic South Africa may be, nonetheless, it is a potential rival as well as a collaborator for the states to the north' (Clapham, 1994: 50). The possible future impact of this fact is not yet clear. What has already become clear, however, is the attractiveness of South Africa to many citizens from the north. Problems similar to those listed, above, with regard to southern Africa, may also be detected as part of the changed relations between South Africa and the rest of the continent. Again, the future negative effect of these developments, and in particular of migration, remains to be seen. At present there is great emphasis on South Africa as a part of Africa and on Africa as the natural political home to South Africa. Possible peacemaking and peacekeeping roles for South Africa are much debated and South Africa is championed as a natural leader in Africa. So far the South African government response to fulfilling such roles has been cautious. With isolation at an end, intervention has not taken its place.

South Africa had substantial economic and cultural ties with *western Europe*, including Britain, even at the height of isolation. These were often ascribed to historical and cultural ties. The fact is that western European states were also some of the most active penetrating and even intervening states as well (Geldenhuys, 1989). The extent to which western European states utilized isolation, penetration and intervention in order to effect

---

4. Geldenhuys (1989: 283) reported that around 1985 South Africa traded with 49 of the 51 African states.

change in South Africa varied somewhat. Three categories of west European states could be differentiated in this regard. First, Britain, France and (West) Germany, and less obviously so, Austria, Switzerland, Luxembourg and Belgium, maintained a relatively cautious position in the international campaign against South Africa until a late stage. South Africa had strong economic ties with Britain, West Germany and France, which were never entirely dismantled by the sanctions movement. Diplomatic relations were maintained, though Belgium and West Germany suspended their cultural accords with South Africa (Geldenhuys, 1989: 285). Second, and in contrast, the Netherlands and the Scandinavian countries were more openly critical of the South African government. Economic considerations did not play as prominent a role in these cases. The Netherlands, culturally closest to the Afrikaner, was very careful to dissociate itself from the South African government, which was Afrikaner-dominated. Diplomatic ties were maintained, but not cultural ties (Geldenhuys, 1989: 285). Some Scandinavian countries actually discontinued diplomatic relations (Denmark and Norway – Geldenhuys, 1990: 164), and most gave significant support to the anti-apartheid movement and the ANC. Third, and somewhat in the middle of the spectrum, were countries such as Italy, Greece and Spain. Italy had fairly extensive economic relations with South Africa, maintained diplomatic relations, but was fairly critical towards the South African government. Greece and Spain, which had fewer and less established ties with South Africa, were perhaps less openly critical. Portugal presented a special case; having been in 'the same political boat' as South Africa before its revolution of 1974, it made a decisive break with the latter after 1974. Diplomatic relations were maintained, however. Like Greece, many of Portugal's nationals had settled in South Africa.

The above illustrates that all that was really needed, when the longed-for political change occurred in South Africa, was for western European states to abolish sanctions and adopt a laissez-faire approach to the normalization of political and economic relations. However, the fact that western Europe had at more or less the same time itself undergone some momentous changes, meant that this 'minimalist approach' was not adopted (Holland, 1996 [forthcoming]). The former West and East Germany had been re-united in late 1990, and at the end of 1991 the Maastricht Treaty was adopted. These two developments greatly accelerated the transformation of the European Community – and therefore most of western Europe – into a single foreign policy actor (Soetendorp, 1994: 103). Instead of the 'minimalist approach', South Africa was selected as one of the first five 'joint actions' of the new European Union's (EU) Common Foreign and Security Policy (CFSP) launched in November 1993. This 'heightened the attention given to external relations with South Africa, but also made those relations subject to the difficulties, novelty and internal pressures of creating common joint actions' (Holland, 1996 [forthcoming]). Bilateral relations with western European countries would not cease (Pfetsch, 1994: 120), but South African relations with the region in the 1990s and beyond can probably best be dealt with in the context of the EU. This is again referred to below under the heading of South Africa's relations with regional organizations.

North America, and in particular the USA, was very active with regard to the penetration of and intervention in South Africa. At the same time, however, it was very active in the effort to isolate the country by means of disinvestment and sanctions (Geldenhuys, 1989: 282–5). The USA was also in the forefront of enforcing the arms embargo against South Africa. In spite of or perhaps because of its active role in bringing about change in South Africa,[5] the USA maintained engagement in South Africa throughout and this remains true today. South African and US foreign policies had a very important element in common: anti-communism (Landsberg and De Coning, 1995: 1).

The end of the Cold War and the beginning of the process that eradicated apartheid enabled the USA, from 1990 onwards, to play an energetic role in supporting the transition, both economically and politically (Landsberg and De Coning, 1995: 1). Sanctions were lifted (later than in the case of some European states – Grundy, 1996 [forthcoming]) and apart from Egypt, South Africa became the largest recipient of US aid in Africa (Landsberg and De Coning, 1995: 23). The African-American lobby remained an important one in the USA regarding South Africa. However, business, security and other interests are relevant too, and South Africa stands to benefit much more from direct foreign investment, coupled with extensive trade, than from aid (Landsberg and De Coning, 1995: 24–5). It is clear that economics plays an important part in the new relationship between South Africa and the USA (Grundy, 1996 [forthcoming]). However, there are some problem areas.

American enthusiasm for its continued relationship with South Africa depends to a large extent on two factors: South Africa's ability to realize hopes that it will act as a force for regional stability and whether it will remain inviting to investors and/or traders (Landsberg and De Coning, 1995: 29). There are also other factors affecting the relationship. There seems to be some suspicion of the ANC among more conservative groups in the USA – and the Republicans currently have control of both Houses of Congress (Grundy, 1996 [forthcoming]). The US government will want South African cooperation on issues such as the environment, global trade, nuclear nonproliferation, and 'promoting (or exporting) democracy' (Landsberg and De Coning, 1995: 28). From the South African side there is

---

5. It is, of course, possible to interpret United States 'engagement' in South Africa before the transition in different ways (see, for example, Vale [1994]).

some sensitivity within the ANC constituency about too close a relationship with Washington, and the controversy surrounding the 'pariah' states of Cuba, Libya and the Sudan could prompt tension between South Africa and the USA (Landsberg and De Coning, 1995: 26; Grundy, 1996 [forthcoming]). The ANC views such countries as friends who stood by it during its struggle against apartheid, and established full diplomatic relations with Cuba immediately after the inauguration of President Mandela in May 1994 (*The Star*, 26 September 1994).

Before 1990 *Latin American* relations with South Africa were in fact characterized by a good measure of variety and variability. At one end of the spectrum could be found a country like Cuba, which constituted the only significant military threat that the South African state had faced for 45 years and which, at the height of the Angolan confrontation, had some 50,000 men just across the Namibian border, who were involved in a number of clashes with the South African Defence Force (Roelofse-Campbell, 1993: 105). At the other end were to be found countries like Chile, which, during the military government, maintained close diplomatic, cultural and military relations with South Africa, and Paraguay, which, in the days of South African isolation, was one of the few countries willing to host visits by South African heads of state and government (Roelofse-Campbell, 1993: 112–13). Between these extremes could be found countries such as Mexico (which broke off consular relations with South Africa in 1973 and was quite outspoken against the old South African government), Peru (with which limited relations were maintained during the period of isolation), Uruguay (which never severed diplomatic relations with South Africa, but considerably scaled down ties) and Argentina (which broke off diplomatic relations with South Africa in 1986, restored them in 1989, and which was rumoured to have received covert support from South Africa during the 1982 Falklands War, but of which no concrete evidence ever emerged) (Roelofse-Campbell, 1993: 111–14). Brazil was a particularly interesting case and not easy to fit into the scheme of things. Its foreign policy also underwent some radical changes. Brazil was among the first countries to decry the apartheid system, while at the same time upholding a strictly noninterventionist line (Roelofse-Campbell, 1993: 108). 'From the 1960s onwards, the Brazilian government maintained ambiguous relations with South Africa, treading carefully on the political front whilst at the same time fostering trade to an ever increasing degree, Brazil being since then the largest trade partner South Africa has in the whole of Latin America' (Roelofse-Campbell, 1993: 108–9). From the South African side, early and more or less consistent attempts were made to foster relations with (noncommunist) Latin American countries willing to do so.

With political change in South Africa came an immediate normalization of relations with most of Latin America. With the coming to power of an

ANC-led government came friendship with such countries as Cuba, as referred to above. With talk of a South Atlantic Rim, a loose economic area to benefit all the countries concerned (Roelofse-Campbell, 1993: 117), came more possibilities regarding the structuring of relationships between South Africa and its neighbours across the Atlantic in Latin America.

The *Middle East* may be taken to embrace the area east of Suez up to Iran, but excluding Turkey (Dadoo, 1996 [forthcoming]). For purposes of this discussion the *Arab* states of *North Africa* (Algeria, Egypt, Libya, Morocco, Sudan and Tunisia) may also be included. Similar to its relationship with Africa, South Africa never really had substantial direct and open relations with most of these countries until the internal political changes of 1990–94. This did not mean that there was little going on at the covert level (Dadoo, 1996 [forthcoming]). Covert contact excluded, the Middle Eastern and Arab countries generally adopted a very strong anti-South African stance and gave support to the liberation movements (Dadoo, 1996 [forthcoming]). The exceptions were Israel and for a time Lebanon and Iran.

Israel and South Africa had a long-standing – dating back to 1953, when the South African Nationalist prime minister was the first head of government to visit the new state of Israel (Cockram, 1979: 55) – and interesting relationship. Much has been written and speculated about it over the years, and military and nuclear cooperation were strongly rumoured (Cockram, 1979: 55–62; Dadoo, 1996 [forthcoming]; Kahana, 1990; Reiss, 1995: 25–6). The relationship, especially from the Israel side, was however subject to contradictory pulls: Israel did not want to alienate Africa by associating with South Africa too openly (Kahana, 1990). However, a variety of formal, open and more informal and covert links persisted (Dadoo, 1996 [forthcoming]).

In 1954 Lebanon became the second Middle East country to forge diplomatic links with South Africa with the primary objective of 'safeguarding the old strong links with the Lebanese community' in the country (Dadoo, 1996 [forthcoming]). Direct relations were severed in the 1970s on the recommendation of the Arab League. Some indirect links were, however, maintained, and in spite of sanctions, bilateral trade occurred (Dadoo, 1996 [forthcoming]).

South Africa and Iran, under the Shah, forged a variety of links, including diplomatic relations. As with Israel, Iran's policies of westernization and anti-communism played an important role in the development of relations with South Africa (Dadoo, 1996 [forthcoming]). Until the overthrow of the Shah in 1979, when all direct relations came to an end, almost 90 percent of South African oil imports came from Iran (Barber and Barratt, 1990: 177).

With political change in South Africa came a radical change in relations with the Middle East and the Arab states. Support for the liberation movements and a religious bond between these countries, and an influential

(Muslim) segment of the new South African government, played an important role in this regard, though economic considerations were also evident (Dadoo, 1996 [forthcoming]). From 1991 onwards (Morocco) diplomatic relations were established with Algeria, Egypt, Sudan, Tunisia, Bahrain (1993); Iran, Jordan, Kuwait, Lebanon, Libya, United Arab Emirates, Qatar (1994); and Iraq, Saudi Arabia, Palestine, Mauritania (1995) (Dadoo, 1996 [forthcoming]). Formal trade relations were established with Oman in 1994. A wide variety of relations now exist between South Africa and the Middle East and the Arab states of North Africa. Formal relations with some of these (such as Morocco) are contentious on the grounds of human rights and self-determination, and others (with Libya, Sudan, Iraq) may complicate relations with the USA to some extent (FGD and CPS, 1995). As a result of vastly improved relations with the Arab countries, relations between South Africa and Israel have become a little less cordial. South Africa has, of course, also declined in importance as a market for Israeli military technology (Dadoo (1996) [forthcoming]).

South Africa's relations with *East Asia* have always been dominated by trade, and this continues to be the case (Carim, 1994: 21; Jones, 1994: 15; Kobayashi, 1994). This applies particularly to such countries as Japan and Singapore. India represents a rather special case, as do the two Chinas.

Though Japan did, eventually, institute some sanctions against South Africa, continued trade relations were made possible by Japan's principle of the separation of economics and politics, *seikei bunri* (Carim, 1994; Custy and Van Wyk, 1994; Sono, 1993: 311–47). 'In 1988 and 1989 Japan was South Africa's largest trading partner; and South Africa Japan's largest African trading partner, and their two-way annual trade was in billions of dollars (Sono, 1993: 311). Sanctions had only imposed a psychological barrier to expanding South African–Japanese trade even further (Carim, 1994: 32). As early as October 1991, Japan lifted all sanctions on South Africa with the exception of the arms embargo and the sale of computers to the police and defence forces (Carim, 1994: 32). Though there are signs that Japanese firms are keen to re-enter South Africa in terms of investment, it is already clear that the new South African government will have to convince investors, with viable development strategies which foster both economic growth and redistribution (Carim, 1994: 32, 35). The South African government is probably aware of the importance to this process of Japan's participation. However, it would prefer to design policies and incentives to direct Japanese intervention in ways that are 'compatible with the state's overall economic objectives both in South Africa and throughout the region'. (Carim, 1994: 35). President Mandela's state visit to Japan manifests the need to overcome some economic caution on the Japanese side; it would seem that *seikei bunri* is still the paradigm for Japanese foreign policy towards a new South Africa (Custy and Van Wyk, 1994: 76–7).

South Africa's relations with the Asian Commonwealth (Pakistan, Bangladesh, Sri Lanka, India, Malaysia, Singapore, Brunei [Lyon, 1994]) were far less cordial before 1990. Lyon (1994: 64) states that it would appear as though 'apart from political and propagandistic opposition to apartheid', South Africa's relations with these countries were 'well nigh non-existent'. It is true, however, that prior to India's active isolation of South Africa from 1946 onwards, that country had in fact had meaningful economic and family ties with South Africa. (There were, of course, a sizeable number of people of Indian origin in South Africa, who were politically speaking treated much on a par with the indigenous black population [Sawant, 1994].) The price paid by India for its moral stance against apartheid was therefore not cheap on an economic or personal level (FGD and CPS, 1995; Sawant, 1994: 6, 28). Nevertheless, India spearheaded much of the international criticism of South Africa's racialist policies from the 1940s onwards (Lyon, 1994: 66; Sawant, 1994). Political change in South Africa not only removed the single big obstacle to cordial relations between the two countries, but also put in power a political grouping (the ANC) in which the local Indian population is well represented. India started lifting sanctions against South Africa, in tandem with the Commonwealth, from 1991 onwards (Sawant, 1994: 31).

In addition to Japan and India, South Africa now has formal (often diplomatic) relations with most countries in East Asia, including South Korea, Malaysia, Pakistan, the Philippines, Singapore, Thailand and Vietnam. It also has, at present, formal relations with both Taiwan and Mainland China. The former is still, as was the case before 1990, full diplomatic relations, while the latter consists of 'cultural' (special interest) relations (South African Department of Foreign Affairs, information supplied by, 1 August 1994). As fellow 'pariahs', South Africa and Taiwan had over the years built up a strong and varied relationship (Geldenhuys, 1995), and this has not been terminated. Current relations with Mainland China originated when democratization in South Africa first commenced. Taiwan would gladly continue in the present vein; however, Beijing insists that South Africa makes a choice: no state has yet been able to maintain diplomatic links with both the Peoples' Republic of China (PRC, or Mainland China) and the Republic of China (ROC, or Taiwan) (Geldenhuys, 1995). The future of these relations is currently much debated, outside and inside government (Breytenbach, 1994; Geldenhuys, 1995; television interview with the deputy minister of foreign affairs, Mr Aziz Pahad, June 1995; two conferences held in August 1995 in Pretoria and Johannesburg, respectively) and it would not be wise to speculate on the outcome. It may however be said that economic and human rights considerations play a part on both sides of the argument (Geldenhuys, 1995). It may also be remarked that South Africa was, in 1995, only one of some 30 countries still maintaining diplomatic and consular relations with the ROC (Mengin, 1995: Appendix A).

Central and eastern Europe may be defined to include 27 countries stretching from the Baltic to the Pacific and from the Arctic to the Himalayas (Pienaar, 1996 [forthcoming]). This includes a number of independent states which were previously part of the former Soviet Union and central European countries such as Poland and Hungary. These countries are in many ways different, but there are common denominators: a history of Russian/Soviet domination and/or that they were 'communist' from 1945 or thereabouts (Pienaar, 1996 [forthcoming]). These also hold the key to South Africa's relations with the region prior to 1989. South Africa was vehemently anti-communist and eventually broke off all ties, such as they were, with the region in the course of the 1940s, 1950s and 1960s on these grounds (Muller, 1976: 170–71). Some trade with eastern Europe and even with the Soviet Union did, however, continue (Geldenhuys, 1989: 283). The countries of the region were perceived by the South African government as some of the worst protagonists against it. And indeed, they were some of its most vehement critics in international forums and gave active support to liberation movements in South Africa and southern Africa generally.

Though much of interest can be said about the eventual development of the relationship (see Pienaar, 1996 [forthcoming]), suffice it to say here that historical and not entirely unrelated changes overtook central and eastern Europe and South Africa more or less at the same time. This led to probably the most dramatic and sudden improvement in South Africa's foreign relations ever recorded. South Africa forged diplomatic and other ties with many of these countries virtually overnight, and the rest were to follow quite soon. Together with new ties forged with African countries, the speed with which South African ties with the former communist countries of Europe happened was quite staggering. By the time the Government of National Unity was in place, most of the changes with regard to these relations had already taken place (*Department of Foreign Affairs List*, October 1993). This could probably be attributed to the fact that change came from both sides, and that the former communist countries were as keen to start building new relationships as was the previous South African government. These ties have been maintained since the new government came to power, in spite of the fact that the ANC-led government has a strong South African Communist Party component. It may, however, be assumed that central and eastern Europe will not be a foreign policy priority for a future South African government and a long-rumoured invitation to President Mandela to visit Russia has not yet materialized (Pienaar, 1996 [forthcoming]).

The relationship between South Africa and *Australia and New Zealand* originated in a common membership of the British Commonwealth and continued based on cultural ties and in particular sporting ties. As international pressure mounted, these two countries joined the campaign against apartheid in largely cutting these ties. Their restoration followed speedily in the wake of moves towards democratization in South Africa. Cricket and rugby internationals, close to the heart of white South Africans, have been much celebrated as rewarding signs of South Africa's reacceptance into the world.

Regional organizations. For purposes of this discussion, regional organizations may be taken to include such institutions as the South African Development Community (SADC), the Organisation of African Unity (OAU), the Commonwealth and even the Non-Aligned Movement (NAM). The European Union (EU) needs also to be referred to, not because of South African membership of it, but due to the fact that European relations with South Africa will apparently be largely regulated through the institution (Hamill and Spence, 1993/94; Singh, 1993). Again, it is not possible to given an in-depth or complete discussion of South Africa's relations with regional institutions. It need only be mentioned that by 1990 South Africa had either lost its membership of institutions it had previously been a member of (the Commonwealth) or had not been able to gain membership of such organizations as had been formed and could possibly, under different political circumstances, have included it (the OAU, NAM). It retained membership only of one or two institutions, such as the Southern African Customs Union, which it dominated (Geldenhuys, 1990: 184).

SADC, originally formed as an economic counter-alliance against South Africa (Esterhuysen et al., 1994: 58–65; Mills et al., 1995: 199–279), welcomed the new, democratic South Africa into its ranks on 29 August 1994 (Hamill and Spence, 1993/94: 124). From the 'enemy' against whom all effort was made, South Africa became the 'great hope' of southern Africa. There was much talk at the time whether South Africa would be joining the SADC or whether SADC would be joining, but the fact is that South Africa is by far the stronger member and will, by its sheer relative power, dominate the institution, as it unavoidably dominates the region. The new South African government has emphasized repeatedly that it will not play hegemon in the region or in SADC, and it certainly regards the region as a primary area in terms of foreign policy interest and objectives (Hamill and Spence, 1993/94: 125). For the time being at least, 'dominates' simply refers to an objective situation and not a foreign policy goal. 'Initially, there was the expectation that the Republic would act as an "engine of growth" stimulating developments throughout the region' (Hamill and Spence, 1993/94: 125) and it was widely expected that the framework provided by SADC would be instrumental in this. On the other hand, it has also become clear that South Africa will have its hands full in just dealing with the task of internal social and economic reconstruction (Hamill and Spence, 1993/94: 125). For the time being, there is, however, still much optimism within

SADC of good intentions on the part of the new South Africa.

When the OAU was established in 1963, South Africa was not only excluded from membership, but a number of existing regional institutions in Africa, of which South Africa had up until then been an active member, were 'absorbed' by the new organization and South Africa excluded from continued membership (Muller, 1976: 143–44). Though it was largely ineffective in many areas (Hamill and Spence, 1993/94: 116–17), the OAU played a role in the liberation struggle in South Africa through the financial support provided by its Liberation Committee to both the ANC and the Pan Africanist Congress (PAC), as well as rhetorical support in other forums. With decisive political change in South Africa came immediate admission for South Africa (May 1994) as the 53rd member of the OAU. It assumed its seat for the first time on 13 June 1994 at the 30th annual summit of heads of state and government in Tunis (Hamill and Spence, 1993/94: 117). Though this was the culmination of a long struggle against colonialism and white majority rule, it also meant that the organization lost its principal unifying theme (Hamill and Spence, 1993/94: 117–18). It is now faced with some very pressing realities on the continent, and South Africa is expected to play its part in seeking solutions to some of these. Though the new South African government is certainly proud of the country's return to 'the African family', and is constantly emphasizing its gratitude to the OAU and the continent, it is already becoming clear that even more emphasis is being placed on southern Africa (Hamill and Spence, 1993/94: 119). Thus far it has avoided direct intervention in African trouble spots.

South Africa joined the NAM, a seemingly anachronistic organization in the post-Cold War world, as its 109th member, on 31 May 1994 at the 11th Council of Ministers meeting in Cairo, Egypt (Hamill and Spence, 1993/94: 122). This was without a doubt a milestone in the history of the NAM and in a sense the end of an era. Over the years the movement had become identified with opposition to and criticism of colonialism, imperialism, neo-colonialism, racism, apartheid and other forms of domination and hegemony (Singh, 1993: 27). In 1992 it had initiated a reformulation of its objectives to focus much more on the economic sphere at the expense of high international politics (Hamill and Spence, 1993/94: 122; Singh, 1993). The new South African government identifies with the NAM's new focus and it may well seek to campaign, as best it can, for a more equitable economic deal for the developing countries. It is, however, already clear that dealing with the problems of the southern African region and to a lesser extent with upheaval in Africa, and obtaining a sizeable economic input from the West, have higher priority as South African foreign policy concerns than the broader cause of the NAM (Hamill and Spence, 1993/94: 122–23).

South Africa had left the Commonwealth in 1961 due to the institution's opposition to apartheid, and with the demise of the latter, the country duly rejoined – officially on 20 July 1994 (Anyaoku, 1993; Hamill and Spence, 1993/94: 110, 112–13). The Commonwealth is also currently in the process of reassessing its role in international society, but some benefits to South Africa of its resumed membership are apparent: the prospect of providing a degree of leadership and enthusiasm for rejuvenating the Commonwealth ideal, given South Africa's peculiar placement in the association as a bridge between the rich and the poor members; a sense of solidarity with its third world neighbours in Africa and elsewhere – the Commonwealth provides South Africa with an 'inside connection' to one of the three main trading blocs which are presently 'congealing' within the international economy, namely, the East Asian, Pacific Rim or Asian-Pacific Economic Co-operation (APEC) (Lyon, 1994: 69); and the direct benefits to be derived from various Commonwealth programmes (Anyaoku, 1993; Hamill and Spence, 1993/94: 114-15). The benefits to the association are also evident from the above.

In concluding the discussion of South Africa's changing relations with regional organizations, brief mention should be made of the EU, another of the three main trading blocs. It has already been asserted that this relationship is truly one between two international actors. It was brought about by historical developments in both Europe and South Africa, and it is a relationship which is at present being defined. The detail of South African status vis-a-vis the EU is therefore not a matter which can be pronounced on as yet. The new relationship is very much in the process of being made (Holland, 1996 [forthcoming]). The importance of this relationship both for South Africa and the EU (as well as the southern African region and perhaps even Africa) should not be underestimated, however.

Global organizations. Included in the category of global organizations are the United Nations (UN) and its specialized agencies such as the International Atomic Energy Agency (IAEA), the Universal Postal Union (UPU), the World Health Organization (WHO), the International Labour Organization (ILO), the General Agreement on Tariffs and Trade (GATT) and the World Trade Organization (WTO), as well as a large number of comprehensive inter-governmental institutions outside the UN system. South Africa's position with regards to global institutions, and the change which this has undergone since early 1990, need only be sketched in the broadest outline. In the centre of this stands relations with the UN.

At the time when the UN and many of the specialized agencies, as well as a host of other global inter-governmental institutions, had been established, South Africa was still respected as a valuable member of the international community. In time this changed and South Africa was gradually barred or suspended from or prevented from participating in many of these institu-

tions (Heunis, 1986; Muller, 1976: 140–3, and 144–7). By 1989, in the entire
UN family, South Africa still actively participated in only the GATT, the
World Bank and the International Monetary Fund (IMF) (but had effectively been denied access to IMF loans) (Geldenhuys, 1990: 184). The other
global inter-governmental organizations to which it belonged were functional bodies and few in number (Geldenhuys, 1990: 184). South Africa
actually became the subject of numerous resolutions passed each year in the
UN General Assembly (in which it was not allowed to participate since
1974) ('Discussions and Resolutions on South Africa in the United Nations',
1976–1991/92), and the brief of a number of subsidiary organs created
within the UN, specifically for dealing with the problem of South Africa. No
doubt in reaction to this barrage of negative attention in international
forums, South Africa repeatedly emphasized that it preferred bilateral
relations to multilateral relations ('South Africa's Foreign Policy and International Practice as Reflected Mainly in Speeches, Statements and Replies
by the Government in Parliament', 1976–1992/93).

One of the most marked changes in South African foreign policy and
relations occurred in this regard: with democratization came a triumphant
return for South Africa to all possible global institutions, and the new
government has adopted a very strong emphasis on 'multilateralism' in its
foreign relations. South Africa is now an active participant in numerous
international conferences and several important institutions have opened
missions in South Africa. With 'democratization' in the UN, South Africa
may in the future play an increasingly prominent role as a leading African
nation.

An Issue-oriented Approach

The following salient themes may be used in order to record changes in
South African foreign relations: the North–South dialogue; human rights;
issues of nuclear and general disarmament; refugees and migration; the
environment. The list is not exhaustive, but can serve to illustrate the most
important changes since early 1990. An issue-oriented approach perhaps
underlines the development of a more active or enterprising South African
foreign policy under a new government. Some very brief comments will
suffice.

South Africa is in many respects an interface between the developed
North and the developing *South*; there are elements of both these realities in
the South African situation. This has been the case for many years and will
no doubt remain so, to a greater or lesser extent, for many years to come.
White South Africa, which dominated foreign policy under the old regime,
positioned itself as a Northern–Western society in a Southern–Third World
geopolitical setting. While various policy initiatives were launched with

regard to the South–Third World and especially vis-a-vis other states in a similar situation, such as certain Latin American states (Maré, 1983: 1), the strongest element of its self-perceived identity was that of a Northern-Western society. As was noted before, South Africa hoped to promote itself as a 'leader through service' in Africa, but the rationale for this was its identity as a (relatively) developed state in an underdeveloped continent.

The new South African identity under its Government of National Unity, and doubtless under any future government, is that of a Southern-Third World country, with certain important elements of 'developedness' (FGD and CPS, 1995). The emphasis is quite different from before. South Africa's community of interest with the South is stressed, at the same time as its willingness to play a meaningful role there. This is, as has already been mentioned, manifested in its association with the socio-economic problems of southern Africa and Africa in general, as well as, though to a lesser extent, by the role it would play in the NAM. It is, however, already clear that not all actors will unconditionally recognize South Africa as a 'developing' country. Negotiations currently under way with the EU attest to this.

Human rights used to be something of a dirty word in the old South Africa. Mention of it was usually interpreted by the old government as just another way of 'getting to' its domestic policies (see Muller 1987/88: 303; Van Vuuren, 1976: 273). That government, therefore, refused to sign the Universal Declaration of Human Rights, and preferred in its rhetoric to emphasize the need for the recognition of group, rather than individual human rights.

With moves towards democratization came an immediate shift in policy, and in 1992 during the state president's opening address to Parliament, this was already evident (Kriek, 1992/93: 174):

> A new constitution cannot be separated from a bill of fundamental rights. The Government is committed to the principle of a justiciable bill of fundamental rights as part of a new constitutional dispensation ...
>
> (T)he Government (is) also ... making a study of international conventions on fundamental rights, including the rights of women and children, and the United Nations Declaration on Human Rights ... in the realisation that it is necessary for South Africa to come into line with the international community ...

With the ANC-led Government of National Unity in May 1994 came a very decisive move towards support for human rights in domestic and international affairs. In fact, it may quite safely be said that the promotion of human rights is a cornerstone of current *articulated* foreign and domestic policy (see FGD and CPS, 1995; Maluwa, 1993/94). Coupled with the promotion of human rights internationally is support for the liberation of suppressed peoples and their self-determination, and democratization. These principles, strongly as they are supported by the new decision-makers, are already presenting the latter with some difficult choices: the

promotion of human rights, liberation, self-determination and democratization does not always come in neat packages, and one's long-time friends and
erstwhile supporters may not always be great champions of these lofty
principles when it comes to their own affairs. It is in this context that the new
government has already been subject to criticism from some of its supporters (and opponents), with regard to the establishment and maintenance of
diplomatic relations with states such as Indonesia and Morocco (FGD and
CPS, 1995). As was indicated above, the choice between the ROC and the
PRC can also not be made by simply applying these principles (see Geldenhuys, 1995: 5).

In the light of the previous perceptions that the country was being
threatened mainly by outside (communist) forces wanting to bring about its
downfall, as well as the increasing isolation to which it was subjected,
military preparedness was hardly surprising. After the imposition of the
arms embargo against South Africa by the UK and the USA in 1963,
followed by the mandatory UN embargo in 1977, and while South Africa
was embroiled in campaigns in Namibia and Angola, it was hardly likely
that it would be a champion of *arms control and disarmament*. It once again
developed its own arms industry and also found ways to circumvent the
arms embargo (Landgren, 1989). In time this also included cooperation in
the area of nuclear technology and the clandestine development of a nuclear
weapons capability (Landgren, 1989: 153–71; Muller, 1996 [forthcoming];
Rabert, 1995; Reiss, 1995). Though it denied nuclear testing and did not
admit to having a nuclear weapons capability, South Africa refused to sign
the Non-Proliferation Treaty (NPT). The government was no champion of
nuclear nonproliferation. In the meantime the liberation movements, and in
particular the ANC, had been attacking the South African government on
this score and had in the process built up a reputation as champions of
disarmament and nuclear nonproliferation.

On 24 March 1993 President de Klerk announced that South Africa had
indeed produced a limited number of nuclear weapons but that they had
since been destroyed under strict control. This was decided, he said, in early
1990, and by July 1991 South Africa had been able to sign the NPT. This
meant that South Africa, under the former government, became the first
and only example of nuclear 'rollback', voluntarily and unilaterally dismantling its nuclear arsenal (Reiss, 1995: 7). In his statement, F. W. de Klerk
emphasized his hope that 'this chapter of the past (could) be closed and that
a new one of international cooperation and trust (could) be opened' (Reiss,
1995: 7). Though this resurrected many questions about South Africa's
nuclear activities and also raised new ones about the original motives
behind South Africa's decision to build nuclear weapons *and* about the real
motives behind the decision to choose the 'rollback' option, it did mean the
end of South Africa as a nuclear power. (Many elements of its capability

have since been dismantled and many nuclear scientists and technicians have in fact left the country.) It also meant South African support for international efforts at nuclear nonproliferation and disarmament.

Under its new ANC-led government, South Africa has recently taken a strong stand in these matters. It also played a unique role in the recent NPT extension negotiations when it made a proposal which facilitated a compromise between the Franco-American position and the Third World position (see Statement by the Foreign Minister, 19 April 1995). Though some commentators in South Africa and elsewhere thought that South Africa had not pushed hard enough for the Third World position, which aspired to limited extension of the treaty only in order to put more pressure on the nuclear powers to disarm, South Africa's position was certainly in favour of nonproliferation and nuclear disarmament.

The South African government's position on disarmament generally has not been put to the test publicly as yet. However, there is every reason to believe that it will support, at least rhetorically and in principle, disarmament and arms control. South Africa still has a fairly strong arms industry, a 'left-over' from the previous era, which can earn valuable foreign currency and provides jobs domestically. Though it has been stressed that South Africa will be a 'responsible arms producer', the government has not undertaken to terminate the production of arms or to stop export of such commodities. As in many other areas of foreign policy, the principle and hard economic realities often do not coincide. It is clear that the debate on these issues within South Africa, and within the government, has only begun (Dippenaar, 1995).

Under previous South African governments, practice if not the policy with regard to the treatment of *refugees and migrants* was generally indisputably racist. (It was often said that the policy was to treat refugees in the most humane way, irrespective of race or colour [Van Vuuren, 1976: 282].) Though the South African mining industry made use of large numbers of (black) migrant workers from the neighbouring states, immigration into South Africa was clearly regulated along colour lines (Barber, 1973: 52, 71, 137, 219). The treatment afforded refugees was mostly determined by the same criteria.

With a 'non-racial' government in place, all refugees and migrants should be treated the same. And now that South Africa has been cooperating with the UN High Commissioner for Refugees, persons in this category will be treated more or less in line with acceptable international practice. This does not, however, solve all the problems relating to how freely migrants should be allowed into the country and what their status will be once they have arrived in the country. The new government is somewhat reluctant to deal too harshly with illegal migrants from neighbouring states and further afield in Africa. However, the sheer numbers of these people, and some serious 'security risks' which they bring with them (see the discussion of relations with southern Africa above) have already complicated the matter considerably. In June 1995 the minister of defence, Mr Joe Modise, called for the erection of an additional electric fence on South Africa's borders with its neighbours. It has also been proposed that the existing fence on the border with Mozambique be switched to lethal levels of current. South Africa's policy with regard to the treatment of refugees and migrants has changed, but the extent remains to be seen.

A heightened awareness of *environmental issues*, both nationally and internationally, came to South Africa at about the same time as democratization happened. Exactly in what way these two occurrences are connected is not quite clear, but it would seem as though the new South Africa's position on environmental issues will be shaped, at least in broad outline, by its positioning within NAM. It is bound to adopt a 'Southern' viewpoint on environmental issues as they surface in international forums though it may also be careful not to alienate the West. In southern Africa environmental affairs have already and will in future come to the fore in the context of cooperation with regard to such important matters as soil erosion and water.

Continuities in South African Foreign Relations

Continuities in South African foreign relations may generally be attributed to four types of factors: relatively permanent, mainly material factors; fundamental change in the international system which in some cases act to cancel out the removal of negative factors which used to influence South African foreign relations; the slowness with which perceptions about South Africa, held by some in the international community, change; and the fact that some of the 'old' decision-makers remain in position in South Africa, due in no small measure to the nature of the transition process.[6] Some clarification of these factors for continuity is in order.

It is generally regarded as a cliche in foreign policy analysis that some

---

6. The transition process in South Africa has been characterized as 'transition by transplacement' (Nel, 1995). This implies that the break with the past was not as clear as in a case of 'transition by replacement' (e.g. East Germany, 1989), nor as limited as in the case of 'transition by transformation' (e.g. USSR, 1985–). It may also be characterized as a particular subtype of 'transition by transplacement', which may be called 'transition by erosion', as it entailed a gradual erosion of the power of the reforming government to control the process till the end (Nel, 1995: 85). Coupled with the Nelson Mandela-led government's intention of 'putting white fears to rest', an agreement was reached whereby civil servants from the old regime were given some assurance that they would not lose their jobs. Though many did choose retirement, many remained in place.

'determinants' of foreign policy are more or less permanent and not subject
to rapid or frequent change. A very good example of such an influence on
South African foreign policy and the foreign policies of other actors is South
Africa's dominant power position within southern Africa and its favourable
power position within Africa as a whole. This factor of 'giantism' continues
to influence South Africa's relations with southern Africa and Africa, much
as it did before (Clapham, 1994; Mills, 1995; Muller, 1993: 79; Spicer and
Reichardt, 1992). This is equally true with regard to South Africa's unfavourable position vis-a-vis the developed countries of the world. To a large
extent this position pre-dates the unrest and sanctions of the mid-1980s, and
consequently persists after the political transition (McGowan, 1994, 1996
[forthcoming]). Such 'facts of life' have ensured a measure of both positive
and negative continuity in South African external relations, and will probably continue to do so for some time.

Repeated mention is made in the literature of the fact that changes in
central and eastern Europe, while having had a very positive effect on South
African external relations, have also meant that western Europe and other
actors will be diverting resources from Africa to these parts (Mills, 1994;
Mills et al., 1995; Spicer and Reichardt, 1992). This has manifested in the
often remarked upon phenomenon that the lifting of sanctions and the
cessation of an imperative for disinvestment have not had the dramatic
effect on, in particular, economic relations. If Africa is being marginalized,
it is all the more important to note that South Africa is now truly part of
Africa. In some sense isolation has been replaced with marginalization.

The 'effects upon bureaucratic and business mindsets of decades of
apartheid and isolation' (Van Nieuwkerk, 1995: 258) should be cited as a
factor for continuity. This is particularly true with regards to business
people in the developed countries of the world, who will only in time truly
change their perceptions of South Africa as a business nonprospect. This
has contributed to the sluggishness with which reinvestment in South Africa
has occurred, and has given rise to the urgent need not to scale down South
African missions in potential investor countries too rapidly. Though the
political focus of the new South Africa points away from the North to Africa
and the rest of the South, economic considerations have already acted as a
counterinfluence to this. Though many new missions have been opened
outside of western Europe and North America, missions in the latter two
regions have not been scaled down correspondingly.

Although a new minister and deputy minister of foreign affairs have
taken over political control of the department, and although many new
people (both from the ANC's overseas service and the foreign ministries of
the former independent homelands) have joined the department, many of
the 'old' members of the department are still there. This is also true for
other state departments active in the area of foreign affairs and giving

direction to it. The perceptions and values of the old guard have probably already undergone some change and will continue to do so, but their presence will at least see to some measure of (desirable or undesirable) continuity in South African foreign policy. The impact of the realities of incumbency on ANC 'foreign policy' has also been a factor for continuity, as had already become apparent before April 1994. By 1993 '(l)iberation politics, directly linked to the Cold War era and the exigencies of the anti-apartheid struggle, have given way to the "geo-economics" and concerns of a government-in-waiting' (Alden, 1994: 77–8). Though this should not be overestimated, some convergence between 'old' and 'new' decision-makers has already occurred. This is a factor for continuity.

Future Prospects

Further changes in the international system might bring about more changes in the very nature of international politics and the way in which inter-national relations are conducted. As such, it will of necessity impàct on South African foreign relations. It will be recalled that this is precisely what happened when the international system underwent substantial changes after the Second World War. Most commentators are of the opinion that the changes we have recently seen, and of which the full effects are not clear yet, are even more fundamental than those after 1945. Hopefully, their impact will not be as negative for South Africa as those of 50 years ago. If South African decision-makers are able to adapt their perceptions and values so as to render a constructive South African foreign policy possible, this should be the case. Certainly, the very nature of international interactions will be shaped by these 'structural factors'.

Further developments in other actors themselves will probably bring more immediately visible changes in or further crystallization of South African external relations. The shape of things to come in the EU is a case in point, as well as internal political developments in Mainland China. International institutions today, such as the UN, are not static and there are constant moves to shape and change them in new directions. Such changes could mean that new demands could be made on South Africa as member country (Urquhart, 1993). This could also lead to the further development of South Africa's role in Africa with regard to peacekeeping for example (see Nathan, 1994: 116). Changes within the OAU could have a similar effect on South African foreign relations (see Legum, 1994). NAM may also be cited in this regard, as it is finding a new role for itself in the post-Cold War world (Singh, 1994). Another important aspect is the development of 'new' actors in international politics, and in particular of new groupings of states. Various possibilities are mentioned in the literature, for example the formation of an economic grouping based on the Indian Ocean rim, including possibly India, Singapore, other Association of South-east Asian Nations (ASEAN) states, Australia and South Africa (Jones, 1994: 17).

Further developments in South Africa could change the country's style of diplomacy and the way in which foreign policy is formulated. The role of public opinion and Parliament, and of the democratization of foreign affairs generally, are much debated currently (Van Nieuwkerk, 1994: 104–7). More immediately, the new government will in due course address aspects of its foreign relations which have not as yet been dealt with. As Van Nieuwkerk (1995: 258) remarks, 'the "re-evaluation" of South Africa's foreign policy objectives takes place at a rather slow pace'. South African relations with the two Chinas is a good case in point. A new direction in the relationship is likely to come soon on the basis of a re-evaluation of South African foreign policy objectives (Geldenhuys, 1995). Perhaps the most fundamental influences to emanate from 'future developments in South Africa' will be those of political stability and the ability of government to deal with problems of law and order. There can be little doubt that developments in this sphere will be decisive for the economic aspects of South Africa's external relations in particular, but as such it will also affect most other dimensions as well.

REFERENCES

Alden, C. (1994) 'From Liberation Movement to Political Party: ANC Foreign Policy in Transition', *The South African Journal of International Affairs (SAJIA)* 1(1): 62–81.
Anyaoku, E. (1993) 'The Commonwealth and South Africa: Restoring A Relationship', *The South African Journal of International Affairs (SAJIA)* 1(1): 1–8.
Ballinger, M. (1969) *From Union to Apartheid. A Trek to Isolation.* Cape Town, Johannesburg and Wynberg: Juta.
Barber, J. (1973) *South Africa's Foreign Policy 1945–1970.* Oxford: Oxford University Press.
Barber, J. and J. Barratt (1990) *South Africa's Foreign Policy. The Search for Status and Security 1945–1988.* Johannesburg: Southern in association with the South African Institute of International Affairs (SAIIA).
Benjamin, L. and C. Gregory (eds) (1992) *Southern Africa at the Crossroads?* Rivonia: Justified Press.
Breytenbach, W. (1994) 'The Chinese Dilemma: Dual Recognition is the Ultimate Solution', *The South African Journal of International Affairs (SAJIA)* 2(1): 50–61.
Carim, X. (1994) 'Economic Relations Between Japan and South Africa', *The South African Journal of International Affairs (SAJIA)* 2(1): 21–36.
Carlsnaes, W. (1986) *Ideology and Foreign Policy: Problems of Comparative Conceptualisation.* Oxford: Blackwell.
Carlsnaes, W. (1983) 'On Analysing the Dynamics of Foreign Policy Change: A Critique and Reconceptualization; *Cooperation and Conflict* 28(1): 5–30.
Carlsnaes, W. and M. E. Muller (eds) (1996, forthcoming) *Change and South African External Relations.* Halfway House: Thomson International/Southern.

Cilliers, A. (1993/94) 'Reincorporation of Bophuthatswana and Certain Other States into the Republic of South Africa', in *South African Yearbook of International Law* vol. 19, pp. 93–109. Pretoria. VerLoren van Themaat Centre for Public Law Studies, University of South Africa.

Cheru, F. (1994) 'The Prospects for Expanded Trade and Investment Between Kenya and South Africa', *The South African Journal of International Affairs (SAJIA)* 1(2): 19–31.

Clapham, C. (1994) 'The African Setting', in G. Mills (ed.) *From Pariah to Participant: South Africa's Evolving Foreign Relations, 1990–1994*, pp. 37–51. Johannesburg: SAIIA.

Cockram, G. M. (1970) *Vorster's Foreign Policy*. Pretoria and Cape Town: Academica.

Custy, M. C. and J. J. Van Wyk (1994) '*Seikei Bunri* and Apartheid: An Analysis of the Japanese-South African Relationship 1985–1991', *Politikon* 21(2): 64–79.

Dadoo, Y. (1996, forthcoming) 'Relations with the Middle East and the Arab World', in W. Carlsnaes and M. E. Muller (eds) *Change and South African External Relations*. Halfway House: Thomson International/Southern.

Department of Foreign Affairs List (February 1989; September 1989; August 1990; February 1991; September 1991; March 1992; September 1992; March 1993; October 1993). Pretoria: South African Department of Foreign Affairs.

Dippenaar, N. (1995) 'The Future of the South African Arms Industry', paper delivered at the 45th Pugwash Conference, Hiroshima, Japan, 23–9 July.

'Discussions and Resolutions on South Africa in the United Nations', (1976–1991/92) in *South African Yearbook of International Law*. Pretoria: VerLoren van Themaat Centre for Public Law Studies, University of South Africa.

Donaldson, A., J. Segar and R. Southall (eds) (1992) 'Undoing Independence: Regionalism and the Reincorporation of Transkei into South Africa', *Journal of Contemporary African Studies* 11(2).

Esterhuysen, P., D. Fair and E. Leistner (eds) (1994) *South Africa in Subequatorial Africa: Economic Interaction. A Factual Survey*. Pretoria: Africa Institute of South Africa.

Foundation for Global Dialogue (FGD) in conjunction with the Centre for Policy Studies (CPS) (1995) 'Workshop: Democratic South Africa's Foreign Relations – One Year Later', Johannesburg, 30 June 1995; proceedings to be published by FGD and CPS.

Geldenhuys, D. (1984) *The Diplomacy of Isolation. South African Foreign Policy Making*. Johannesburg: Macmillan, for SAIIA.

Geldenhuys, D. (1989) 'The International Community and South Africa: a Framework for Analysis', in A. Venter (ed.) *Foreign Policy Issues in a Democratic South Africa*, pp. 35–49. Johannesburg: PWPA.

Geldenhuys, D. (1990) *Isolated States. A Comparative Analysis*. Johannesburg: Jonathan Ball.

Geldenhuys, D. (1995) 'South Africa and the China Question: A Case for Dual Recognition', Working Paper Series No. 6, East Asia Project, Department of International Relations, University of the Witwatersrand.

Grundy, K. W. (1973) *Confrontation and Accommodation in Southern Africa. The Limits of Independence*. Berkeley, Los Angeles and London: University of California Press.

Grundy, K. W. (1996, forthcoming). 'Stasis in Transition: United States-South African Relations', in W. Carlsnaes and M. E. Muller (eds) *Change and South African External Relations*. Halfway House: Thomson International/Southern.

Hamill, J. and J. E. Spence (1993/94) 'South African Participation in International Organisations', in *South African Yearbook of International Law*, vol. 19, pp. 110–126. Pretoria: VerLoren van Themaat Centre for Public Law Studies, University of South Africa.

Heunis, J. C. (1986) *United Nations Versus South Africa. A Legal Assessment of United Nations and United Nations Related Activities in Respect of South Africa*. Johannesburg and Cape Town: Lex Patria.

Holland, M. (1996, forthcoming). 'European Union and South Africa', in W. Carlsnaes and M. E. Muller (eds) *Change and South African External Relations*. Halfway House: Thomson International/Southern.

Jaster, R. S. (1988) *The Defence of White Power. South African Foreign Policy Under Pressure*. London: Macmillan in association with the International Institute for Strategic Studies.

Jones, D. S. (1994) 'Singapore: An Overall View of the Country and its Relations with South Africa', *The South African Journal of International Affairs (SAJIA)* 2(1): 1–20.

Kahana, E. (1990) 'Israel's Changing Policy Towards South Africa, 1948–1988', unpublished D. Litt et Phil thesis, University of South Africa, Pretoria.

Kobayashi, H. (1994) 'Economic Development of Pacific Rim Countries and Southern Africa', *The South African Journal of International Affairs (SAJIA)* 2(1): 37–49.

Kriek, A. (1992) ''n Analise van die aard van die magskonfigurasie in die Suider-Afrikaanse Regionale Stelsel, 1969–1990', unpublished D. Litt et Phil thesis, University of South Africa, Pretoria.

Kriek, A. (1992/93) 'South Africa's Foreign Policy and International Practice as Reflected Mainly in Speeches, Statements and Replies by the Government in Parliament', in *South African Yearbook of International Law*, pp. 173–216. Pretoria: VerLoren van Themaat Centre for Public Law Studies, University of South Africa.

Landgren, S. (1989) *Embargo Disimplemented. South Africa's Military Industry*. New York: Oxford University Press.

Landsberg, C. and C. De Coning (1995) *From 'Tar Baby' to Transition: Four Decades of US Foreign Policy Towards South Africa*, (*International Relations Series, Policy: Issues and Actors* 8(6)). Johannesburg: Centre for Policy Studies.

Legum, C. (1994) 'South Africa's Potential Role in the Organisation of African Unity', *The South African Journal of International Affairs (SAJIA)* 1(1): 17–22.

Lyon, P. (1994) 'South Africa and the Asian Commonwealth', *The South African Journal of International Affairs (SAJIA)* 2(1): 62–72.

McGowan, P. J. (1994) 'The "New" South Africa: Ascent or Descent in the World System?', *The South African Journal of International Affairs (SAJIA)* 1(1): 35–61.

McGowan, P. J. (1996 forthcoming) 'The Global Informational Economy and South Africa', in W. Carlsnaes and M. E. Muller (eds) *Change and South African External Relations*. Halfway House: Thomson International/Southern.

Maluwa, T. (1993/4) 'International Human Rights Norms and the South African Interim Constitution', in *South African Yearbook of International Law*, pp. 14–42. Pretoria: Verhoren van Themaat Centre for Public Law Studies University of South Africa.

Marais, D. (1991) *South Africa: Constitutional Development. A Multi-disciplinary Approach*, 2nd rev.edn. Halfway House: Southern.

Maré, J. H. E. (1983) 'South Africa in the Polarised International Context of the Post-1945 Period. South Africa's Foreign Policy vis-a-vis the East-West Issue as Expressed in Dimensions of the North-South Issue', unpublished D. Litt et Phil thesis, University of South Africa, Pretoria.

Mengin, F. (1995) *Taiwan's Non-Official Diplomacy (Discussion Papers in Diplomacy*, Diplomatic Studies Programme, no. 5), Centre for the Study of Diplomacy, Department of Politics, University of Leicester.

Mills, G. (ed.) (1994) *From Pariah to Participant. South Africa's Evolving Foreign Relations, 1990–1994*. Johannesburg: SAIIA.

Mills, G. (1995) 'The History of Regional Integrative Attempts: The Way Forward?' in G. Mills, A. Begg and A. Van Nieuwkerk (eds) *South Africa in the Global Economy*, pp. 214–44. Johannesburg: SAIIA.

Mills, G., A. Begg and A. Van Nieuwkerk (eds) (1995) *South Africa in the Global Economy*.

Johannesburg: SAIIA.

Muller, M. E. (1976) *Suid-Afrika se Buitelandse Verteenwoordiging (1910–1972)*. Pretoria: J. L. Van Schaik.

Muller, M. E. (1989) 'The Department of Foreign Affairs', in A. Venter (ed.) *South African Government and Politics. An Introduction to its Institutions, Processes and Policies*, pp. 241–71. Johannesburg: Southern.

Muller, M. E. (1989/90) 'South Africa's Foreign Policy and International Practice as Reflected Mainly in Speeches, Statements and Replies by the Government in Parliament, in *South African Yearbook of International Law*, pp. 215–86. Pretoria: VerLoren van Themaat Centre for Public Law Studies, University of South Africa.

Muller, M. E. (1993) 'South Africa and its Regional Neighbours: Policy Options for Regional Cooperation', in A. Venter (ed.) *Foreign Policy Issues in a Democratic South Africa*, pp. 75–88. Johannesburg: PWPA.

Muller, M. E. (1996, forthcoming) 'South Africa Crisscrosses the Nuclear Threshold', in W. Gutteridge (ed.). *South Africa's Defence and Security into the 21st Century*. Aldershot: Dartmouth.

Muller, M. E. (1996, forthcoming) 'The Institutional Dimension: the Department of Foreign Affairs and Overseas Missions, in W. Carlsnaes and M. E. Muller (eds) *Change and South African External Relations*. Halfway House: Thomson International/Southern.

Nathan, L. (1994) 'With Open Arms': Confidence- and Security-Building Measures in Southern Africa', *The South African Journal of International Affairs (SAJIA)* 1(2): 110–26.

Neack, L., J. A. K. Hey and P. J. Haney (1995) *Foreign Policy Analysis. Continuity and Change in Its Second Generation*. Englewood Cliffs, NJ: Prentice-Hall.

Nel, P. (1995) 'Transition Through Erosion: Comparing South Africa's Democratisation', *Aussenpolitik* 46(1): 82–93.

Nolutshungu, S. C. (1975) *South Africa in Africa. A Study in Ideology and Foreign Policy*. Manchester: Manchester University Press.

Pfetsch, F. (1994) 'Tensions in Sovereignty: Foreign Policies of EC Members Compared', in W. Carlsnaes and S. Smith (eds) *European Foreign Policy. The EC and Changing Perspectives in Europe*. London: Sage.

Pienaar, S. (1996, forthcoming) 'Relations with Central and Eastern Europe', in W. Carlsnaes and M. E. Muller (eds) *Change and South African External Relations*. Halfway House: Thomson International/Southern.

Pitswane, J. (1992) 'Namibia. Challenges of the First Decade', in L. Benjamin and C. Gregory (eds) *Southern Africa at the Crossroads?*, pp. 105–124. Rivonia: Justified Press.

Rabert, B. (1995) 'South Africa's Defused Nuclear Weapons – Trend Reversal in the Third World?', *Aussenpolitik* 46(1): 71–81.

Reiss, M. (1995) *Bridled Ambition. Why Countries Constrain their Nuclear Capabilities*. Washington DC: Woodrow Wilson Center Press.

Roelofse-Campbell, Z. (1993) 'Misperceived Neighbours: South Africa and Latin America', in A. Venter (ed.) *Foreign Policy Issues in a Democratic South Africa*, pp. 105–19. Johannesburg: PWPA.

Rosenau, J. N. (1995) 'Signals, Signposts and Symptoms: Interpreting Change and Anomalies in World Politics', *European Journal of International Relations* 1(1): 113–22.

Sarakinsky, I. (1992) 'South Africa. Changing Politics and the Politics of Change', in L. Benjamin and C. Gregory (eds) *Southern Africa at the Crossroads?*, pp. 125–59. Rivonia: Justified Press.

Sawant, A. B. (ed.) (1994) *India and South Africa. A Fresh Start*. Delhi: Kalinga.

Schoeman, E. (comp.), assisted by C. Schoeman (1992) *South Africa's Foreign Relations in Transition 1985–1992: A Chronology*. Johannesburg: SAIIA.

Shaw, T. M. and C. E. Adibe (1994) 'South Africa, Nigeria and the Prospects for Complementary Regionalism after Apartheid', *South African Journal of International Affairs (SAJIA)* 1(2): 1–18.

Singh, S. K. (1993) 'Non-Alignment: Past, Present and Future', *The South African Journal of International Affairs (SAJIA)* 1(1): 23–24.

Soetendorp, B. (1994) 'The Evolution of the EC/EU as a Single Foreign Policy Actor', in W. Carlsnaes and S. Smith (eds) *European Foreign Policy. The EC and Changing Perspectives in Europe*, pp. 103–19. London: Sage.

Solomon, H. (1993) 'In Search of Canaan: A Critical Evaluation of the Causes and Effects of Migration within Southern Africa, and Strategies to Cope With Them', in *Southern African Perspectives*, Working Paper Series, no. 24, August, Centre for Southern African Studies, University of the Western Cape.

Sono, T. (1993) *Japan and Africa. The Evolution and Nature of Political, Economic and Human Bonds, 1543–1993*. Pretoria: HSRC.

South African Department of Foreign Affairs, information supplied by, 1 August 1994.

South African Yearbook of International Law (SAYIL) vol. 15, (1989/90); vol. 16 (1990/91); vol. 17 (1991/92); vol. 18 (1992/93); vol. 19 (1993/94). Pretoria: VerLoren van Themaat Centre for Public Law Studies, University of South Africa.

'South Africa's Foreign Policy and International Practice as Reflected Mainly in Speeches, Statements and Replies by the Government in Parliament (1976–1992/93) in *South African Yearbook of International Law*. Pretoria: VerLoren van Themaat Centre for Public Law Studies, University of South Africa.

Spicer, M. and M. Reichardt (192) 'Southern Africa. The International Community and Economic Development in the 1990s', in L. Benjamin and C. Gregory (eds) *Southern Africa at the Crossroads?*, pp. 255–80. Rivonia: Justified Press.

'Statement by the Foreign Minister of the Republic of South Africa, Mr Alfred Nzo, to the 1995 Review and Extension Conference of the Parties to the Treaty on the Non-Proliferation of Nuclear Weapons (NPT)' (1995) 19 April.

Urquhart, B. (1994) 'The United Nations and the Future Peace', *The South African Journal of International Affairs (SAJIA)* 1(1): 9–16.

Vale, P. (1994) 'Review Article: Crocker's Choice: Constructive Engagement and South Africa's People', *The South African Journal of International Affairs (SAJIA)* 1(1): 100–6.

Van Aardt, M. (1994) 'In Search of a More Adequate Concept of Security for Southern Africa', *The South African Journal of International Affairs (SAJIA)* 1(1): 82–99.

Van Aardt, M. (1996, forthcoming) 'Factors Influencing Development Prospects for Southern Africa', in W. Carlsnaes and M. E. Muller (eds) *Change and South African External Relations*. Halfway House: Thomson International/Southern.

Van Nieuwkerk, A. (1994) 'Where is the Voice of the People? Public Opinion and Foreign Policy in South Africa', *The South African Journal of International Affairs (SAJIA)* 1(2): 98–109.

Van Nieuwkerk, A. (1995) 'Big or Small, Open or Closed? A Survey of Views on Regional Integration', in G. Mills, A. Begg and A. Van Nieuwkerk (eds) *South Africa in the Global Economy*, pp. 245–64. Johannesburg: SAIIA.

Van Vuuren, D. J. (1976) 'South Africa's Foreign Policy and International Practice as Reflected Mainly in Speeches, Statements and Replies by the Government in Parliament', in *South African Yearbook of International Law*, pp. 270–319. Pretoria: VerLoren van Themaat Centre for Public Law Studies, University of South Africa.

Van Wyk, K. (1994) 'Foreign Policy Options for a New South Africa', *The South African Journal of International Affairs (SAJIA)* 1(2): 78–97.

Venter, A. (ed.) (1989) *South African Government and Politics. An Introduction to Its*

Institutions, Processes and Policies. Johannesburg: Southern.

Venter, A. (ed.) (1993) *Foreign Policy Issues in a Democratic South Africa*. Johannesburg: PWPA.

Venter, D. (1993) 'South Africa and Africa: Towards Reconciliation', in A. Venter (ed.) *Foreign Policy Issues in a Democratic South Africa*, pp. 52–71. Johannesburg: PWPA.

9. THE NEW SOUTH AFRICA AND THE ARMED FORCES

Deon Fourie

Introduction

An important and unexpected feature of the changes taking place in South Africa since April 1994 has been the way in which the South African National Defence Force (SANDF) has adapted both to the new government and to the integration of forces against whom they had previously been ranged. The manner in which this has taken place has been in contrast to the expectations of many observers and also to the comparative difficulties apparently experienced in the civil service. Indeed, the adaptation of personnel from the armed forces of Umkhonto we Sizwe (MK) and the Azanian People's Liberation Army (APLA), the armed branches of the African National Congress and the Pan-African Congress respectively, has been equally surprising. An important feature of the adaptation has also been the loyalty which the SANDF has demonstrated in its peacekeeping role in the strife-torn parts of the country in which the killing has not yet stopped, particularly KwaZulu-Natal, where soldiers, including the part-time forces, continue to place their lives at risk in the interests of peace and stability.

This chapter describes the system, origins, development and character of the South African National Defence Force; the way in which the process of transformation was dealt with prior to the 1994 elections; and some problems and uncertainties that may make for a difficult road ahead.

Structure and System

The SANDF was previously (1912–94) the Union Defence Force (UDF) and then the South African Defence Force (SADF). It consists of the professional Permanent Force (PF), the Citizen Force (CF, which forms the bulk of the conventional fighting forces), and the Commandos, a voluntary home guard of infantry units for local defence and guarding vulnerable points. There is a South African Air Force twin, the Volunteer Air Squadrons, in which members use their own private aircraft for reconnaissance, liaison and other light aircraft missions. Both the CF and the Commandos are active militia forces, not reserves.

A new national service scheme was introduced by the Defence Amendment Act 1993, for citizens to be drawn by ballot unless sufficient were to offer themselves for service. However, in 1994 the new minister of defence came under pressure to abandon compulsory service and although the provisions for compulsion remain in the law, he has declared a moratorium on prosecutions for failure to report for duty. The effect is to remove compulsion and to rely on volunteers entirely. However, even before the moratorium there was a large-scale failure among part-time forces to report for the election mobilization in April 1994. This might have been caused by anxiety in the country regarding the atmosphere in which the election might take place: rumours were rife of impending riots and disorders. Since then, however, there has been a notable increase from the 10 percent reporting figure for April to 39 percent for an exercise later in the year.

The Defence Amendment Act 1993 provided that the CF servicemen should contract to undergo 12 months' continuous training, with CF part-time service for 30 days per year during the succeeding eight years, or longer periods for operational needs. After compulsory service members may continue as volunteers in the CF or the Commandos. Women may serve as volunteers for national service and in the CF or Commandos. At the end of July 1995 numbers in the part-time forces were as follows: short-term service, 2184; Commandos, 78,161; CF, 550,358, of whom 453,000 are in the Army. The remainder are in Air Force, Navy and Medical Services CF units (Committee on Integration, SANDF).

Historical Review

Early South African Wars

It is only natural that a country with a long history of colonization, imperial competition and political development should have been involved in a variety of wars and rebellions involving whites against whites as much as blacks against whites and blacks against blacks.[1] The first actual war between whites and San (otherwise known as Bushmen) under Chief Gonnema took place in 1673. There were small campaigns from time to time between 1770 and 1800 when engagements took place between colonial authorities and the Khoikhoi (whom the whites called the Hottentots). The first encounter between the colonists and the Xhosa began late in the 18th century, but peaceful commerce was interrupted at various times by nine wars with the Xhosa between 1778 and 1878.[2] During these periods the Cape was involved when the Netherlands fought in various wars against or in alliance with Spain, France and England in the religious and dynastic wars, in the American War of Independence and in the French Revolution and the Napoleonic wars. From the arrival of the Dutch in 1652 the fortification of the Cape and the institution of military service were meant to prevent other European powers from capturing the Cape.

Inevitably, as the British took over the Cape and Natal and republics were formed in the interior of southern Africa, British and colonial soldiers fought against the Boers – as the Dutch came to be called – and both fought the Zulus and other black nations. These were the times of wars such as the Transvaal–Pedi War (1876–7), the 'Gun War' with the Sotho, and the Anglo–Zulu War of 1879. Ultimately, the Anglo–Boer War (1899–1902) was fought, ending with Britain's annexing the Orange Free State and Transvaal republics. Although that was a war primarily between whites, many blacks became involved on both sides. South African involvement in wars of the 20th century is referred to later in this chapter.

Militia, Commandos, Volunteers

Of particular significance in an understanding of the armed forces in South Africa is the reliance that was always placed on part-time soldiers or militia in various forms almost from the beginning of colonization. Accordingly, the presence of professional or career armed forces was always minimal and almost always confined to command and support roles. However, more than 25 years after the Second World War, while the campaigns in Namibia and

---

1. The expression 'black' is now used for all people who are not 'white'. This includes the indigenous San, Khoi and the Bantu-speaking peoples (e.g. the Nguni – Xhosa and Zulu), the descendants of the slaves who were imported between the 17th and 18th centuries from countries such as Madagascar, Angola, Ghana, India and the Dutch East Indies (Indonesia), the Indian immigrants who came to Natal from 1862 onwards, and people of mixed race. Previously there were blacks (or Bantu), Coloureds, Asians (or Indians) and whites.

2. On this period see Davenport, T.R.H., *South Africa: A Modern History*, 3rd edn, Johannesburg, Macmillan, 1987, pp. 124–6 and Boeseken, A.J., 'Die Nederlandse Kommisarisse en die 18de Eeuse Samelewing aan die Kaap', *Argiefjaarboek vir Suid-Afrikaanse Geskiedenis, 1944*, 7e Jaargang, Staatsdrukker, Kaapstad, 1945, pp. 97–8.

Angola were under way between 1972 and 1989, the numbers in the PF grew dramatically to somewhere between 40,000 and 60,000, including civilian employees. Relatively few PF servicemen were in fighting units except for those in the Special Forces or in the command cadre of the National Service units. For active operational service reliance was still placed primarily on an annual establishment of some 23,000 National Servicemen, serving for two years, and on the part-time forces periodically mobilized to serve in operations for periods of 90 days annually. This was an unusual system for any country directly involved in warlike operations.

The concept of part-time citizen service began during the period of Dutch United East India Company (VOIC) rule (1652–1795). Initially, the regular forces were either the Company's own soldiers – including locally recruited Khoi and later Fengo soldiers – or specially raised mercenary regiments. However, when in 1659 the Company granted permanent settlement to all male *vrijburgers* between 16 and 60 rendering compulsory military service, companies of uniformed *militie* or *burgermacht* (militia or citizen forces) of infantry and dragoons were established.[3] Subject to regular compulsory training, the force was summoned to Cape Town castle by the firing of guns and the lighting of signal fires in times of threat from suspect foreign vessels.[4]

As the Cape Colony's frontiers extended, an irregular military system became more practicable for the rural areas for frontier conflict. The result in the outlying regions from 1715 was an additional but unorganized and temporary militia called the *commando*. Each commando was an irregular mounted company, mainly farmers, serving only for a specific task, usually with the local magistrate as 'commandant'. The system continued after the coming of the British who used commandos in the Cape as well as in Natal. In the Orange Free State and Transvaal Republics the commando system became the primary military system and was used in the republican forces that fought from October 1899 to May 1902 against the British army in the Anglo–Boer War. A strong emotional connotation resulted.[5] Indeed, in his *The Second World War*, Churchill (who served in that war) describes how their rugged determination to continue fighting after the British occupation

---

3. Diary of the Commander, Jan van Riebeeck, 1 May 1659 in Leibrandt, H.C., *Report on the Cape Archives*, 1907. Theal, G.M., *The History of South Africa 1691 to 1795*, Vol. II, Sonnenschein (s.l.), 1888, p. 91. The Dutch *Vrijburgers* (free burgers), VOIC employees conditionally released from their indentures, were the first of the colonists, mainly Dutch but later a Franco-German-Dutch combination who became known as the Boers or Afrikaners.

4. Theal, G.M., op. cit. note 3; Theal, G.M., *The History of South Africa Since September 1795*, Vol. I, Sonnenschein (s.l.), 1908, p. 130.

5. See Tylden, G., *The Armed Forces of South Africa*, Johannesburg, Africana Museum, 1954, Appendix; Theal, Vol. I, op. cit. note 4, pp. 15–17, 130; *Journal for Army Historical Research* XXIII, pp. 34–8.

of 1900 decided him to choose the title 'commandos' for the amphibious elite forces organized in 1940 as the only possible means of striking on land in raids against the German army of occupation in Europe.[6]

Forms of organized and compulsory service were also known among the black peoples of South Africa, especially the Nguni nations, at various times.[7] Especially well known is the system developed by the Zulu king, Chaka (1787?–1828), for a massive and successful long-service conscript army at the beginning of the 19th century. Organized by age group in regiments (*amaButho*) drilled to control deployment, they were used in a characteristic form of tactics for encirclement which, combined with the use of open, set-piece warfare, enabled a Zulu force to kill 1300 British soldiers in less than four hours in the Anglo–Zulu War of 1879.

On their second occupation of the Cape in 1806, the British dissolved the militia which had fought side by side with the Dutch regulars and mercenaries in 1795 and 1806. Henceforth, the garrisons of the Cape and later of Natal consisted of the professional British imperial army and small locally recruited colonial gendarmery forces. A British land forces command remained in South Africa until 1922 and a naval headquarters was kept at Simonstown until 1957. When the British units were withdrawn for the Crimean War in 1855 uniformed militia reappeared, this time as units of the Volunteers – which had developed in England, particularly during the

6. Churchill, W.S.L., *The Second World War*, Vol. 2, *Their Finest Hour*, Book 1, *The Fall of France*, Ch. 12 'The Apparatus of Counter-Attack, 1940', London, Cassell, 1949. After 1945 the term was retained by the Royal Marines to designate their amphibious battalions. The romance of the name also led organizations like the PLO's Fatah to designate their bands 'commandos'. See Macksey, K. et al., *The Penguin Encyclopaedia of Modern Warfare*, London, Penguin, 1991, pp. 81–2; Parkinson, R., *Encyclopaedia of Modern War*, London, Granada, 1979, p. 93 and Luttwak, E., *A Dictionary of Modern War*, London, Allen Lane, 1972, p. 58. The Anglo–Boer War had a profound emotional influence on South Africans for decades after. Once the set-piece campaign ended in early 1900 the Boer forces continued an irregular war, called the guerrilla campaign, closer in methods to T.E. Lawrence's campaign against the Turks than to the campaigns fought, for example, in Asia, Ireland or Greece after 1945. Nevertheless, in their attempts to force a conclusion the British used a scorched-earth campaign, burning farms, killing livestock and incarcerating women, children and black labourers and tenants in 'concentration' camps: some 22,000 whites and 14,000 blacks died in the camps: Warwick, P., *Black People and the South African War, 1899–1902*, New York, Cambridge University Press, 1983, p. 4.
7. A wide-ranging description of the age-regiment systems among various South African tribes is given in Davenport, op. cit. note 2, pp. 64–9. Donald Morris in *The Washing of the Spears*, London, Jonathan Cape, 1966, Chs 2, 3 and 8, gives probably the most comprehensive examination of any African military system. See also Becker, P., *Path of Blood: Mzilkazi – Founder of the Matabele*, London, Longmans Green, 1962, Chs 3, 7, 8, 14, 19 and Appendix II.

Napoleonic threat.[8] They supplemented the few remaining imperial and regular colonial forces in the Cape and Natal, providing part-time infantry, mounted infantry, artillery, engineers, medical services and logistic services. This was the foundation of a strong tradition that was to enable the country to participate, solely with volunteers, in both world wars.

Many of the so-called Dutch (Boer or Afrikaner) colonists served to-gether with the British colonists in the Volunteers, and in the Cape some units included Coloured volunteers. Membership of the Volunteers had considerable social significance for Cape and Natal colonial society. Some of the prominent Boer leaders of the Anglo–Boer War gained their first military knowledge in red coats in the Victoria College Volunteer Rifle Corps, today the Stellenbosch University. They included the Boer generals Barry Hertzog and Jan Smuts, and also Daniel Malan – who all became prime ministers of the Union.[9] From 1877, uniformed, disciplined volun-teers also appeared in the Transvaal, first under the brief British rule (1877–81) and then in Kruger's South African Republic.

Union and a Common Defence Force

In 1912, after the four colonies were unified in the Union of South Africa, Parliament passed the South African Defence Act to establish the Union Defence Force (UDF) with the forces of the four colonies as the foundation. The new system combined elements from South Africa and other countries and was to lay the foundations of the various forms of military service that continued in essence until 1994.

The inefficient and undermanned purely volunteer system was replaced with the liability to serve until the age of 55. However, expecting to need much less than available manpower, compulsion was eased by a ballot to be applied only if insufficient citizens offered themselves for service each year.

---

8. There is a wide range of works on the Volunteer regiments and their successors in the Citizen Force. Tylden, op. cit. note 5, contains an encyclopedic summary of almost every unit that ever existed in South Africa. Among numerous other regimental histories are Neil Orpen's *Gunners of the Cape* and *The Cape Town Highlanders*, A.C. Martin's *The Royal Durban Light Infantry*, Stanley Monick's *Clear the Way – the South African Irish* and James Mitchell's *Tartan on the Veld*, about the Transvaal Scottish, established in 1902.

9. Smuts, a barrister and Attorney-General of the Transvaal Republic at 28, fought as a commando general in the guerrilla phase of the Anglo–Boer War. He became Minister of Defence in 1910, commanded in the field in German South West Africa in 1914–15 and held supreme command of Allied forces in German East Africa in 1916 before joining Lloyd George's War Cabinet in 1917–18. He chaired the committee that established the independent Royal Air Force. In the Second World War he was made a Field Marshall in the Imperial Army and was frequently asked for military advice by Churchill. In his diaries Alanbrooke, wartime Chief of the Imperial General Staff, frequently refers to Smuts's counsels in remarkably flattering terms. Yet Smuts was never a professional soldier.

The Act provided for black men to serve in war, but only white males were compelled to serve for 120 days' 'continuous training' divided among four years in the various branches of the Citizen Force (CF) and to attend weekly parades for training, musketry practice and administration. Forty-four mounted and infantry battalions together with services, a South African Division of the Royal Naval Volunteer Reserve and an Aviation Corps were established in the Active Citizen Force (ACF, equivalent to today's CF).

Although only some 30,000 posts were established, 44,193 volunteered to serve out of the 64,000 men eligible for CF service in 1913.[10] An explanation for this could probably be sought in the tradition of volunteer military service, the first flush of the birth of a 'new' country and the presence in the country of many veterans of the Anglo–Boer War for whom and for whose sons military service might have had a degree of sentimental attraction.

It was the conscious drawing together in the UDF of personnel both of Boer and British origins that makes the period of particular interest and concern for the present developments in South Africa. Then also there was a need to integrate members of erstwhile enemy forces. Among the officers on the first course held in 1913 to train the district staff officers who were to administer the UDF's military districts were Anglo–Boer War veterans from both sides, since colonial forces fought alongside the British army. This required adaptations of all – although in the end it was more of the British military culture that shaped the UDF than anything specifically drawn from the Afrikaner military past.

The Two World Wars and Korea

South Africa became involved in both world wars and in Korea using only volunteers, since the Defence Act prohibited the deployment of citizens outside South Africa.

South African soldiers served in the First World War with a final strength of 231,209 volunteers, of whom 16,000 were casualties. After the brief anti-war Afrikaner rebellion in 1914, some 100,852, including the Commandos, served in German South West Africa (Namibia). Two divisions (60,322) then went on to volunteer to serve in German East Africa (Tanzania) with British forces under South African supreme commanders, first J.C. Smuts and then van Deventer, both former Boer field commanders. The 1st SA

10. Collyer, J.J., *The Campaign in German South West Africa*, Pretoria, Government Printer, 1936, p.16. On the two wars see also: Collyer's *The South Africans with General Smuts in German East Africa*, Pretoria, GPW, 1939; Buchan, J., *The South African Forces in France*, London, Nelson, 1920; *Official Year Book of the Union* No.5 (1922), Pretoria, Government Printer, 1923, pp. 397–411 and No. 23 (1946), 1946, Ch. 29.

Infantry Brigade took part in the Turkish-initiated Senussi uprising in Egypt
before going on to fight in France and Belgium. The brigade was destroyed
three times, at Delville Wood and Butte de Warlencourt in the Somme
Campaign in 1916 and at Ypres in 1917. Accordingly, although it was only a
brigade, ultimately 30,719 men passed through its ranks. The SA Field
Artillery and the Cape Corps served in Palestine in Allenby's campaign
against the Turks.[11]

South Africa entered the Second World War by a resolution of Parliament on 4 September 1939, with the Permanent and Citizen Forces reduced
respectively to 3353 and 14,631 both by the economic depressions and by the
acceptance in South Africa of the '10-year rule' instituted in 1919 by the
British government to the effect that Britain would not be engaged in a
general war for the next 10 years. The rule was renewed year by year for the
next 20 years. During the years preceding the war strict financial economy
had been imposed, and often the soldiers in the ACF regiments had paid the
costs of holding training camps out of their own pockets. Of the 122,000
Defence Rifle Associations (Commando) men registered only 18,300 had
been trained. The Defence Force possessed two old tanks and two 1925
armoured cars. There were some 75 obsolete artillery pieces; the only
modern pieces were six 2-pounder anti-tank guns and eight 3-inch anti-
aircraft guns together with 15 Bren light machine guns. Soon after the war
began six of the anti-aircraft guns were sent to protect the harbour of
Mombassa. The SA Air Force had 11 fighters and 82 obsolete light bombers.
The permanent SA Naval Service had been disbanded in 1923. There was
insufficient artillery ammunition and few aircraft bombs.[12]

Despite the lack of preparation in 1939, by the end of the Second World
War 406,133 volunteers, including 24,975 women, had served in Ethiopia,
the Western Desert including Alamein, Italy, and Madagascar (342,792)
and in the 3rd SA Division at home as well as in various part-time home-
guard formations in South Africa. Thirty-five South African Air Force
(SAAF) squadrons (44,569) flew 34,000 sorties in the Desert Air Force,
destroying 340 enemy aircraft as well as engaging in bombing operations.

---

11. Adler, F., Lorch, A. and Curson, H., *The SA Field Artillery in German East Africa and
Palestine, 1915–1919*, Pretoria, Van Schaik, 1958. The role played by black, Coloured and
Indian servicemen in the two world wars has recently been the subject of study by Lt-Gen. Ian
Gleeson, former Chief of Defence Force Staff, *The Unknown Force*, Rivonia, Ashanti, 1994.

12. The condition of the defence force and the efforts put into preparing it for war are to be
found in Martin, H.J. and Orpen, N., *South Africa At War*, Vol. VII of the series *SA Forces in
World War II*, Cape Town and London, Purnell, 1979. There are also three volumes of the
official history published by the Union War Histories Division, closed by the prime minister in
1961. Published by Oxford University Press under the general editorship of Agar Hamilton,
they were: *Crisis in the Desert*, 1952; *The Sidi Rezegh Battles*, 1957; and *War in the Southern
Oceans*, 1961.

The SAAF went on to fight in Italy and its Liberator bombers flew 41 sorties over 2500km from Foggia, Italy to Poland to aid the Warsaw Uprising in August 1944, losing 11 aircraft. Under the Empire Air Training scheme South Africa housed 32 air schools and trained 21,126 air crew for the Royal Air Force and Allied forces and 12,221 for the SAAF. After the end of the European war in May 1945, 23,391 South Africans offered themselves for service in the Far Eastern theatre; of course, the surrender of Japan made their service unnecessary.

The SA naval forces (SANF), organized in 1939 with 96 corvettes and minesweepers (converted trawlers and whalers) and other small vessels, and 9455 men and women, served to counter the German, Italian and Japanese submarines in the South Atlantic and Indian Oceans. Through these seas men and material were conveyed to the Middle East war until 1943, and to the Japanese theatre, while supplies were conveyed to Britain. Some 5 percent of all Allied shipping tonnage sunk by submarines was sunk around South African coasts. This included 7500 merchant ships and 2600 naval vessels. The SANF also engaged in operations with units in the Mediterranean.

Some 38,000 SA servicemen became casualties, including 12,354 who lost their lives. In 1943 in the midst of war a general election was held with the servicemen abroad also voting, and, despite some vociferous opposition to South African participation in a war alongside Britain, the Smuts government was returned with 110 seats against the mainly National Party's (NP) 43.

A defence industry had to be set up during the war to supply the forces' needs as the British were quite unable to provide anything. Armoured cars, artillery pieces, radios, optical sights, small arms, a wide range of artillery and naval gun ammunition, tyres, food and clothing, all were provided for the campaigns in Africa and Italy until the USA was able to produce armaments for the Italian campaign. Much of the equipment went to the British forces in North Africa and Asia as well.[13]

Two years after the NP acceded to power the Korean War began. Despite their previous opposition to overseas wars they now took the view that the country should demonstrate her anti-communist sentiments. Already in 1948 a transport squadron had been sent by the air force to participate in the Berlin air lift in which 1240 sorties were flown. Accordingly, the 2nd Fighter Squadron of the SAAF was sent with 208 volunteer pilots to Korea in 1950. There they flew 12,067 fighter-bomber sorties during the Korean War (1950–3), losing 74 aircraft and 34 pilots in action. Several South African

13. *Record of the Organisation of the Director-General of War Supplies (1939–1943) and Director-General of Supplies (1943–1945)*, Johannesburg, L.S. Gray & Co. (n.d.). *Military Veterans News*, June 1991, official publication of the Ministry of Defence.

army officers also gained experience serving in the British Commonwealth Division.[14]

Campaigns in Africa

The NP's determination to retain Namibia, perhaps as a fifth province, resulted eventually in the SADF's engagement from 1972 in counter-insurgency operations against the South West African Peoples' Organization (SWAPO) who were based in Angola and Zambia. This was the first campaign in which conscripts as well as volunteers were employed. Initially the South African forces only responded to incursions into Namibia. Since this left the initiative entirely in the hands of the insurgents, a general strategy of striking at SWAPO bases inside Angola and Zambia was adopted. Eventually in the aftermath of the demise of the Portuguese empire this strategy led to small South African units participating at various times in the civil war in Angola on the side of UNITA (National Union for the Total Independence of Angola) against the MPLA (Popular Movement for the Liberation of Angola) regime.

Participation in the civil war began during late 1975 with Operation Savannah. In this operation aid was given to UNITA and the FNLA at the request of the American, Zambian and other governments on the collapse of the tripartite Angolan government established in 1975 by the Alvor Agreement. To avoid the stamp of association with South Africa she was asked to conduct the operation in secret. Thus it was undertaken with a mere 1200 men – the first foreign campaign in which volunteers were not used. They used only liaison aircraft and helicopters together with light Panhard armoured cars and Second World War 25-pounder and 5.5-inch artillery. Outmatched and outranged by the Soviet T-54/55 tanks and artillery which the 11,000 Cuban forces deployed to aid the MPLA, resort was successfully made to stratagem, surprise and courage. Despite the disadvantages, the South African–UNITA–FNLA forces saw the lights of Luanda. But the resolution of 19 December 1975 by the US Congress forbidding aid to the two movements led to a South African decision to withdraw rather than risk engaging in a full-scale battle for Luanda.

After the MPLA allowed the establishment in Angola of SWAPO bases for operations in Namibia, the South African government considered its interests threatened and national service was extended from 12 months to two full years. The two years were then followed by annual periods of training or operations during the succeeding 12 years in the CF or in the Commandos. During that period it was customary for the CF and even the

---

14. Moore, D. and Bagshawe, P., *South Africa's Flying Cheetahs in Korea*, Johannesburg, Ashanti, 1991.

Commandos to be called upon to fulfil up to 90 days' operational service each year.

Subsequently, the SADF was engaged in a variety of operations inside Angola. Several, such as Protea and Smokeshell, were well publicized abroad. These operations included considerable participation by CF units temporarily mobilized to serve in various roles. The first was Operation Reindeer in May 1978. Immediately prior to the operation a number of prominent Namibian politicians had been murdered by SWAPO and the RSA government felt vulnerable and unable to dominate Namibia's political scene. The operation was a parachute landing of a CF battalion at Cassinga, 250km inside Angola, combined with an armoured car strike close to the border. It was aimed at destroying SWAPO facilities rather than awaiting further cross-border incursions by guerrilla bands. After several such operations had followed over a period of years, the American government prevailed on the South African government to stop in the interests of a negotiated settlement.[15]

In the meantime ARMSCOR, the government's armaments supplier, had been engaged in a large-scale renewal of the stock of conventional armaments. A heavy infantry combat vehicle called the Ratel, a multiple rocket launcher, Kukri – a copied improvement of one captured during Operation Savannah – and the G-5 155mm gun-howitzer with a range of 40km were developed under the aegis of ARMSCOR, frequently with foreign help. The South African government had been manufacturing arms since 1963, when Britain and the United States began embargoes in response to a UN call. This time they were far more sophisticated than they had been during the Second World War, however, and included a variety of missiles, electronic equipment and other features.

When in 1987 the MPLA regime commenced a large-scale conventional campaign in the south east of Angola directed at capturing Jamba, UNITA's capital, Savimbi asked for help to prevent UNITA's being overwhelmed.[16] Consequently, some 1500 South Africans were forced to help stop the advance across the Lomba River towards Jamba – again with a pretence to secrecy. The success of the operations was dramatic. When the MPLA's 47th Brigade was destroyed on 3 October and 16, 21 and 59 Brigades withdrew to Cuito Cuanavale the campaign ground to a halt. The government then ordered that the region to the east of the Cuito river be cleared in an endeavour to prevent the launching of any further offensives

---

15. Crocker, Chester, *High Noon in Southern Africa*, Johannesburg, Jonathan Ball, 1994 (1993), p. 181.

16. Fred Bridgland's work *The War for Africa*, Gibraltar, Ashanti, 1990, contains full details of this campaign. Bridgland relied heavily on SADF sources but as a former supporter of Savimbi who changed his mind during this period, he seems a fairly reliable source.

by the MPLA in 1987 or 1988. This order took the South Africans to the neighbourhood of Cuito Cuanavale where several battles were fought in early 1988. An advance to Cuito Cuanavale had not been part of the original intention, which had been only to stop the MPLA and Cuban advance. South Africa's seeking to keep operations secret enabled the Cuban ambassador Jorge Risquet to proclaim a Cuban victory, thus robbing the South African government of political advantage despite the forces' having achieved successive dramatic victories. For example, during one 58-minute battle at dusk in February 1988, a CF tank squadron of Olifant tanks (redesigned Centurions) destroyed eight MPLA tanks, several artillery pieces, armoured cars and lorries, with no South African casualties at all. The Cuban generals Rafael del Pino and Ochua both later described this campaign as a disaster for MPLA and Cuban arms. Indeed, Fidel Castro himself took command of the campaign when, as he put it in a speech explaining Cuban involvement, he believed 'the revolution was in danger of being lost in Angola'. When the Cuban 50th Division was deployed in western Angola in 1988, CF units were combined with full-time units to form the 10th Division to meet the anticipated invasion of Namibia. The ability of the Cubans to get away with claiming victory, however, probably made a considerable contribution to enabling a settlement to be reached over the vexed question of the withdrawal of Cuban forces by saving face for the Cuban government.

Between 1966 and April 1989, 788 South African servicemen lost their lives in operations in Namibia and Angola. In addition, from 1981 in the SWA Territory force, the Namibian military establishment, 108 men died; 32 Battalion, consisting of Angolans serving in a unit of the SADF, lost 181 men between 1976 and 1989.[17]

Aid to the Civil Power

At various times since 1913 the Defence Force, including the CF and Commandos, had been used to support the inadequate police force as an aid

---

17. The casualties are the official figures obtained from the Military Veterans Administration of the Ministry of Defence. They represent the names marked with an asterisk on the memorial to the fallen at Fort Klapperkop, Pretoria. For accounts of the main campaigns see Bridgland, op. cit., note 16, passim, Heitman, H.R., *War in Angola*, Gibraltar, Ashanti, 1990 and Spies, F.J. du T., *Operasie Savannah, Angola 1975–1976*, Pretoria, SA Weermag, 1989. After the imposition of the British and American arms embargoes in 1963 the South African government returned to the local manufacture of all kinds of armaments, far more sophisticated than those made during the Second World War. See Landgren, S., *Embargo Disimplemented – South Africa's Military Industry*, Oxford, Oxford University Press, 1989.

to the civil power during internal disturbances.[18] The most prominent
occasions include the industrial strikes by whites in 1913 and 1914, the
Afrikaner Rebellion of 1914, and the so-called Rand Revolution of 1922
when white labour unions rose in armed revolt and Johannesburg was
subjected to artillery fire and aerial bombing. The armed forces were also
called to serve in the states of emergency of 1960, 1976 and 1984. During the
years 1990 to 1994 the political conflicts among the various contenders for
power in the events leading to the first nationwide election again necessitated employment of military forces, part-time as well as full-time, to assist
the police in their attempt to keep the peace. By the end of April 1994, some
5000 CF and Commandos, as well as full-time soldiers, 10,000 in all, had
been mobilized for service throughout the country to enable the election to
take place in safety. According to a SANDF information release, 'on the
election days this peaked at 143 companies or 20,500 full and part time force
members'.[19] The policy of calling up part-time soldiers to supplement the PF
and the police proved to be very successful. The marked decline in the level
of violence bore testimony to the ability of the military forces to enable the
elections to take place in an atmosphere untrammelled by intimidation and
fear. The significance of this role can best be understood when the numbers
of people killed in the political violence in South Africa since 1984 are
considered. Between September 1984 and February 1990, 5539 people died
as a result of political violence, while another 4699 had died by the end of
April 1991. Toward the end of 1993 the numbers killed in some 90,000
incidents of political violence since 1984 were estimated at around 11,000.
Between January and 17 May 1994, there were 4415 incidents and 1416

---

18. The recent history of the South African Police is that of a neglected, ill-led, misused,
underpaid, undertrained and dispirited force. For several years they have been the targets of
deliberate assassinations: during 1995, 212 were murdered; in 1994 the number exceeded 260.
Despite their repeated role in internal disturbances as well as the steady population growth,
both of which would have justified a larger police force, they remained numerically small and
virtually untrained for riot control. The effect was to make several relatively low-level public
disturbances uncontrollable. Examples were Sharpeville (1960), Soweto (1976) and Uitenhage
(1985). In each case the police, outnumbered, unprepared and untrained for correct mob
control, opened fire without orders or in desperation. In 1983–4, for an area of over 1 million
square km, there were 44,615 professional policemen and women distributed among 808 police
stations, headquarters and training schools – a ratio of 1.6 policemen per 1000 people. In
Northern Ireland the proportion was 4.4, in Scotland 2.4, in France 3.4, in the Netherlands 2.5,
in Israel 2.7, in West Germany 2.6, in Botswana 2.5. In each case the area served has to be taken
into account for the figures to be emphasized. There was also a Reserve Police Force of about
14,000 unpaid part-time volunteers. *Information Digest*, Johannesburg, South Africa Foundation, 1987, pp. 24–6.

19. SANDF, 'The Defence Force and Election 1994', *Information Bulletin*, Chief Directorate of Communications (n.d.).

deaths – more than in any single year since 1990.[20]

Rule by the Soldiers?

During the period when the SADF was engaged in Angola and in the counter-insurgency operations at home, a myth was propagated by a variety of writers, some South African but mostly foreign, that a form of military coup d'etat had taken place in South Africa. In summary, the allegations were that the country was being run by armed forces in the interests of irresponsible militarism and conservative resistance to change. The allegations were the work of people who had no access to primary sources and who had almost without exception neither met nor interviewed the officers alleged to have been the leaders of the supposed military junta; names were never mentioned, suggesting that the writers did not know to whom they were referring. This was the period in which the campaigns in Namibia and Angola were at a climax while the black townships burned, the 'necklace' (a petrol-filled tyre around the neck) seemed the highest form of political discourse, and the SADF was trying to conduct a number of counter-insurgency operations to assist the administration of the townships because of the inability or unwillingness of the civilian departments to come to grips with the disasters that accompanied the half-hearted reforms of the Botha government. In an effort to stabilize the situation within the country as well as in Namibia, use was made of an instrument introduced not by the SADF but by parliamentary legislation in 1970, namely, the State Security Council (SSC). Derived from the system of federal and state 'war' committees in Malaya during the insurgency between 1948 and 1960, this was an instrument for overseeing and coordinating not only the security but also the administrative arms of government in accordance with contemporary approaches to counter-insurgency. Since the civil servants were untutored in staff methods and reluctant to learn anything about counter-insurgency, the SSC and its subordinate regional committees were almost without exception chaired and staffed by military officers. This situation also contributed to the myth that they were the ultimate decision-makers in South Africa. In fact, their actions could more properly be seen as attempts to apply – and to

---

20. The following selection gives an impression of the extent of the problem of violence and the SADF's role: the data comes from De Kock, C.P., 'Dynamics of the Present Political Violence and Suggested Solutions', unpublished paper, Human Sciences Research Council, 1990, p. 1, and 'The Potential for Violent Conflict in a Democratic South Africa', unpublished paper, HSRC, 1994, p. 2, Table 1; also Olivier, J.L., 'Violence: Achilles Heel of Democracy in South Africa', *HSRC in Focus* 2(6), July/August 1993, p. 2; Kentridge, M., 'Root Cause of Natal Violence', *The Star*, 18 April 1990, p. 12; Nicolson, M., 'The Issue Behind the Natal Blood-letting', *The Star*, 18 April 1990, p. 13; Linscott, G., 'SADF Has to Walk a Fine Line to Keep the Peace', *The Star*, 18 May 1990, p. 8.

push the civil servants into applying – the axiom propounded during the Malayan emergency by Sir Gerald Templar, who wrote that 'any idea that the business of normal civil government and the business of the Emergency are two separate entities must be killed for good and all. The two activities are completely and utterly interrelated.'[21]

No doubt the myth of a military assumption of power was very useful to the opposition to the government, especially while the armed forces were engaged in a counter-insurgency programme which relied very much on the British approach of 'winning hearts and minds' in contrast to the harsh methods of the police which, if anything, had the opposite effect. Some of the writers were undoubtedly engaged in an interpretation in which they genuinely believed, but others were merely climbing on what had become a profitable publishing bandwagon. What is interesting is the absence of analysis on the part of those members of the South African press without a political axe to grind. The silence of the NP government, especially under P.W. Botha, at the suggestion that it had lost control of the country was as remarkable as it was inexplicable. It was perhaps an indication of the convenience of the myth at a time when the government was employing police and armed forces in covert operations, the full extent of which may only be revealed once the Truth and Reconciliation Commission has completed its work.[22] If the armed forces were running the country, how was it that F.W. de Klerk was able to overturn the supposed warlike, conservative military government and hand the Defence Force over to the new government? The various allegations have been analysed by Annette Seegers in her review article which discusses the conclusions of several writers. Rocklyn Williams, an ANC publicist, has also written that the SADF 'never formally challenged either the civilian or political authorities ... A strong constitutionalist identity, a reliance on conscripts for the bulk of its operational manpower, and a tradition of subservience to elected government constituted restraining factors in this regard.'[23]

---

21. Quoted by McCuen, J.J., *The Art of Counter-Revolutionary War*, London, Faber, 1966, p. 189.

22. See, for example, Boraine, A., Scheffer, R. and Levy, J. (eds), *Dealing with the Past*, Johannesburg, IDASA, 1994 and Minaar, A., Liebenberg, I. and Schutte, C. (eds), *The Hidden Hand: Covert Operations in South Africa*, Johannesburg, IDASA, 1994.

23. Seegers carefully examines the defects in the 'analyses', and the absence of sources, in 'The Military in South Africa: A Comparison and Critique', *South Africa International* 16(4), April 1986, pp. 192–200; Williams, R., 'SANDF in Transition', *MPD News* 3(3), September 1994, p. 5.

The Process of Transformation Since 1990

Transition for the Defence Force was beset by challenges and difficulties almost from the moment de Klerk delivered his speech to Parliament in February 1990.

Following decades of government pursuit of the policy of preventing at all costs the accession to power of the ANC and the South African Communist Party, the question naturally arose of how the services would face up to the government's reversal of its previous position. The mere decision to embark on negotiations expected to result in the accession to power of their erstwhile enemies was likely to result in unfavourable reaction from the services – at the least, a serious crisis of loyalty, even though these movements' forces had hardly ever been engaged by the SADF.

In particular, the process of transformation after the change in government could also be expected to hold great potential for conflict between the government and its armed forces. The SADF had developed its own character, albeit one rooted in the British military tradition. Although many members had a loyalty to the governing party, the part-time character of the majority meant that large numbers of active members were not NP supporters. On the other hand, MK and the APLA had been trained mainly by the Soviet bloc or Chinese forces and had developed as the armed wings of political movements.[24] Fundamental changes to values, traditions, customs and symbols could be expected to cause friction.[25]

Brief Encounters

The earliest moves towards dealing with the problems of bringing the armed forces of the negotiating parties together in preparation for transition were made by the Institute for a Democratic Alternative for South Africa (IDASA), which invited the SADF, individual members of the Citizen Force and Commandos, the ANC, the PAC and others to participate in discussions in Lusaka in May 1990 regarding the future of the SADF. At the political level permission to participate was refused to members of the SADF. Accordingly, only officers serving in the 'homeland' forces, and retired or low-profile part-time forces officers attended. Nothing was accomplished and some of the discussions became acrimonious. Then in 1993 several officers of the PF and of MK were invited to visit the armed forces in the USA. In October of that year the Institute for Defence Policy and the

---

24. There is a brief review of MK in Motumi, T., 'Umkhonto we Sizwe', *African Defence Review* No.18, August 1994, pp. 1–11.

25. A fuller discussion of what follows may be found in Gutteridge, W., *The Military in South African Politics – Champions of National Unity*, London, RISCT, June 1994.

Bavarian Hanns-Seidel Foundation took a larger group of high-ranking civil servants, SADF (PF and CF), homeland forces and MK to Germany to learn about contemporary German training, approaches to command and the concept of *Innere Führung*. The group included the deputy minister of defence. Finally, early in 1994 a similar group was taken by IDASA to Denmark, Belgium and Austria to learn about the functioning of the Danish Defence Ministry, their permanent and part-time forces and civil defence structure, NATO and the Commission for Security and Cooperation in Europe (CSCE). The latter visits were highly successful in enabling former opponents to meet.

Stage Managing Change

Among political leaders official discussions had begun in February 1992, when the issue of 'private armies' was raised at the Convention for a Democratic South Africa (Codesa). Within days, Minister of Defence Roelf Meyer and the Commander of MK, Joe Modise, commenced the process of discussing the future of the armed forces under the control of the various parties. Their motive was simply the need for the SADF and the police to gain almost instantaneous legitimacy so as to be able to provide a form of guardianship under which the democratic process, the new constitution and the election could develop.

Failing to understand or to accept the ethic of political obedience extant among both career and part-time members of the SADF, the liberation movements feared that the armed forces would rise against the coming transformation. There was also a belief that the forces would interfere with the election process and prevent it being free and impartially administered. Consequently there was a great deal of pressure throughout the negotiations for the institution of a form of joint or multi-party control over the forces. This was achieved, ultimately, through the establishment by Act of Parliament in December 1993 of the Transitional Executive Council (TEC), whose object was to provide for a form of joint transitionary control over government as a whole.[26]

The TEC's tasks were to ensure the transition's taking place without interference, and to serve as a precursor of the Government of National Unity. Among the seven sub-councils established was the Sub-Council on Defence (SCD). Its least successful undertaking was the establishment of the so-called National Peace Keeping Force. For a variety of reasons, including impatience on the part of some of the principal actors, this was a disaster, wholly unable to fulfil its purpose of replacing the police and SADF

---

26. 'Ticklish Tasks of the TEC Sub-structure', *Negotiation News* No.14, 15 March 1994, pp. 6–9. Transitional Executive Council Act, 1993.

in maintaining order during the elections. On the other hand, a very successful enterprise was the Joint Military Coordinating Council (JMCC) directed at planning a national defence force acceptable to all parties that would simultaneously house the SADF, the disestablished 'homeland' forces and the political armed forces. The Sub-Council on Defence itself was constituted at a semi-political level with Deputy Minister of Defence Wynand Breytenbach, Joe Modise and Ronnie Kasrils (the subsequent minister and deputy minister of defence) and the retired Chief of the SADF, General André Liebenberg, among the members. Although some envisaged that it would take effective command of the SADF, this never really happened. The JMCC was more of a working group with the Chief of the SADF, General Georg Meiring, and the Chief of Staff of MK, Sipiwe Nyanda, as co-chairmen. Subordinate to the JMCC were six working groups dealing with the future character of National Defence Force personnel, intelligence, operations, logistics, finance and miscellaneous subjects. Their concerns ranged from the integration process and requisite organizations, through the re-establishment of a civilian defence secretariat, to insignia and uniform. Despite an atmosphere of mistrust at the beginning, cooperation developed so well that conflicts among those serving on the subordinate working groups could be amicably resolved at the two higher levels. Unlike the civil service departments, who for the most part had taken no preliminary steps towards preparing for the fundamental changes that were about to follow, the JMCC was able to wind up its work formally on 22 April 1994, five days before the election.

Table 1. South African National Defence Force: % on Full-time Service (PF, VMS), 31 May 1995

	Men	Women
Black	50.9	1.7
Coloured	9.0	0.5
White	29.6	7.1
Asian	1.0	–

Source. Committee on Integration, SANDF.

Instituting Transformation

Integration and its implications for the appointment of officers from organizations outside the SADF and from the homeland forces has naturally proved to be one of the hardest problems (Table 1). During the two world wars many blacks served in non-combatant roles. In the campaigns in Tanganyika and Palestine, however, there were Coloured troops who were combatants. Once the NP had begun to institute apartheid from 1948, Minister of Defence F.C. Erasmus ended the use of black soldiers. After that they were employed only in an auxiliary semi-civilian establishment. This was in contrast to the police in which they formed some 50 percent of the strength. Integration of black citizens into the predominantly white SADF began in the 1970s. When General Magnus Malan (later minister of defence) became chief of the army he began the integration of black, Coloured and Indian citizens into the forces. There were numerous differences from the past, however. Malan believed in full integration and he gradually changed the identity of the PF to one consisting of many more blacks than ever before as well as introducing the commissioning of blacks as officers. Since this was to all intents and purposes a contradiction of the government's policies it was not until 1993 that the first Coloured brigadier was appointed as a director in the personnel division at army headquarters. This progress was not seen by the liberation movements as being acceptable.

Clearly a fundamental change in the SANDF as a reflection of the constitutional changes elsewhere in the country would be in the composition not only of the substructure of the force but of the officer corps. This was a particularly strong expectation because during their underground history the black opposition movements were preparing for a campaign of violence. Many members, male and female, had been given some form of military training in Africa, Asia or eastern Europe. It was inevitable that this kind of training would condition people to expect to be absorbed into a new defence force, even if only for a brief period. Algeria, where armed formations marched into the towns, may have been a dominant image for many, despite the fact that such events did not occur in Zimbabwe or Namibia.

Initially, MK and APLA apparently conceived of the SADF's being dissolved, to be replaced either by their members or by a selection of acceptable personnel from all parties. Patently, this was impracticable. The SADF point of view was that the 'non-statutory forces', i.e. MK and APLA, having been trained as guerrillas, could not have enjoyed standards of training equal to those of the SADF or the homeland forces – that is, the small forces maintained in the Transkei, Bophutatswana, Ciskei and Venda (TBCV) who were also to be brought into the new SANDF. Indeed, there remains an impression that Soviet bloc training often fell short of western levels.[27] In addition, there was the problem that many of the returning exiles

27. During the visit of the mixed group to the Bundeswehr the defects in the development of officers and NCOs in the Nationale Volksarmee of the GDR was graphically described in lectures and briefings by the DBW. A detailed exposition appears in Millotat, C.O.E., 'The Bundeswehr in the New Federal States', *Defense Analysis* 9(3), 1993, pp. 311–18. In this article the description of the absence of an NCO's corps and the employment of officers in the NVA in inferior roles might serve to explain the impression given by the non-statutory forces integrated into the SANDF.

lacked the educational qualifications required of modern military officers and even NCOs. There were some strenuous debates before the final recommendations were made in April 1994. However, the wise decision had been taken to invite the British government to send the military Advisory and Training Team (BMATT) to adjudicate and to resolve disputes on the levels of training and capacities of individuals and the ranks to which they were capable of being appointed. Also, a system of 'bridging training' was introduced for the newly entered personnel. This enabled numerous appointments to be made on 28 June 1994, including two lieutenant-generals (one was Sipiwe Nyanda, the Chief of Defence Staff who was formerly MK Chief of Staff), nine major-generals and several brigadiers and colonels and other officers. These appointments were all according to the norms acceptable to neutral observers, so all parties could be reasonably satisfied. Figures a year later can be seen in Table 2.

Table 2. Integration by Rank, at 30 June 1995

Lt-Gen.	2	Colonel	51
Maj.-Gen.	9	Lt Col.	114
Brigadier	17	Major	247
Junior Officers	867	Chaplain	1

Total 1308 (excluding SADF and TBCV)

Source. Committee on Integration, SANDF.

The appointment of these officers was intended to mark a genuine change from white hegemony. At the same time there was a great deal of dissatisfaction and delay due to the absence of accurate prior information on the numbers that would report at the assembly areas. There were shortages of bedding, uniforms and tents; and since there was an insistence on self-sufficiency, contracts for catering were given outside the SANDF with some disastrous results. Administration was also somewhat tedious. All these matters were taken in hand in October 1994, in attempts to speed up integration and improve morale and discipline. Nevertheless the last personnel will not be taken in until August 1996. In the meantime, another product of the discussions, the Service Corps, intended to provide training in trades to enable former members to follow careers outside the forces was also set in hand. At the end of 1995, however, it had not proved very successful, apparently because it could not offer large enough incentives for personnel to give up salaries in favour of the uncertainties of the outside world. The budget for integration in 1994/5 was R597,170 million.

The working groups had not anticipated all the problems of integration. The process found the organizers surprised by numbers far in excess of what had been expected. This could largely be ascribed to poor record-keeping by

MK, the late decision of APLA to participate, and the arrival at bases of numbers of people whose connection with the movements was doubtful and probably more related to unemployment.[28] There was also a failure to anticipate that many MK and APLA members would have preferred demobilization with cash gratuities to 'seeking the bubble reputation/Even in the cannon's mouth'.[29] Demobilization at first proved to be more successful than the plan to accept all former guerrillas, and by the end of September 1995 some 1500 had agreed to accept demobilization with gratuities.

Problems, including hitherto unknown strikes and demonstrations, have arisen from the fact that many black short-term soldiers who helped keep the peace during the elections have been angered at the refusal to allow them to renew their contracts so that room could be made for the newcomers. Moreover, as time has passed more and more middle- and lower-level whites have begun to seek careers elsewhere, considering that the introduction of officers over their heads on the seniority lists, coupled to the intention to diminish overall numbers in the peacetime forces, would effectively close careers. The most serious effect has been the loss of instructors who would have been able to raise the professional levels of the newcomers. This has slowed the pace of integration since the SANDF is determined to keep standards to previous levels. Table 3 shows SANDF numbers at the end of June 1995.

One important working group dealt with the question of re-instituting the civilian Secretariat of Defence which had been absorbed into the various

Table 3. Permanent SANDF Numbers, 30 June 1995

Origins	Present Numbers
SADF	65,000
Civilians	20,000
APLA	6,000
MK	29,000
TBCV	11,000
Total	131,000

Note. It was planned to reduce total numbers to 91,000.
Source. Committee on Integration, SANDF.

28. Motumi, op.cit. note 24, p. 10, says that 23,000 names were submitted to the TEC but that not more than 10–12,000 were formally trained outside South Africa. Some of the data on the JMCC are derived from the writer's own participation and some from the unpublished paper delivered at a conference of Lecturers in Governmental Sciences by Maj.-Gen. D.J. Mortimer, vice-chairman of the Integration Committee, 'Integrating the Armed Forces: Planning and Realities', University of South Africa, Pretoria, 2 November 1995.

29. (Shakespeare, *As You Like It*) For a comparison with a similar situation see Rupiah, M., 'Demobilisation and Integration: "Operation Merger" and the Zimbabwe National Defence Forces, 1980–1987', *African Security Review* 4(3), pp. 52–64.

general staff branches of the SADF in 1966.[30] There appear to have been two reasons for re-instituting the secretariat. Firstly, there was a belief in the ANC that the absence of the civilian secretariat had led to a disregard for civilian control of the armed forces. Secondly, as the implications of integration of the MK and APLA leaders into the militarily more sophisticated SANDF became clearer during discussions and familiarization with the SADF, it also became more attractive to many MK members to aim at being taken into the civilian establishment rather than into the uniformed forces. Consequently, although the re-institution had been left out of the terms of the constitution, a great deal of discussion and planning was devoted to organizing a civilian secretariat 'to control the Defence Force'. The planning procedures made it possible to commence developing a secretariat of defence from the time that the work of the JMCC ended in April 1994, and although the process was slower than expected a secretary, Lt-Gen. Pierre Steyn, a retired chief of staff of the SADF, was appointed at the end of March 1995. Since then the secretariat has been developed with the utilization of officers seconded from the various staff divisions, such as finance, management and logistics, together with MK personnel. The purpose in absorbing these officers is to return to the old functions of the secretariat – although it is to be hoped that it will be better employed as a source of expert advice on political and economic matters. Lack of adequate advice was a serious defect in SADF decision-making once uniformed military intelligence personnel had become the only source of such advice. Indeed, the former secretariat, absorbed by the various General Staff divisions after 1966, suffered from many serious defects. Not only did it fail to provide political and economic advice, but it tended to employ personnel able to undertake only financial control and accounting, while their contemporaries in the uniformed services were trained at sophisticated foreign training establishments. After several conflicts over prerogatives between the secretary and the chief of the SADF, the latter was given the office of secretary in 1966. There should, of course, have been a concerted effort to find a practicable solution instead. A serious consequence has been that the chief of the SADF has been burdened with the non-military problems of his office rather than being able to concentrate on substantive military questions, as most of his foreign counterparts can. It will be important for the new secretary and the chief of the SANDF to realize that the secretariat should be concerned with more than just financial policy and control.

---

30. The article by the recently appointed Defence Secretary Lt-Gen. Pierre Steyn, 'Striking a Balance Between Civil Control of the Armed Forces and Effective Defence', *African Defence Review* No. 14, January 1994, pp. 14–17, sets out the problems of reintroducing a secretariat after 30 years. Fourie, D. 'A Ministry of Defence for the New South Africa', in Gutteridge, W. *South Africa's Defence and Security into the 21st century*, Dartmouth, Aldershot, 1996, pp. 19–27, provides an historical survey projected into the future.

Defence by Constitution

While steps were being taken toward bringing the forces together under a new government, the terms of the interim constitution were being negotiated. This constitution is to be replaced but it is of some interest because it influenced subsequent thinking, set certain demands for Parliament, the government and the SANDF, and included terms intended to set a variety of constraints in place. The provisions reflect the belief of at least one major party to the negotiations that the SADF had acted outside the control of the civilian political authority. They were also intended to provide a way of changing the government without interference from the forces and to prevent, moreover, the SADF from 'running wild' in the southern African region. The defence provisions reflect a variety of attitudes and preconceptions held by the constitutional negotiators. The result is probably a notable contrast to the majority of constitutions throughout the world.[31]

In contrast to the constitutions that had been in effect in South Africa since 1910 which had simply stated that the head of state was the commander-in-chief and assumed the existence of an armed force and everything that would be attendant upon that, a chapter of five articles of the interim constitution was devoted to the National Defence Force (NDF) (i.e. the SANDF).[32] In terms of articles 82(4) and 228 the president is designated commander-in-chief, able to declare 'a state of national defence' – not a state of war – subject to the duty to inform Parliament, who may terminate the employment of the NDF. This is reminiscent of the French Constitution of 1791 and the American War Powers Act of 1975. Indeed, much of the wording of these clauses entitles the reader to think that texts were taken over almost verbatim.

According to article 226 the president was to appoint a chief of the NDF to exercise military executive command subject to the minister's direction and to the direction of the president during a 'state of national defence'. These arrangements simply made an existing state of affairs explicit. In the colonial practice the governor-general always held command as representative of the sovereign with professional officers as the executive functionaries. There were exceptions. During the Second World War the Governor-General had made Smuts, as prime minister and minister of defence,

---

31. See the examples in Blaustein, A.P. and Sigler, J.A. (eds), *Constitutions that Made History*, New York, Paragon House, 1988, and Fourie, D., 'Constitutions and Defence', unpublished paper delivered to the Constitutional Assembly Committee on Security Apparatus, Cape Town, 8 May 1995.

32. Cf. the SA Constitution Act 1910 (9 Ed.VIII, Ch.9) and the Constitutions of 1961 and 1983 as well as the Defence Acts 1912 and 1957. Articles 224 to 228 of the interim constitution constitute Chapter 14. The final constitution (May 1996) returned to sparse provisions and instituted a secretariat. Articles 200–203.

commander-in-chief. In the First World War Prime Minister Gen. Louis Botha had himself taken command in the field in the campaign in German South West Africa. The interim provisions had the effect of reining in the relatively unchecked control held in the past.

Despite the emphasis by the ANC on having a civilian secretariat of defence to 'control' the armed forces, there was no provision in the constitution – an apparently strange omission, but it did not prevent the creation of a new secretariat.

Articles 227 and 228 provided for similar controls in that the roles of the NDF were narrowly defined and apparently restricted in an attempt to ensure that the country would be manifestly peaceful. The minister was also explicitly made accountable to Parliament, and the Joint Standing Committee on Defence, previously created by the rules and conventions of parliament, was established. The system of committees, quite unlike previous committees of parliament, proved to have a great deal of promise, provided members could be enticed to attend sittings, a default which has yet to be mended. Officials and ministers have discovered a need to be very much more careful with their work than before – even though select committees existed in the past.

Article 224 is curiously worded since it provides that the NDF shall be the *only* defence force. The reason for this becomes clear from article 224(2) which provides that the NDF shall consist of the SADF, the Homeland Forces and any armed forces as defined in the Transitional Executive Council Act 1993. This was intended to provide for the entry into the NDF of the armed wings of the ANC, PAC, Azanian People's Organization (AZAPO), the Afrikaner Weerstandsbeweging (AWB) and any other group claiming to be an armed wing of a political party or movement. In the curious constitution-speak that developed during 1993 they are the 'non-statutory forces'. However, the article also provides for the exclusion of any such force whose 'political organization' did not participate in the 1994 election. Patently, this was aimed at ending political violence by compelling the participation of all parties and movements in the election. By the end of 1993 South Africa could have been compared to the Weimar Republic in which political thugs from all sides ruled certain townships. This clause was reasonably effective and it mattered not that the AWB stayed out, since the defeat of an armed foray into Bophuthatswana destroyed their credibility as a political as well as a military force before the election.[33]

Article 226 goes onto prescribe the composition and roles of the NDF, in particular that there should be a permanent and a part-time reserve component, that the force should provide balanced, modern and technically

33. Sass, Bill, 'The Might of the Right', *African Defence Review* No.15, March 1994, pp. 37–41. IFP protection units began to be accepted in 1996.

advanced military forces, and that it should be trained to 'international standards of competency'. Moreover, no member should hold political office and members 'shall be entitled to refuse to execute any order if [it] would constitute an offence or would breach international law'. These provisions reflect in part the desire of the other negotiators to retain a defence force which would not be constituted solely of former 'terrorists', that it should retain sufficient former members of the SADF to ensure that they could not simply be cast off and that it should be of a high quality. This opened the door for the BMATT to be brought into the adjudication of appointments of the 'non-statutory' personnel. Moreover, there remained a strong desire to retain a defence force that consisted mainly of part-time, citizen soldiers, with careers outside the armed forces, so that there would be minimal danger of coups d'etat taking place. This was also the basis of the requirement that no one should hold political office – although considering the origins of the non-statutory forces and the history of forces such as those in Zimbabwe, political neutrality would not be easy to achieve.

The provision relating to refusal to obey unlawful orders – again, merely the repetition of provision in the military laws in South Africa – was another attempt to ensure that service personnel would not engage in operations ordered by politicians which would conflict with domestic or international law. The difficulties courts have had in settling these principles makes it very difficult to know how a soldier – even an officer – would deal with these provisions in heated circumstances. Although the Bundeswehr teach this as a principle they admit its impracticability. The easiest decision would be for a senior commander to resign if asked to embark on a manifestly illegal war. But generally, servicemen brought up in an atmosphere of discipline would regard this article as an invitation to mutiny.[34]

In the light of the experience of the year and a half in which the results of the negotiations in the JMCC began to take effect and the interim constitution could be seen in a less suspicious atmosphere, the constitutional sub-committee has proposed far less all-embracing provisions on defence for the final constitution. There are still provisions requiring a disciplined professional military force; political responsibility and accountability to Parliament with the aid of a multiparty committee, which shall make recommendations on the budget, functioning, organization, armaments, policy, morale, and state of preparedness of the defence force; the subordination of the chief of the SANDF to the minister and the president; and the establish-

---

34. Woetzel, R.K., *The Nuremburg Trials in International Law*, London, Stevens, 1962, Ch. 5 and pp. 96–121; ibid, p. 3, German (Imperial) Military Code of Justice 1872 (II Reich), Article 47, states that 'a subordinate who obeys an order which is clearly contrary to law, is liable to prosecution and punishment'. In applying this rule the Supreme Court of Leipzig (1920–2) found both for and against accused in the Submarine Cases.

ment of a civilian secretariat, this time with a less detailed specification of its relationship to the SANDF. The primary employment of the defence force has been broadened to being 'in the national interest' rather than in a state of national defence.

Glimpsing the Future – Prospects or Problems?

The SANDF, while it appears to have progressed the best of all the government institutions in moving toward the kind of transformation desired by its political heads, is far from free of problems and disputes. It has to justify its identity as a strong, modern force; it faces a strong anti-military lobby; it continues to experience difficulties with integration of forces and the consequent 'rationalization'; there is a shadow over the future of the part-time forces; and there is the threat of its equipment, especially in the navy and air force, becoming obsolete.

In Search of a Future

At this stage in the history of South Africa the SANDF faces the dilemma not necessarily of justifying its existence, but certainly of justifying its expenditure, size, sophistication and significance. While the object proposed for the new constitution is that it 'shall be the defence and protection of the Republic, its territorial integrity and its people ... guided by the principle of nonaggression', there is little reason at present to anticipate the need for such defence. There is a strong lobby in the ANC, but not only there, for virtual unilateral disarmament, partly because of opposition to anything military, partly because many still feel that the SANDF is too white, and partly because it is thought that the Reconstruction and Development Plan requires money far more than the services who are seen as privileged, wasteful, unproductive and unnecessary. The SANDF faces demands, frequently repeated in the media, for the identification of threats to South Africa as justification for renewal or modernization (sanctions cause many of the larger items of equipment such as ships and aircraft to deteriorate or become obsolete). Indeed, this writer has often (fruitlessly) attempted to influence the services to abandon the customary tendency among armed forces to look for threats to justify their training, equipment and establishments, in favour of the more rational and permanent definition of roles. Excellent examples of permanent role definition rather than nebulous threat identification are to be found in the Swiss defence system and the Chilean navy's definition of all-embracing maritime roles.

At the same time, thinking about the SANDF's purposes generally has continued to be influenced by the terms of the interim constitution. In that document the objects defined include statements of policy as well as missions usually included in defence legislation. Thus they provide for aid to the police, assistance during disasters, border protection, internal stability and commitments in terms of treaties and membership of international organizations. These views as to the employment of the SANDF, as well as views outside South Africa as to the ability of the country to accept a leading role in the region, have led to considerable discussions on possible roles. Indeed, UN officials visited South Africa in 1995 to discuss the possibilities of South African forces being sent to the Yugoslav region; and during the brief coup in Lesotho, the SAAF and a parachute battalion were used in response to foreign pressure to demonstrate the possibility of military intervention to put down the coup.[35] Again, the problem is related to the cost of the SANDF. International peacekeeping or enforcing roles require the kinds of equipment needed for primary or fighting roles. On the other hand, the other internal secondary roles require completely different kinds of equipment, such as that for search and rescue and similar tasks. South Africa has never given the SANDF the kind of budget that provides for secondary roles, and these have always had to be catered for by using tents, vehicles and food stockpiled for the primary role.

The Part-time Forces

Despite promises made during the earlier constitutional negotiations that the part-time forces were not negotiable, and also despite the minister's good relations with the Part Time Forces' Council, the fact remains that their future remains uncertain – certainly in the form that they will take in the future. They are overshadowed at present by the largest permanent force the country has ever seen – expected to be 130,000 instead of the planned 91,000. They continue to be the subject of suspicion among many of the more radical politicians and their supporters. The provisions on defence recommended for the final (1996) constitution do not mention the dual permanent–part-time establishment. Perhaps the door to this was opened by the apparent lack of enthusiasm for service once the government had imposed a moratorium on prosecutions and constitutional change was in the offing. But absenteeism should be seen in perspective: the citizen soldiers, paid below PF rates, were misused as a cheap means of continuing the campaign in Namibia when the government lacked courage to take the inevitable decisions; employers are still frustrated by the effects they experienced; and employers and servicemen alike are frustrated because despite

---

35. See the account in Seery, B., 'Africa's Reluctant New Policeman Twirls his Truncheon', in Shaw, M. and Cilliers, J. (eds), *South Africa and Peacekeeping in Africa*, Vol.1, Halfway House, Institute for Defence Policy, 1995, pp. 87–97.

their effort and sacrifices the government they served failed politically. This influences their response when they are called to risk their lives in keeping the peace in the townships, when they see no reason for the political parties to continue the killing. Nevertheless there is still a strong nucleus of devoted part-time servicemen, and also a strong influx of black part-time servicemen – and women.

Rationalizing Loyalty

In order to adjust to peacetime conditions, to make room in the SANDF for those to whom the liberation movements made promises about the future both of the defence force and their employment, as well as to secure the funds to keep a reasonable proportion of their followers in the forces, a programme euphemistically called 'rationalization' has been in progress since 1990. This means that several thousand people have been pensioned off or discharged from the services. In addition, the Variable Military Service (VMS) scheme, which allowed personnel to serve for renewable periods of two years, has been used to make room for the numerous MK and APLA candidates for employment over the heads of many VMS personnel who expected to be re-engaged. The result has been to raise the question of loyalty. Soldiers who served during the various campaigns and in the 1994 election have been disillusioned by the way in which they have been discarded, albeit legally. Many have taken part in demonstrations and even threatened to make the coming local government elections impossible to carry through. The president himself has had to give his personal attention to some of these demonstrations. Loyalty is naturally affected by the way in which the government handles the SANDF, by the way in which amalgamation is dealt with, and by the conservatism of members of the SANDF. Success or failure in persuading the government and part-time servicemen to accept the transition of the CF and Commandos to the new SANDF will be of critical concern. Yet, contrary to predictions, members of the former SADF, professional and part time, have displayed loyalty and have served the government very well since the change in June 1994. Certainly, suggestions made by the uninformed and the malevolent that the SANDF could be expected to resort to a coup d'etat have been shown to be wrong. But the government still needs to learn how to deal with the labour problems resulting from rationalization.

Conclusion

The future of the SANDF is not easy to predict. In 1910 South Africans experienced a similar state of euphoria with the passage from four Crown colonies to the Union. There was much good will and much optimism. There was a spirit of cooperation among people who but eight years before had been engaged in a tragic and unnecessary war. Two years after union a realignment took place in politics. The good will began to evaporate as the Afrikaners grouped around General Barry Hertzog argued that the spirit of conciliation advocated by Prime Minister Louis Botha was to their disadvantage in practice. At the same time the English party, the Unionists, accused Botha of favouring the Afrikaners, while they accused Hertzog of 'racialism' (Afrikaner nationalism). Within 12 years the moderate Afrikaner South African Party had been defeated by the more intensely Afrikaner nationalist National Party who, with a relatively short break between 1933 and 1948, went on to rule South Africa until 1994. This history is not without its warning for South Africa in the coming years. The spirit of reconciliation evinced by Nelson Mandela does not please or satisfy everyone – in the ANC or in other parties relying for the most part on black support. This affects the armed forces as well. There are, for some black politicians and youth, too many white faces, too many concessions to past practices. If South Africa is, in the terms of Charles Tilly, in a revolutionary situation, the government may have a long way to go to be sure that the revolutionary outcome has been left far behind.

The changes in progress now resemble those of 1913 when former enemies in war came together to create the Union Defence Force to replace the British Imperial Army and the colonial forces. There was remarkable acceptance in those days – at least outwardly. When the rebellion against joining in a European war on Britain's side came in August 1914, few soldiers refused to serve and few actually rebelled. But much bitterness developed among the Afrikaners and was cultivated by politicians. Yet in the course of subsequent history there was a coming together of the English and Afrikaner whites. In some ways, the differences today are greater and there is much more bitterness. True, the officers have already begun to find common ground. The most difficult adaptations are likely to be those among people who should be the closest – 'the other ranks' – to use a characteristic British and South African term. They are perhaps the people who feel the greatest threats to their security and dignity and the least compensation for the past.

The SADF always gave the appearance of resilience in the past. It was the only government department in which the rule of using English and Afrikaans in alternate months was religiously maintained as a gesture of good will. But it was also the most visible object of attack by the first NP minister of defence in 1948 when he sought to transform the armed forces from what he considered British to what he saw as a purely South African model. In fact, he was wrong: they were already a South African force. Nevertheless, uniforms and regimental names were changed, symbols were altered, per-

sonalities were forced out of the services, ranks were changed. Most of the
resistance to this came from within the Citizen Force, but even there the
part-timers were too disciplined to disobey the political head. Within
months of the appointment of a successor, J.J. Fouché (from the same
party), the reversal of the process began. Today the SANDF's identity as a
military force can be said to be virtually as it was in 1948. The question to be
asked continually during the changes taking place now is: what will become
the ethos of the SANDF? Will it remain true to its past, or will it become
another Third World military establishment with officers who believe they
have better answers to the country's and their own needs?

It is significant that there is at present a confidence in the forces expressed
by their political heads even if there are doubts elsewhere. Ministers have
been surprised by the loyalty, the quality of work, the professionalism
among the services they now head. If there *are* people who expect the
services to become involved in coups, they are not the political heads, the
president and the ministers.[36] This is very different from the aggressively
anti-defence force attitude adopted by the NP in 1948 when they bitterly
resented the UDF's presence by the side of the British in two world wars.
The examples presented by the services now – as indeed in 1924 and 1948 –
of unqualified loyalty and business as usual may provide a model for the
continuation of a force free of party political influence and free of prae-
torianism.

36. At the conference 'Preparing the SA Army for the 21st Century', Pretoria, 19 October
1995, Minister of Defence Joe Modise and the Premier of Mpumelanga Province, Mathews
Phosa, praised the loyalty and devotion to the democratic state of the SANDF.

10. ADMINISTRATIVE JUSTICE IN THE PUBLIC SERVICE: A PUBLIC ADMINISTRATION INTERPRETATION OF SECTION 24 OF THE CONSTITUTION

Dirk J. Brynard

Daily allegations of irregularities in government, on the one hand, and optimistic expectations of the present constitution, which has justice for everybody as a goal, on the other, are opposing scenarios. In these circumstances, can administrative justice be a possibility or will it remain an improbability? It is the aim of this chapter to explore the nature and scope of this dilemma against the background of the provision that section 24 of the constitution makes for the attainment of administrative justice in public administration.

Background

In a new South Africa the reconstruction and development of communities, the promotion of national unity and the continued governance of the country while the elected Constitutional Assembly draws up a 'final' constitution are necessities. The present constitution endeavours to create a sovereign and democratic constitutional state in which the fundamental rights and freedoms of citizens are protected. The continued existence of a substantial public administration to realize these ambitions is inevitable. Rawls (1988: 195–228) views a constitutional state as the most basic governmental structure to ensure justice. It should however be realized that such ideals will depend on the existence of a governmental structure with integrity to curb the inevitable onslaught of corrupt, authoritarian and arbitrary government. Expectations in terms of the current constitution include, *inter alia*, that officials remain within their lawful authority and act fairly. It is therefore essential to create a system of justice which attempts to ensure that justifiable decisions are made through the use of fair procedures.

Despite their yearning for justice, human beings remain only human, and are therefore plagued by the sins of avarice and desire, influenced by self-interest, victims of prejudice, and affected by pride and the desire for authority (James, 1968: 322). Human beings are also trapped within a web of complex governmental institutions from which they cannot escape. The hallmark of these institutions is, on the one hand, a multitude of rules designed to achieve institutional goals as efficiently and effectively as possible, resulting in the entrapment of human beings in a rule-dominated society (Hart, 1974: 9). On the other hand, the possession and exercise of discretionary authority by public officials and institutions remains an essential commodity in the public administration of a democratic society (Cooper, 1992: 113). Administrative discretion, however, is often stigmatized as antithetical to the notion of justice, and is often considered the 'scourge of justice' as a result of its unpredictability, arbitrariness, uncertainty and inconsistency (Boulle, 1986: 138; Burns, 1994: 350). One possible solution to rule-domination and the inherent danger of administrative discretion is to maintain a balance between adherence to formal rules and the use of discretion in decision-making. A lack of meaningful discretionary authority (i.e. excessive pursuance of rules) is likely to produce unjust decisions. Conversely, too broad a discretionary authority may lead to violations of the principle of justice. Unjust decisions are therefore more likely to occur when the balance is tipped in either direction (Pavlak and Pops, 1989: 935).

The transitional constitution contains a chapter on fundamental rights in which the right to administrative justice is entrenched (section 24). This chapter constitutes a bill of rights. The Constitutional Assembly must also incorporate a bill of rights in the 'final' constitution (Schedule 4, Principle 2) which should also serve as a framework for future public administration.

From Justice to Administrative Justice

Justice has been defined by many people in many societies over a long period of time. A concise definition of the concept of justice remains elusive, however, because of its complexity and susceptibility to a multitude of meanings. Justice tends to be interpreted differently by different people. The resultant jumble of literature on the topic only causes more confusion about the 'real' meaning of the notion. It is hoped that this contribution will not add to the existing confusion.

As a result of the multiplicity of meanings attached to the idea of justice it is difficult to define the notion with certainty in terms of a single human way of life and experience, such as public administration. In addition to this, one has to realize that public administration is but one of the domains in which justice can take place. An attempt will however be made to define and circumscribe justice within the context of public administration. It is the aim of this contribution to shape this vague and disputed concept in an empirically useful mould for the purpose of public administration.

Administrative justice, too, may be susceptible to different meanings. Firstly, administrative justice and administrative law cannot be used interchangeably since that would be to confuse and equate law with justice (Boulle, 1986: 137). Secondly, administrative justice is often used to refer to the formal structure of administrative justice, meaning those non-judicial institutions (such as ombudsmen and administrative tribunals) that exist to adjudicate between the state and the citizen away from the courts of law (Bradley, 1981: 8; Elcock, 1990: 33). For the purpose of this chapter the latter is not the primary meaning which will be attached to justice, because justice is not only an institutional principle, but also a matter of individual moral responsibility (Stackhouse, 1989: 894). Justice is such a commodious notion that, thirdly, it is possible to circumscribe this particular configuration of justice, namely, administrative justice, as those principles which the public official should uphold in order to be able to act fairly. The most basic principles that can be raised and with which acts of the authorities should comply in terms of the social contract are reasonableness, fairness and impartiality (Davis, 1993: 26). Administrative justice thus provides the basis for consistent and fair public official response to legitimate citizen demands for fair treatment (Pops, 1992: 228). This also implies fair treatment by the authorities of individuals and groups in terms of the methods and procedures being used for the making of and implementation of decisions. The basis for this circumscription of administrative justice is the Rawlsean notion of 'justice as fairness' (Rawls, 1988: 3–53). Rawls's 'justice as fairness' establishes an ethical standard which is not only justifiable, but also applicable by public officials in a public-sector environment. The fact that justice is but one aspect of the complete ethical paradigm does not detract from the idea that justice ought to be the central virtue of governmental institutions, because it sets the ethical parameters for such institutions (Hart, 1974: 5). Justice establishes the essential principles for the orderly functioning of governmental institutions and thus furnishes the arena within which all other values find expression.

Administrative Justice in Terms of the Constitution

Section 24 of the Constitution of the Republic of South Africa, 1993 (Act 200 of 1993) sets the scene for the exercise of administrative authority by defining the parameters within which the public administration ought to function. This section makes provision for the right to administrative justice as a justifiable fundamental right. This means, in short, that every person shall have the right to: lawful administrative action (section 24a), procedurally fair administrative action (b), be furnished with reasons in writing for administrative action (c), and administrative action which is justifiable in relation to the reasons given for it (d). The continuous reference to 'administrative action' includes administrative decision-making and the acts performed on the strength of those decisions (section 7[2]). A brief exposition of the contents of each of the four subsections follows.

Right to lawful administrative action. Under the first subsection (24a) every person shall have a constitutional and fundamental right to lawful administrative action where any of his/her rights or interests is affected or threatened. The contents of this subsection should be accepted as implicit because everybody is always entitled to lawful administrative action, as a principle of common law. It is thus a mere confirmation of the common-law position. The clause makes more sense if it is interpreted as a specific obligation to lawful action by the public administration (section 7[1]). This implies that administrative action should be exercised within the bounds of a vested authority (i.e. the enabling or empowering statute) or a prerogative authority pertaining to common law (i.e. which does not have a statutory base) (Carpenter, 1994: 469). The fact that this clause effectively prohibits the promulgation of the challenged ouster clause (which excludes judicial review) by the public administration (Burns, 1994: 352), leaves more scope for judicial review of administrative action, but does not lift the inherent moral obligation of the public administration to ensure administrative legality.

Right to procedurally fair administrative action. Under subsection 24b every person shall have a constitutional and fundamental right to procedurally fair administrative action where any of his/her rights or legitimate expectations is affected or threatened. This subclause constitutionalizes a fundamental principle of justice, namely, the pursuance of the rules of natural justice. The significance of the rules for public administration boils down to two principles, namely, the right of an affected person to be granted the opportunity to be heard (*audi alteram partem*), and the requirement that the deciding authority must be free from bias and unprejudiced (*nemo iudex in sua causa*). Procedural fairness demands also that the authority complies with other procedural requirements for valid administrative action, i.e. with the statutory provisions of the enabling act (Du Plessis and Corder, 1994: 169). The establishment of this general obligation for fair administrative procedures to be used implies that justice must be done and be seen to be done. The criterion against which administrative justice is thus evaluated at the hands of public officials depends on whether the procedures followed are used to promote fairness and are perceived, by the public, as promoting fairness (Pops, 1992: 233). An important last element of procedural justice offered to the citizen involves the opportunity to correct the inevitable errors, i.e. the right to appeal. Provision is made hereto in the sense that justifiable disputes can be settled by a court of law or another independent and impartial forum, like the Public Protector (ombudsman) (section 24 read together with section 22).

Right to be furnished with reasons in writing for administrative action. Under the third subsection (24c) every person shall have a constitutional and fundamental right to be furnished with reasons in writing for administrative action which affects any of his/her rights or interests, unless the reasons for such action have been made public. The obligation created by this right and its importance in establishing a climate of accountability, transparency and accessibility in public administration cannot be overemphasized. In practical terms the obligation has the potential to ensure decision-making which is well thought through, and safeguarded against arbitrariness. It will also foster increased public confidence in administrative decisions, and yield greater legitimacy (Basson, 1994: 34; Craig, 1994: 283). The obligation is however restricted to instances where rights and interests of a person concerned are affected. It is not clear what the scope of the subclause will be in terms of its interpretation of the word 'interests'. Another limitation of this right is that reasons cannot be claimed if they have already been made public. Neither is it clear what amounts to 'publicity' and how and through whom this publicity is to occur. The other side of the obligation, especially for the public administration, is less attractive in terms of cost, time, workload and skills, particularly as the reasons have to be supplied in writing (Barrington, 1980: 180; Glazewski, 1994: 10).

Right to administrative action which is justifiable. In terms of the fourth subsection (24d) every person shall have a constitutional and fundamental right to administrative action which is justifiable in relation to the reasons given for it where any of his/her rights is affected or threatened. This subclause has the potential to lift the veil of the inner workings of administrative decision-making by exposing it to the lights of the ethic of justification. The fact that a justifiable decision is one based on reason (which means that all the jurisdictional facts must be considered), implies that the decision must be capable of objective substantiation (Burns, 1994: 356). This implies that public officials, in an effort to justify their actions, will have to take their decisions with care in order to adhere to the standards of rationality and logic. Subclause 24d may thus render the public administration exceedingly vulnerable. If it is read as referring back to the written reasons which may be called for in terms of section 24c, it might put an unreasonably heavy burden on the public administration. The reason for this is that it would require of public officials to supply reasons under section 24c which are drafted carefully enough for the administrative action or decision to pass the test of judicial review as required under section 24d. In the interest of sustainable public administration, it can only be hoped that the courts would interpret section 24d in a rather less demanding way, i.e. the provision of adequate reasons, which implies that the subclause is not read together with section 24c (Hoexter, 1994: 708). An interpretation which keeps section 24c and section 24d separate is therefore to be preferred. The latter interpretation implies that the reasons against which the justifiability of administrative action is to be measured should read in such a way as to include all reasons advanced and not only the reasons in writing required under section 24c (Du Plessis and Corder, 1994: 169). Seen against the backdrop of the current vulnerability of the public administration as a result of the great tide of demands, expectations and volume of work associated with the transformation that South Africa is undergoing, a desirable solution is one that will not frustrate, but improve orderly public administration.

Closer Analysis of Section 24

The other side of a right is an obligation. The right to administrative justice, which is guaranteed expressly in chapter 3 of the constitution, bestows an obligation on the bearers of authority, such as the public administration (in terms of section 7[1]), to treat individuals with dignity and with respect. The spirit and values which underlie the charter of fundamental rights are prescriptive of the general obligation to fair action by the public administration towards the public, and not only where certain rights, interests or legitimate expectations are affected or threatened. The contents of section 24 not only confirm certain principles which are already entrenched in our law (sections 24a and b), but also introduce new principles (sections 24c and d). The formulation of the new principles displays some unusual features and has already been contested in academic circles. The pronouncement of the Constitutional Court is eagerly awaited on these matters before a general pattern can take shape. Although constitutional entrenchment of administrative justice is rather unusual, it is not being questioned. There are those, however, who argue that the formulation of the clause in the constitution has introduced more problems than it has solved (Carpenter, 1994: 468–73; Glazewski, 1994: 11–12). As a possible solution to the many questions that remain, it was proposed, among others, that a separate, clarifying parliamentary act on administrative justice be promulgated (Corder, 1994: 400). If decisive answers can be found to the remaining questions, and if the relevant principles are properly followed by the public administration, then South Africa could be at the forefront of the search for a culture of justice and fairness in public administration. Seen against the backdrop of the transitional nature of the constitution and within the structural context of reconstruction and development, the charter of fundamental rights does not pretend to be the final word on human rights in general and administrative justice in particular, but should be acknowledged as a powerful instrument on the road thereto.

Implications of Section 24 for public administration

Section 24 has other implications for public administration. Fairness, transparency, accountability and participation merit specific mention. The latter are all closely related. They also serve as the underlying values of the constitution and must be interpreted in the spirit of the constitution.

Fairness is a responsibility of the public administration to the public which is acquired by the adoption of a clear procedure (Rawson, 1984: 606; Robson, 1958: 16), the preservation of high ethical and moral standards and the availability of public officials of integrity. This procedural fairness in administrative action is acquired through compliance with the rules of natural justice (section 24b).

A *transparent*, accessible and responsive public administration is an indispensable element of a true democracy: a closed or secret public administration will, sooner or later, give rise to decadence and corruption. Transparency or openness is therefore one of the values which underlie the constitution and which find expression in the obligation to provide reasons in writing for administrative action (section 24c) and in the functioning of the rules of natural justice (section 24b).

Accountability or answerability implies the obligation to account to others. Accountability ought to be the aspiration of each public official and is also an important value underlying the constitution. In terms of administrative justice the aspiration to accountability translates into a call or demand for the provision of reasons for administrative action (section 24c), and that the administrative action should be justifiable in relation to the reasons given for it (section 24d). The constitution also extends a right of access to all official information (section 23), essential for accountable public administration.

Participation coheres closely with the transparency of the decision-making that allows citizens to participate in a meaningful way, and that contributes to their dignity (Pops, 1992: 234). Participation in decision-making serves not only to protect the interests of those directly affected by a decision, but also to enhance citizens' sense of being treated fairly (Pavlak and Pops, 1989: 939). Access to administrative justice is being facilitated in particular by the opportunity to procedural fairness (section 24b) in terms of the constitution.

Conclusion

The aim of chapter 3 of the constitution is to foster a culture of respect for human rights. Despite the uncertainties and problems inherent in the administrative justice clause, the inclusion of this clause in the constitution will undoubtedly go a long way towards ensuring and promoting values like fairness, transparency, accountability and participation in public administration. It is evident that the judicial mechanisms of enforcement attached to the constitution, for example judicial revision, can be applied effectively in the prevention and deterrence of injustices in public administration. It is, however, important to realize that administrative justice is not the sole mandate of the legal profession and the courts, but that public officials, too, ought to play a decisive role – particularly because no one can be *compelled* to fair and virtuous action. How, then, is fair and lawful behaviour to be elicited? At best it can only be *encouraged* among those who are sensitive to their own personal responsibility for their actions. Underlying the quest for fair, lawful and justifiable administrative action is a sensitizing to certain values, attitudes and practices that would need to be inculcated within individual public officials and public institutions. Academic departments in South African tertiary institutions, which provide tuition in public administration, need to recognize their important task in this regard. A new awareness of the importance of the moral education of public officials, within the context of the subject of public administration, has become a matter of urgency. An approach like this should, however, be realistic in that it should take account of humankind's limitations and fallibilities. Ethical standards which could be impressed on public officials do not require that the officials be saintly or angelic, but only that they act fairly, honourably and responsibly. The establishment of a culture of human rights through relevant education in public administration has the potential of making the constitution a living document. The bottom line remains that there is no substitute for the personal integrity of each and every member of South African society. Its importance cannot be overestimated. The possibility or improbability of administrative justice is in the hands and on the conscience of every well-meaning South African.

REFERENCES

Barrington, T.J. (1980) *The Irish Administrative System*. Dublin: Institute of Public Administration.

Basson, D.A. (1994) *South Africa's Interim Constitution*. Cape Town: Juta.

Boulle, L.J. (1986) 'Administrative Justice and Public Participation in American and South African Law', *Journal of South African Law* 2: 136–52.

Bradley, A.W. (1981) 'Administrative Justice and the Binding Effect of Official Acts', *Current Legal Problems* 34.

Burns, Y. (1994) 'Administrative Justice', *South African Public Law* 9(2): 347–59.

Carpenter, G. (1994) 'Administratiewe geregtigheid – meer vrae as antwoorde?', *Tydskrif vir Hedendaagse Romeins-Hollandse Reg.* 57(3), August: 467–73.

Cooper, P.J. (1992) 'Conflict or Constructive Tension: The Changing Relationship of Judges and Administrators', in R.B. Denhardt and B.R. Hammond (eds) *Public Administration in Action*. Pacific Grove, CA: Brooks/Cole Publishing Company.

Corder, H. (1994) 'Administrative Justice', in D. van Wyk, J. Dugard, B. de Villiers and D. Davis (eds) *Rights and Constitutionalism*. Cape Town: Juta.

Craig, P.P. (1994) 'Reasons and Administrative Justice', *The Law Quarterly Review* 110(1), January: 12–15.

Davis, D.M. (1993) 'Administrative Justice in a Democratic South Africa', *Acta Juridica*.

Du Plessis, L. and H. Corder (1994) *Understanding South Africa's Transitional Bill of Rights*. Cape Town: Juta.

Elcock, H. (1990) 'Administrative Justice and the Citizen', *Teaching Public Administration* 10(1), Spring: 33–46.

Glazewski, J. (1994) 'The Environment and the New Interim Constitution', *South African Journal of Environmental Law and Policy* 1(1), March: 3–16.

Hart, D.K. (1974) 'Social Equity, Justice, and the Equitable Administrator', *Public Administration Review* 34, January–February: 3–11.

Hoexter, C. (1994) 'Administrative Justice and Dishonesty', *South African Law Journal* 111(4), November: 700–19.

James, N. (1968) 'Law and the Idea of Justice', *Tydskrif vir Hedendaagse Romeins-Hollandse Reg.* 31(4): 321–9.

Pavlak, T.J. and G.M. Pops (1989) 'Administrative Ethics as Justice', *International Journal of Public Administration* 12(6): 931–46.

Pops, G.M. (1992) 'Securing Citizen Rights through Administrative Justice', *International Review of Administrative Sciences* 58(2), June: 227–37.

Rawls, J. (1988) *A Theory of Justice*. Oxford: Oxford University Press.

Rawson, B. (1984) 'The Responsibilities of the Public Servant to the Public: Accessibility, Fairness and Efficiency', *Canadian Public Administration* 27(4), Winter: 601–10.

Republic of South Africa (1993) *Constitution of the Republic of South Africa, 1993* (Act 200 of 1993).

Robson, W.A. (1958) 'Administrative Justice and Injustice: A Commentary on the Franks Reports', *Public Law*, Spring: 12–31.

Stackhouse, S.B. (1989) 'Upholding Justice in an Unjust World: A Practitioner's View of Public Administration Ethics', *International Journal of Public Administration* 12(6): 889–911.

11. RELATIONS BETWEEN STATE, CAPITAL AND LABOUR IN SOUTH AFRICA: TOWARDS CORPORATISM?

Louwrens Pretorius

The transition to democracy in South Africa brought with it renewed attention to relations between the state and interest organizations representing capital and labour respectively. This article reviews some tendencies, describes salient dimensions and functions of selected forums for interest intermediation and attempts an assessment of the future of corporatism in South Africa.

The scope of discussion is limited in three ways. First, evolving modes of interaction between the state, capital[1] and labour should ideally be traced within a long historical view. This paper provides, however, only a brief overview of events and tendencies over, primarily, the past 35 years. The second limitation concerns arenas of interaction. Relations between the three interest groupings have been and are being shaped in different but connected arenas. The most important of these are specific production units, whole industries and the arenas of local, regional and national politics. Relations within these arenas are, moreover, influenced by the linkages between capital and labour and interest organizations operating in other spheres of society (e.g. cultural and community affairs), political parties and

---

1. In this paper the terms 'capital' and 'business' are used loosely to refer to industrial, commercial and service sector corporations and companies as well as organized business. 'Organized business' refers specifically to interest organizations ('organized interest groups' or 'associational interest groups') which represent the interests of capital. The interest organizations cited in this paper are all federal-type associations of chambers of commerce and industry, and the like, which themselves could have individual companies and/or individual entrepreneurs as members. The interest organizations cited here are all associations which are dominated by relatively large corporations.

social movements. While a variety of interactions and arenas are noted as important, the primary concern of this paper is with interactions between the state and the peak organizations of capital and labour within the arenas of industrial and national political action.[2]

The third limitation is in some ways the most important one. Any assessment of the future of corporatism should take cognizance of *noncorporatist* relations between the state and interest groups. In this paper it is claimed that relations between state, capital and labour have for some time been evolving in a corporatist direction. This evolution has not, however, pushed aside direct, one-on-one interactions between the state and individual interest organizations representing capital or labour. Nor is it replacing bilateral and multilateral interactions between trade unions and organized business. Moreover, the ascendancy of corporatism in state-capital-labour relations has not displaced noncorporatist relations among the vast array of interest groups outside the economic domain. In fact, a rich diversity of interest organizations and modes of interaction have sprung up since 1990. Whether or not these are the harbingers of a post-apartheid pluralism or some other type of interest representation and interest intermediation is as important a theme for consideration as the possible advent of corporatism.

The discussion begins with reference to some general features of the South African system of interest representation. It is suggested that we have been witnessing the gradual ascendance of corporatist interest *representation* and that the trend has, at least since the early 1990s, also been taking on shades of corporatist interest *intermediation*.[3] The prospects for corporatism are explored by reviewing the history of corporatism in South Africa and by considering the views of activists and analysts, as well as some salient structural features of the participating organizations.

The suggestion that we are witnessing the ascendance of corporatism is subject to a number of qualifications. First, it is not being suggested that the political system as a whole is tending towards corporatism. The label *corporatism* is used to describe interactions which take place outside (but not independently from) electoral and parliamentary politics. In this regard, it is well to remember that a focus on relations between state, capital and labour is 'theoretically predestined' to find traces of corporatism. This is

---

2. Following Skocpol (1979: 29), the concept of 'state' is defined as 'a set of administrative, policing, and military organizations headed, and more or less well coordinated, by an executive authority'. In this paper the active agent of the state which is most often referred to is 'the government', which in South Africa usually refers to the chief executive and his ministers.

3. 'Interest representation' is used here to identify interactions between the state and interest organizations which have *policy advice* as their major outcome. 'Interest intermediation' conveys the idea that the interactions are intended to result in *authoritative policy decisions* and that the participating organizations take joint responsibility for the execution of the policies.

because the concept of corporatism has been formed specifically with regard to interactions between these three sets of organizations. Precisely for this reason, it is important to use *corporatism* in a fairly strict sense. It is advisable to consider not only the composition of policy-making or advisory bodies but also the structural features of organizations and the dynamics of policy processes on the 'input' as well as the 'output' sides of the system. In particular, it is the involvement of organizations in interest intermediation and not only interest representation which should be regarded as definitive. In this paper the label *quasi-corporatism* is used to indicate processes and institutions which involve the state and the interest organizations of capital and labour, but which have no more than advisory functions. *Corporatism* without the qualifier 'quasi' identifies processes and institutions with an explicit and authoritative policy-making function, and which involve not only interest representation but also interest intermediation.

The second qualification has already been mentioned, namely that corporatism in South Africa has never and is unlikely ever to encompass all relations between the state and interest organizations. Even while corporatism seems to be gaining strength under the post-apartheid regime, direct lobbying of the state executive and legislative branches also seems to be intensifying and gaining in influence (Edmunds, 1995). The third qualification pertains to theoretical explanations for the ascendance of corporatism. Much of the literature on corporatism contains strong structuralist leanings. This literature presents corporatism as being associated with the development of (monopoly) capitalism and as a way of containing the fiscal and legitimacy crises of capitalist states. It is not a primary purpose of this paper to offer explanations for the corporatist trend. Nevertheless, its theoretical learnings are towards political action approaches rather than structuralist approaches. Political action approaches credit political agents, including organized formations of leaders and masses and broad social movements, with the shaping of state-society relationships. While such approaches acknowledge the influence of material and other structural conditions on human action, the evolution of state-society relations, including patterns of interest representation and intermediation, are seen as processes which are driven by human agency (Pretorius, 1994b).

General Features of the System

The State and African Trade Unions

From 1924 to the late 1970s, the state's attempts to shape relations between itself, capital and labour was manifested in various forms of statutory and conventional racial segregation and, from 1948, in the form of apartheid. This was true for both the industrial relations system and the encompassing political and social system. Limiting our attention to the apartheid period, two features of industrial relations as governed by the Industrial Conciliation Act of 1956 are particularly germane to the theme of this paper. The first is the exclusion, until 1979, of African persons from trade union rights while granting those rights to whites, Indians and Coloureds. The second feature was the prohibition of all trade union and employer organizations from involvement in party political activities. African workers' relations with employers were also governed by the Native Labour Settlement of Disputes Act of 1953. This limited the workers' opportunities for dispute settlement to plant-level works committees, only 24 of which existed by 1973 (Maree, 1985: 286).

Beyond the above measures, which were designed to control Africans' involvement in both industrial and political affairs, African workers' ability to organize was restricted by a wide range of statutory and administrative measures. These in fact inhibited the evolution of black interest organizations of all kinds. The measures cannot be listed here. Suffice it to say that they were measures which stunted black organizations because they restricted the economic and social resources available to such organizations and because they subjected leaders and followers to diverse forms of administrative and police harassment and persecution.

Formal exclusion invites reaction. The attempts of the state to exclude African trade unions from formal or legal participation in the industrial and the political arenas achieved the opposite: it created fertile conditions for the rise of a vigorous, highly politicized union movement. The South African Congress of Trade Unions (Sactu), for example, was formed in 1955 to pursue the related objectives of worker organization and political liberation (Lambert, 1985, 1987; Maree, 1985). However, Sactu's overt alliance with the African National Congress and the Pan Africanist Congress (PAC) invited, in turn, the repression of its leaders and activists. Given the close alliance between Sactu and the Congress movement, the banning of the ANC and the PAC also resulted in the decapitation of Sactu.

Throughout the 1960s the state's repression of radical anti-apartheid opposition was largely successful. Consequently, the decade was one of relative industrial peace. However, the advent of the 1970s brought the rapid growth of independent African unions. The movement was precipitated by the 1971–2 'Ovambo strikes' in the then South West Africa and the 1973 strikes in the then province of Natal. The visible growth of worker activism and unionization encouraged both the state and organized business to move in the direction of recognizing union rights for Africans. The formal device for achieving this was the Wiehahn Commission of Inquiry into Labour Legislation. According to Maree (1985: 295), the commission

... was appointed in 1977 for a number of important reasons. In addition to the reemergence of African trade unions, this included the shortage of skilled manpower that became apparent during the boom years of the 1960s and threatened to put a stranglehold on economic growth. It was a matter of great concern to the state since it required a strong economy to ensure that it had the resources available to ensure white and capitalist domination. Other important reasons were the high levels of industrial and political conflict in the country that erupted in the 1970s, and the international pressure against apartheid with the possibility that it could disrupt investment in and trade with South Africa.

An influential conventional interpretation of the work of the Wiehahn Commission is that the legalization of African unions was a result of the recommendations of the Commission. It is, however, more likely that the Commission served as a post-hoc legitimator for previously decided policy. The Commission was appointed against the background of increasingly strained industrial relations and the Soweto student rebellion. Its membership included representatives of a number of trade unions and trade union federations, of the Association of Chambers of Commerce (Assocom), the Federated Chambers of Industries (FCI), the Steel and Engineering Industries Federation (Seifsa), and the state Department of Labour. With the exception of the 'mixed unions' affiliated to the Trade Union Council of SA (Tucsa), black workers were not represented. The purpose of the Commission seems to have been to cultivate the agreement of key interest groups, including conservative white unions, to the introduction of a state-sanctioned system for collective bargaining which would incorporate African unions (Friedman, 1986b; Pretorius, 1994a).

The Commission achieved a remarkable degree of consensus, thus limiting, but not preventing, opposition from conservative white trade unions. As part of an attempt to institutionalize the Commission's preference for a tripartite mode of reaching agreements on issues concerning industrial relations, a permanent consultative and advisory forum, the National Manpower Commission (NMC), was established. As in the case of the Wiehahn Commission itself, the NMC's membership included representatives of state agencies, trade unions and organized business (Pretorius, 1982).

The reforms brought to the surface a new trend in relations between the state and interest organizations. Previously, government was not inclined to bring 'outside bodies' into policy-making processes other than for the purposes of giving advice. The most prominent exceptions were organizations linked into the Afrikaner network, but even these were more influenced by government than the other way around. The processes around the Wiehahn Commission signalled growing influence on policy-making of tactics such as the African workers' strikes and the FCI's 'quiet lobbying'. Moreover, the government *purposely* used a commission of inquiry consisting of interest group representatives as a vehicle for involving business associations and trade unions in the legitimation of such reforms. This was an instance of what was becoming a more generally employed 'practice of assembling the leaders in a particular field . . . in confidential meetings where [ministers] argue the case for reform. After consensus has been established, everyone is bound to these decisions' (Giliomee, 1979: 210). The process was *quasi-corporatist* in that it involved members of the government and the leaders of interest groups in policy bargaining outside the parliamentary and party political processes. It also bound the relevant interest organizations to the policy reforms and, in this limited sense, indicated early traces of corporatist interest intermediation.

The incorporation of African unions into the official industrial relations system was intended to

> bring them under the same state regulation and control exercised over other unions. These controls placed obligations on the unions to keep audited accounts, to supply the industrial registrar with regular information about the union, and to draw up its constitution in accordance with the specifications laid down in the Industrial Conciliation Act. (Maree, 1985: 296)

Contrary to the state's intentions, the reformed industrial relations system did not succeed in controlling the new wave of independent unions. From the late 1970s onwards, the government was to introduce a number of 'reforms', all of which were intended to control opposition forces by incorporating them into a subsystem of the state without fundamentally changing the central political system. All such attempts were met by resistance from organizations which were intent on destroying apartheid. In the case of many independent unions the response to attempted co-option into a restrictive official industrial relations system was to avoid registration and to concentrate on building their organizations and expanding their membership. The state reacted by extending official controls to the unregistered unions. This included the extension of prohibitions of union involvement in party politics. The unions nevertheless used the imposed legality to advance their own organizations (Maree, 1985).

The growth of the independent union movement virtually compelled 'a small but influential group' of employers to deal with the unions outside of the official bargaining system. The FCI in particular 'worked behind the scenes to lobby the Department of Manpower to relax controls on unions' (Friedman, 1986b: 7). The state's main response to black worker opposition once more became that of repression. Especially since the mid-1980s, the independent unions were increasingly, though eventually unsuccessfully, persecuted by the government. The instruments ranged from restrictive legislation to police harassment. Repression, including the incarceration of trade union leaders, became particularly severe during the states of emergency of 1985 and 1986 (Fine, 1987). In the longer run, both the post-Wiehahn reforms and the state persecution of the unions simply emphasized the decline of the state's and employers' capacities to control organized opposition.

Some analysts and union activists have argued that popular political involvement by unions is undesirable (Friedman, 1986a). The reasoning is that the 1950s' alliance between Sactu and political organizations resulted in the sacrifice of worker organization for populist strategies. The opposing view is that *political unionism* as practised by Sactu was both an unavoidable and a desirable strategy in the struggle against apartheid and for democracy and socialism (Lambert, 1987; Webster, 1988). These two views defined an important ideological and strategic dividing line among the independent unions of the 1970s and the early 1980s.[4] During this period, many independent unions focused their attention on workplace organization, while others allied themselves with broad political movements. For some unions the choices were strategic: avoidance of popular politics was chosen with the hope of avoiding state repression and gaining space for establishing their organizations. For other unions the choices were ideological, between giving priority to working-class interests and subjecting these interests to the 'nationalist' and 'populist' concerns of political liberation (Lambert, 1987; Webster, 1988).

As mentioned above, many independent unions tended to eschew overt involvement in politics in order to avoid state repression. However, political unionism remained an important tendency. By the 1980s, some unions began to branch out beyond the shop floor, both by way of the creation of shop-steward councils in the townships (Maree, 1985; Webster, 1984, 1988) and personal or organizational alliances with community and political organizations. The shop-steward councils facilitated interaction between workers from different factories and unions. Relations between unions and community organizations remained circumscribed by tensions between tendencies which, by the mid-1980s, came to be known as 'populist' and 'workerist' respectively. The former initially found institutional expression in certain unions' corporate membership of the United Democratic Front (UDF – representing the Congress movement) or National Forum (NF – representing the black consciousness movement). By the mid-1980s the trade union movement began to resolve into two organizational and ideological branches. The majority of industrial and general unions, of both workerist and populist orientation, merged into the Congress of South African Trade Unions (Cosatu). A minority strand of black consciousness

---

4. The label 'independent unions' was used well into the 1980s to distinguish black unions, with mainly African members, from black unions affiliated to the former trade union federation, Tucsa. For brief historical overviews, see Maree (1985). A longer study is Baskin (1991). After the formation of Cosatu and other new black trade union federations in the mid-1980s, the label 'independent' was also used to refer to black unions which were not yet affiliated to one of the major federations.

and Pan-Africanist oriented unions merged into Cusa/Azactu, later to become the National Council of Trade Unions (Nactu). By then the split between populists and workerists permeated virtually every black union in South Africa (Fine, 1987).

Meanwhile, the employers had their own disagreements with the state. On the whole, however, employers tended to respond to unions either by treating them as hostiles or by trying to control them through the mechanisms created by state reforms to the industrial relations system.

White Unions and Organized Business

Even though they represent white interests, chambers of commerce and industry, white trade unions and other interest organizations were for long viewed by Nationalist governments as 'outside bodies'. Such bodies have never been allowed much influence in authoritative policy-making processes. The influence of the mixed unions was, in any case, largely limited to the terrain of industrial relations. The influence of unions with predominantly Afrikaner membership derived not so much from unionism as from electoral politics and their position in the interlocking network of Afrikaner organizations.[5]

For most of the duration of the apartheid *regime*, Afrikaner nationalist governments have resisted interest organizations' attempt to influence policy decisions. All interest groups were, however, not equally treated in this respect. Afrikaner organizations, including the *Afrikaanse Handelsinstituut* (AHI – Afrikaans Commercial Institute) and the Afrikaner trade unions, enjoyed privileged and personal access to the bureaux of state. For the primarily English associations, access tended to be regular, but 'official' and largely ineffective. As Afrikaner capital's share in the economy grew, its contacts and common interests with English capital expanded. Especially since the mid-1970s this has benefited English business because the AHI could convey shared positions to the government.

Afrikaner organizations' access to and influence in the state was a benefit accorded to the members of a closely knit political family. Until the early 1970s, LaPalombara's (1963, 1974) notion of *parentela relations* was an apt description of relations between Afrikaner organizations and the state. As he described it, parentela relations 'implies a kind of political consanguinity, a tight family-type relationship where a sharp distinction is made between insiders and outsiders' (LaPalombara, 1974: 333). The National Party (NP) was the electoral and parliamentary head of the family; the political core of a remarkably coherent network of economic, cultural, religious and political

5. See Pretorius (1994a) for more extensive discussion of relations between the government and business organizations.

organizations (Adam and Giliomee, 1979; Slabbert, 1975). Interaction between Afrikaner interest groups and the nationalist governments was greatly facilitated by their interlocking directorates. Through the network, ideological coherence was constructed and maintained and views on policies canvassed and formed.

As a loyal adjunct to the National Party, the *Afrikaner Broederbond* for long played a major role in the establishment of other Afrikaner organizations and in directing and coordinating their activities. It guided the Afrikaner economic movement, created the *Afrikaanse Handelsinstituut* (in 1942), helped to lay the foundations for the establishment, in 1960, of the prime minister's Economic Advisory Council and assisted in the Afrikaner penetration of the state bureaucracy. The Broederbond's purposeful recruitment and nurturing of leaders in key positions of all sectors of Afrikaner society made it an invaluable conduit to the state.

The Afrikaner nationalist network began to unravel from the late 1960s onwards. With this came the expansion of the range of common interests between Afrikaner and English entrepreneurs and business associations as well as a gradual increase in government's permeability to non-Afrikaner business interests.

Although 'outside bodies', particularly those which were marked as being 'English' or sympathetic to the NP's opposition in Parliament, were expected not to interfere in 'politics', their capacities with regard to matters economic were valued. Successive nationalist governments have always been interested in cultivating the productive capacity of industry and commerce to strengthen the economic foundations of the apartheid state. The fact that (English) organized business was inclined to oppose specific apartheid policies, while supporting or tolerating (but not uncomfortably so) the general principles of racial segregation, ensured relatively regular, if not always friendly, relations between state and capital.

The Corporatist Trend

If the incidence of different types of interactions between interest organizations and the state could be counted and used as an indicator of the type of interest representation which prevails in South Africa, the conclusion is likely to be that the system is characterized primarily by *face-to-face lobbying* and, at least during the period 1948 to 1979, by the existence in the Afrikaner sector of a strong *parentela* system of interlocking organizations. However, formally institutionalized interest representation with some quasi-corporatist features has also been around for some years and seems to be gaining strength. *The strengthening of corporatism came with the advent of a democratic regime. A crucial question is how corporatism will relate to the parliamentary institutions of the new democracy.* Among the many other questions which could arise are: what does corporatism imply for the exclusion or inclusion of interest groups in policy processes? How will corporatism affect democratic practices within interest organizations? These are questions concerning the mix of *social* and *state corporatism*[6] which may evolve over the next few years. It is too early to answer them with certainty. We could, however, attempt an assessment of the direction in which influential organizations want to shape the relations between the state, capital and labour. A brief overview of the recent history of corporatism is a useful starting point.

A Brief History of Corporatism in South Africa

Corporatist thinking among Afrikaner nationalists can be traced back to the 1930s. In 1939 an Afrikaner 'Peoples' Economic Congress' adopted a resolution which called on government to establish a Central Economic Council with the purpose of 'guiding and co-ordinating all economic activities' in the country. During the 1940s and 1950s various measures for the protection of the 'legitimate interests of [Afrikaner] producers, distributors, workers and consumers' by the state, and their representation in advisory bodies, were propagated by the NP and Afrikaner nationalist economic interest organizations (Pretorius, 1994a). The first notable institutional manifestation of quasi-corporatism was the establishment, in 1960, by Prime Minister H. F. Verwoerd of the Economic Advisory Council (EAC). It was created as 'a forum for discussion and more or less informal consultation and co-ordination between the State on the one side and private enterprise interests on the other' (Verwoerd, quoted in Pretorius, 1994a). As such, its all-white membership included representatives of state agencies and of business and labour organizations.

The EAC was never intended to be a policy-formulating body. It also fell far short of being an institution for corporatist interest intermediation. There was no expectation and, with the possible exception of the trade unions and Afrikaner organizations, not much likelihood that its advice could have been imposed by the constituent organizations on their own corporate or individual members.[7] The EAC served, at best, as a forum for the cultivation of common economic interests and views between capital, white labour and the state. The major business interests (which at the time

6. Various definitions are available. See, for example, Malloy (1977) and Schmitter and Lehmbruch (1979).

7. The 'employers' organizations' and trade unions which are directly represented on bodies such as the EAC and Nedlac are all federal bodies. While trade union federations have some hold over the federated unions, business federations are likely to be a third layer of association with virtually no authority over the federated units.

included a relatively small but growing Afrikaans component) shared
government's interest in economic growth and political stability and, in
particular, the need to regulate the supply of African labour. The EAC
provided a forum for developing shared views on such issues. It also
provided the government with an opportunity to solicit business support for
the policy of 'border industry development' and other apartheid economic
policies. The exclusionary nature of Afrikaner nationalism did not allow
consultation between the government and English-dominated business to
be seen. Nor would an Afrikaner nationalist government tolerate the
effective intrusion of 'outside bodies' into authoritative policy-making
processes. The institution of a representative *advisory* body facilitated
attempts to solicit private sector support for government policies, but
without doing so in public view and without creating the appearance that
'outside bodies' share in the making of policy (Pretorius, 1982, 1994a).

In 1985 President P. W. Botha reshaped the EAC by replacing the
representatives of organized business, agriculture and trade unions with
corporate notables who were selected by the President himself. Botha's
courtship of the corporate elite was announced with much fanfare on his
ascendancy to the prime ministership in 1979. At the time, this opening to
capital was presented by his own office and by the media as a sign of
imminent liberalization in both access to policy-making and the content of
policies. However, Botha's approaches to leading entrepreneurs (rather
than to the various chambers of commerce and industry) had very little to
do with the effective representation (and much less so with the participation) of economic interests in policy-making processes. Instead, he, like his
predecessors, was intent on harnessing the productive capacity of business
and on gaining their support for policies which were made within the state's
own bureaux. Even so, the events did indicate a general trend in state–
society relations, namely the strengthening of relations between certain
state and business interests, and the weakening of relations between the
state and white unions and organized agriculture (Adam, 1979).

Meanwhile, the growth of the independent union movement and the
consequent policy changes were bringing about a quasi-corporatist industrial relations framework. The framework had the twin objectives of
incorporating the African unions into the official industrial relations system
and, in particular, of bringing them under state control. To the extent that
the post-Wiehahn restructuring of labour relations was an initiative of the
state, the trend could be read as one pointing towards impending state
corporatism. However, the restructuring was itself a response to the increased activism of black workers and, in the broader context, of a variety of
other radical opposition groupings. Furthermore, the opportunities for legal
unionization which were created by the reforms were used with notable
success by the unions to strengthen their own organizations. In this sense,

the trend was one of penetration of the state by organizations of civil society, i.e. social corporatism.

At the level of bargaining between the peak organizations of capital, labour and the state, the NMC was designed as the institutional manifestation of 'tripartism', as the Wiehahn Commission called the system (Pretorius, 1982). However, the NMC never really became much more than a 'think tank' which was apparently dominated by experts rather than by the representatives of interest organizations. When the quasi-corporatist trend was joined by Cosatu and Nactu in the early 1990s, the NMC briefly seemed to be destined for graduation to a greater role in policy-making.[8] However, both the NMC and the EAC were eventually displaced by the National Economic, Development and Labour Council (Nedlac) (see below).

Since the latter half of the 1980s, organized business and labour on various occasions found themselves cooperating, albeit reluctantly, in opposition to government policies. The cooperation did not develop into a firm anti-government alliance of capital and labour, but the publication of a draft Labour Relations Amendment Act (LRA) in December 1986 set in motion a joint effort which, in September 1990, culminated in the tripartite *Laboria Minute*. This agreement between the major union federations (Cosatu and Nactu), an employer federation (Saccola) and the state laid the basis for the rapid passage of the LRA through Parliament and represented the first significant instance of *corporatist interest intermediation*, properly so-called, in South Africa.

Subsequent labour activism, including a stay-away of 3.5 million people in protest against sales tax, precipitated the creation, in October 1992, of the tripartite National Economic Forum (NEF).[9] Although a variety of organizations have over time expressed views in favour of such a body, the forum was largely a product of the demands of Cosatu (BR, 1992, 1993a: 43;

---

8. In early 1991 Cosatu and Nactu demanded that the NMC must be transformed from an advisory body to one which could negotiate labour policy. Cosatu used the body in an attempt to achieve certain policy objectives, but withdrew in September 1991, dissatisfied both with the composition and the functioning of the NMC.

9. Organized labour's representation was made up by Cosatu, the National Council of Trade Unions (Nactu) and the Federation of South African Labour Unions (Fedsal). In 1994 Cosatu had around 1.5 million members in some 17 affiliated unions, Nactu had 330,000 members in 24 affiliates, and Fedsal, a predominantly white-collar union with around 30 percent black members, had some 270,000 members in 17 affiliates (SAIRR, 1994: 583–5). Capital was represented by 12 organizations including the two major black business associations, the Foundation for South African Business and Consumer Services (Fabcos) and the National African Federated Chamber of Commerce and Industry (Nafcoc), as well as the SA Chamber of Business (Sacob), the SA Employers Consultative Committee on Labour Affairs (Saccola), AHI, the Chamber of Mines, Seifsa and others. State representatives were drawn from various departments, usually including Labour and Finance, Trade and Industry. Sacob was formed in 1989 through a merger of Assocom and FCI.

SAIRR, 1992, 1993, 1994). The NEF was the first South African state-created institution for interest representation to include representatives from the predominantly African union federations. However, throughout its brief existence, the NEF was beset by difficulties rooted in reluctant government and trade union support. The unions saw the NEF as the NP government's attempt to legitimize late-apartheid and pro-capitalist economic policies. Government saw the NEF as a front for ANC policies. Other difficulties stemmed from the underrepresentation of black and small business interests. The NEF and other 'forums' which flourished briefly in the early 1990s (De Villiers, 1994; Shubane and Shaw, 1993) nevertheless served as testing grounds for ideas on the composition and functions of their successor, Nedlac.

The National Economic, Development and Labour Council was established by the Government of National Unity in late 1994.[10] Formally, Nedlac is 'a negotiating, not an advisory body, whose brief is to produce agreements, not recommendations, and with government being one of the three partners and not the only decision-maker' (Naidoo, 1995). The intended scope of its policy activities is indicated by the establishment of four 'negotiating chambers' dealing with, respectively, public finance and monetary policy, trade and industry, labour market and general socio-economic development issues. An ambitious interpretation of Nedlac's formal terms of reference would open even more possibilities. Nedlac is charged with, *inter alia*, the duty to 'seek to reach consensus and conclude agreements on matters pertaining to social and economic policy' and 'consider all significant changes to social and economic policy before it is implemented or introduced in Parliament' (Act 35 of 1994, section 5(1)). This wording contains the potential for placing a very wide range of policy issues within the competence of Nedlac.[11] Not surprisingly, its relationship with Parliament is already an issue of concern.

Corporatism and Democracy

Corporatism invariably entails the possibility of encroaching on the terrain of democratically elected legislatures, if not actually undermining them. Corporatism not only tends to operate outside electorally legitimated policy processes, it also predetermines the interests which are to be represented in policy bargaining and policy-making. In terms of relations between various sectors of society and the state, corporatism is exclusionist and tends towards tripartite domination of the relevant arenas of political competi-

---

10. National Economic, Development and Labour Council Act, No. 35 of 1994.

11. I am indebted to Louise Stack of the Centre for Policy Studies for pointing out the implications of the legislation.

tion, usually those relating to aspects of economic policy. Within organizations, corporatism requires strong control of members by leaders. All these features are potentially inimical to democratic and parliamentary systems of governance.

The potential effects of corporatism on the parliamentary system and other democratic institutions and practices are acknowledged by representatives of state, capital and labour in South Africa. They are matters of special concern for, among others, activists working towards the left of the union movement (Von Holdt, 1995: 36). In fact, the potentially anti-democratic features of corporatism are precisely those which mark systems out as corporatist. Schmitter's definition, for example, emphasizes both the exclusivity and the organizational elitism of corporatism:

> Corporatism can be defined as a system of interest representation in which the constituent units are organized into a limited number of singular, compulsory, non-competitive, hierarchically ordered and functionally differentiated categories, recognized or licensed (if not created) by the state and granted a deliberate representational monopoly within their respective categories in exchange for observing certain controls on their selection of leaders and articulation of demands and supports. (Schmitter, 1979: 13)

Although a South African version of corporatism has been a long time coming (Pretorius, 1979), it is unlikely ever to be quite similar to the paradigm cases of either Latin America or Europe. As a union analyst put it:

> ... this is not ... the corporatism of fascist Italy or authoritarian Latin America – with the state controlling or collaborating with puppet unions. The developments here have emerged through struggle and are closer (but different) to the European social-democratic paradigm. The major players retain their organizational independence, and frequently conflict with each other, even as they try to co-operate and find common goals. What is emerging is best described as 'bargained corporatism'. We are not yet a corporatist society, but we are en route to becoming one. (Baskin, 1993b)

Baskin errs in saying that we are becoming a corporatist *society* and he may well be somewhat overoptimistic about the democratic potential of South African corporatism. At most the trend is towards a partially corporatist system of interest intermediation, and it is too soon to predict the balance between state and social corporatist leanings in the developing system.

On the side of the trade unions, awareness of the anti-democratic tendencies of corporatism is expressed in debate and proposals for preventing or countering these. A unionist analyst summarized 'criticisms of corporatism from the left' as follows:

> Corporatism entrenches the power of a centralised and unaccountable bureaucracy in the labour movement.
> Corporatism leads to the demobilisation of the mass base of the unions, and an

alienation of members from the leadership.
Corporatism co-opts labour into accepting the economic perspectives of capital.
Corporatism is anti-democratic in its effects on society, because it centralises power in
the hands of a small elite of labour bureaucrats, businessmen and government officials
...

In South Africa, because so much of the population is outside formal employment,
tripartite forums only represent a minority of the population ...
Corporatism stabilises capitalist society and ensures that the labour movement
cannot struggle for socialism. The labour movement is tied into corporatist institutions
and loses its capacity for independent action. (Von Holdt, 1993: 48)

A typical response to such criticisms is that corporatism may be undesirable in many respects, but that in South African conditions it is a necessary
vehicle for achieving goals such as union power, democracy and a stable
political environment for economic growth (Baskin, 1993a, 1993b).

The concern about corporatism does not only exist on the left of the union
movement. Baskin, who favours corporatism as a means to an end, argues
that centralized bargaining, which is a characteristic of corporatism and
which is supported by Cosatu and other major union federations,

... often requires democratic rupture – a widening gap, especially on the union side,
between leaders and members. Under centralised bargaining, the commissars of labour
meet the captains of industry and negotiate an agreement. Unless the unions are
properly organized, this can take place far from the workplace, with little involvement
from ordinary union members. (Baskin, 1993c: 58–9)

The proposals for countering democratic rupture and other perceived
invidious consequences include those which envisage a continuation of the
tradition of alliances between unions and other 'popular organizations' and
persistent vigilance to ensure the maintenance of democracy within union
structures (Von Holdt, 1993: 49).

In the union movement, at least, there is thus awareness of tensions
between corporatism and democracy. However, assessment of the likely
directions that the corporatist trend could take requires a closer look at
various participants' preferences with regard to three specific themes:
relations between corporatist and parliamentary institutions, the tendency
of corporatism to be exclusivist and the tendency of corporatism to encourage (if not require) hierarchical and authoritarian relations within
participating organizations. It also requires consideration of the composition of Nedlac and of the mid-1995 process of tripartite bargaining on a draft
Labour Relations Act.

Corporatism and Parliament

Because Nedlac is a non-elected body and because it includes representatives of state agencies, the agreements negotiated by the participants cannot
be taken lightly by government. Acceptance of such agreements will,

however, threaten to undermine parliamentary processes. In South Africa the position is complicated by the relationship between the Cosatu unions and the ANC and the South African Communist Party (SACP). Currently, the relationship between these organizations is mediated not only in the chambers of Nedlac but also through ANC and SACP MPs and state bureaucrats who entered their current positions as union members. As was the case with the Afrikaner network, the ANC-SACP-Cosatu linkage is both organizational and sociological. However, it is useful to note that the Afrikaner network was only consolidated *after* the NP took power (Slabbert, 1975); and it was only then that the network became a potent mechanism for ensuring ideological and policy coherence. It is too soon to say whether or not a similar dynamic will develop in the ANC-related network and what the effects could be. For the present, there are signs of tension between parliamentary and corporatist politics, but also of a search for balance between the two processes.

Even strong supporters of corporatism are still careful not to voice opinions which clearly favour corporatism over parliamentary democracy. However, the preferences of some labour activists seem clear. Leading Cosatu negotiator, Ebrahim Patel, for example, has expressed himself as follows:

> ... government obviously would have to give its consent to whatever is finally agreed, or is not an agreement of three parties. To that extent the sovereignty of any parliament will be exercised in the negotiating process. ... Any society is complex, and people's needs are not always best articulated through a member of parliament. They can be articulated through trade unions, or through other organs of civil society. In addition government is not the only power in society. (Patel, 1993: 25–6)

The statements were made in the context of the last year of apartheid and with reference to the NEF. They nevertheless convey the views of an important tendency within Cosatu. It is a tendency which is likely to value its own interpretation of 'the people's needs' over that of Parliament. Not all unionists necessarily share such views. A more cautious formulation is that of former Cosatu negotiator and present executive director of Nedlac, Jayendra Naidoo. Also talking in the context of the NEF, Naidoo seems to have been expressing preference for effective corporatist policy-making, but then in a way which places a relatively high value on parliamentary government.

> In Cosatu we started by saying we wanted a negotiating body and business said, we want to be part of an advisory body. We said advisory and Cosatu never go together. What we agreed then, in principal [sic] ... was we don't want now, or in the future, nor would it be healthy, to have Government subject to an economic forum. A political party goes to the voters every five years or whatever period on a particular policy platform. ... You can't subject governmental processes to a tripartite forum. (BR, 1993a: 39–40)[12]

---

12. See also Naidoo (1994).

The unease about relations between corporatist bodies and Parliament extends to ANC parliamentarians. Member of Parliament Blade Nzimande, for example, expressed concern that 'parliament can become a rubber stamping exercise for civil society agreements which could undermine the legitimacy of representative government' (quoted in Stack, 1995). Government's preferences as articulated by ministerial and other spokespersons are best described as ambivalent (see below).

It is not altogether clear whether organized business has a unified view on the role of tripartite bodies. The South African Chamber of Business (Sacob), for its part, does not seem to favour effective corporatism in policy-making. Its officials have expressed the expectation that the NEF would 'become an institution where consensus can be gained as to the best way to shape the economy' (BR, 1993b: 45). However, Sacob officials' statements on the NEF conveyed relatively clear preferences for an advisory body which does not impinge on the terrain of Parliament:

> Parliament has specific responsibilities to its voters. Other national bodies should not shoulder that burden ... Sacob envisages that the NEF will act as a strong advisory body ... It is ... quite obvious that, however desirable, consensus will not always be possible. Therefore provision will have to be made for minority views. It is also not the goal of the NEF to prevent individual participating members from making their own special pleas and representations to Government. Business lobbying will still be done on the basis of normal organized representation. However, the NEF will have to guard against special pleading on behalf of any of its tripartite members. It will always need to bear overall community interests in mind in the outcome of its deliberations. (BR, 1993b: 47)

That business is uneasy with corporatism is also implied by Raymond Parsons of Sacob, one of organized business's most experienced officials:

> Business is prepared to give Nedlac its best shot. But perhaps we have been too ambitious in our expectations. Perhaps Nedlac should not be asked to formulate legislation. It should rather be seen as a forum in which the stakeholders present their views as a basis for consensus. When there are serious difficulties, it may be more productive if both sides simply make direct representations (outside Nedlac) to the relevant Minister – and the Minister hears them out and makes his own decision. This will avoid the endless delays which could occur when consensus cannot be achieved. (*Financial Mail*, 7 July 1995)

This of course negates the very purpose of Nedlac, but is in line with business's preference for voluntary and decentralized industrial bargaining (see below).

The unavoidable tensions between corporatist and parliamentary policy processes were illustrated by the major issue facing Nedlac during its first few months of existence, namely the 1995 Labour Relations Act (LRA). Suspicions that corporatist deals may overshadow parliamentary democracy were encouraged by the secrecy with which government introduced the LRA into the parliamentary process and by suggestions that the parliamentary committee should not upset what the minister called a 'careful equilibrium' (*Business Day*, 21 July 1995; *The Sunday Independent*, 27 August 1995). A ministerial spokesperson insisted that the agreement should be passed untouched 'in the national interest', while denying that Nedlac agreements are not democratic. The supporting argument was that Nedlac is 'representative'. This of course begs the question as to which interests Nedlac represents – or not. It also misrepresents the relationship between democracy and representation.

The 1995 LRA process, which was in effect driven by negotiators from Cosatu, Business South Africa (BSA) and the state Department of Labour, did not clarify the state's position either with regard to corporatism or, within such a framework, with regard to the organizations of labour and capital. With or without corporatism the likelihood that the executive arm of the state, specifically the government and its bureaucracies, will dominate policy processes, always exists. During the LRA process, some reports indicated that the Minister of Labour placed himself behind union demands. Others, also citing the Minister, said that government would not be supporting union demands. President Mandela and senior ANC officials addressed union demonstrations and supported their right to demonstrate. SACP members of government unequivocally supported organized labour's specific demands (*Pretoria News*, 7 June 1995; *Sunday Times*, 25 June 1995; *The Star*, 6 June 1995). However, the Chair of the Parliamentary Committee on Labour Affairs, and former Vice-President of Cosatu, 'remarked that [Cosatu] should not take it for granted that former unionists in parliament would put Cosatu's interests before national interests' (quoted in Von Holdt, 1995: 33).

All in all, it seems that government contrived the best of an ambiguous stance for itself. While government spokespersons supported labour demands for compulsory centralized bargaining, government also declined to resolve the differences between labour and business. It avoided a clear choice by appealing to technical difficulties in enforcing compulsory centralized bargaining (*Financial Mail*, 30 June 1995). Thus it achieved a tenuous tripartite agreement which left the LRA for the most part with the content which it was originally given by the ministers' own drafting team. This suggests that the state is, for the time being at least, the dominant party, but not one which wants to adopt that position publicly.

Corporatism: Exclusive or Inclusive?

The question of who is included or excluded from corporatist bodies brings to the fore some of the central issues in designing institutions of interest representation and intermediation. Corporatist and quasi-corporatist bodies are often presented by their supporters and members as serving 'the national interest'. However, interest organizations serve sectional interests which are defined by themselves. Furthermore, to the extent that interest organizations advocate definitions of the national interest, these are coloured by sectional interests. As the critical but pro-capital *Financial Mail* put it, bodies such as Nedlac tend to negotiate deals in secret and to create a 'closed shop' of privileged interests. This makes it 'difficult, sometimes impossible for dissenting voices within both the business and labour constituencies to make their views known and their influence felt' (*Financial Mail*, 7 July 1995). Corporatism, like other systems which are geared to achieving agreement among peak organizations and elitist systems in general, always harbours the possibility that social and political cleavages could crystallize around differences in opportunities for access to centres of authority. In particular, relatively weak interest organizations and unorganized interests tend to be marginalized and, perhaps, radicalized.

Being acutely aware of the problem, Cosatu leaders are especially inclined to present their organizations as serving a constituency beyond their paid-up membership:

> Cosatu is a labour movement with a difference. We take the view that we need to promote the interests of our members vigorously, but those interests are best pursued by also looking at the interests of the unemployed, and those who have no voice in society. (Patel, 1993: 26)

These views are not mere ideology. Other actors in and around Nedlac are also aware of the exclusionist and elitist propensities of corporatism. Nedlac has, thus, been designed to extend membership beyond the usual range of capital, labour and state.[13] To a large extent, this arrangement reflects the tradition of political unionism and Cosatu's membership of unions with strong community links. The inclusion of nonunion civil society organizations in Nedlac also recognizes the experience, during the interregnum of 1990 to 1994, of a multitude of quasi-corporatist forums for interest representation.

By September 1995, the National Youth Development Forum (NYDF), National Woman's Coalition (NWC) and South African National Civics Organisation (Sanco) had been granted representation on Nedlac as 'community organizations'. Nedlac's directorate insists that stringent criteria, laid down in the enabling legislation, were used in the selection of organizations for admission. However, the inclusion of these organizations in terms of rules which have to be applied by Nedlac itself (and which were likely designed by the dominant groups in Nedlac), like the inclusion of the peak organizations of capital and labour themselves, prefigures the interests which are worthy of representation. Those interests are virtually always

---

13. With regard to organized business and labour, its membership is much like that of the NEF, with BSA and Cosatu being the dominant participants.

interests which have achieved positions of power in ways other than society-wide democratic elections.

Very little is publicly known about the scope of the NYDF, NWC and Sanco's membership or about their internal decision-making processes. As a mobilizing and coordinating agent for local resistance against the state, Sanco claims to have had some success. However, the extent of this success and, especially, of its ability to represent and control the wider communities for which it claims to speak, are at best debatable (Friedman, 1994). Both representativity and the ability to bind the represented constituency to agreements are essential for corporatist intermediation.

Like the possible effects of their exclusion, the possible effects of the inclusion of these organizations in corporatist forums are difficult to foresee. To the extent that organizations such as Sanco are not representative of significant interests in 'civil society', their inclusion in Nedlac could strengthen rather than weaken the exclusionary and elitist tendencies of corporatism. On the other hand, their inclusion may well dilute the influence of state, labour and capital, albeit without effectively expanding the range of interests represented.

A third possibility is suggested by the recent LRA process. The way in which the process was conducted indicates that negotiations on policy issues will be contained within the respective functionally specific negotiation chambers. One effect of such a procedure would be the creation of different interest sectors within Nedlac, and perhaps in other policy-making bodies. Each such sector could become the privileged domain of a closed, self-perpetuating alliance of powerful interest organizations.

The issues which were raised by LRA 1995 also highlighted, but did not effectively address, the possible exclusivist tendencies of corporatism. A number of clauses were disputed by different interest groups. However, the principal divisions between organized business and labour concern the choice between compulsory centralized and voluntary decentralized bargaining. The unions prefer the former position. Organized business and the large corporations prefer voluntarist and decentralized bargaining. In other words, the unions' positions on the LRA 'are designed to facilitate the emergence of big, centralized unions with a high level of social and economic involvement', while the business position is likely to eventuate into 'a weaker, more fragmented labour movement' (Von Holdt, 1995: 34).[14] Organized business argued that adoption of the union position is likely to reinforce the exclusion of small, micro and medium enterprises' (SMEs)

---

14. The union position is, for the time being at least, shared by the state (Von Holdt, 1995: 34), but its role in reaching agreement between labour and capital also suggested a pragmatic position as a broker rather than as an autonomous party taking its own or another interest's side.

interests from Nedlac and from bilateral negotiations between companies and unions. However, the associations representing SMEs judged the positions of both organized business and labour as being inimical to their interests, and claimed that their submissions were ignored by Nedlac.

It is important to note that organized business's preference for decentralized bargaining is incompatible with corporatism, while the union position favours corporatism. The position taken by organized business may seem to be ironic, given its often expressed preference for a 'social contract' between state, capital and labour. However the terms of the 'social contract' which are favoured by capital are those which support 'free enterprise'. It is, in other words, a contract which itself prefers quasi-pluralist modes of interest representation.

Corporatism, Organizational Coherence and Democracy

Corporatism's possible undercutting of intra-organizational democracy operates at two levels. The first pertains to relations between the peak organizations and their respective corporate members. The second pertains to democracy within particular organizations' own structures.

That corporatist agreements might negate the interests of some trade unions and be undermining of democracy within the union movement is a fear often expressed, notably by the South African Municipal Workers Union (Samwu). After agreement was reached on the LRA, Samwu leaders claimed that they were given little opportunity to consult with their members. In September 1995 branches of this union embarked on wage strikes, soon after the agreement on the LRA was reached by organized business and labour. The strikes were not directly related to the LRA agreement. They do, however, indicate the as yet uncertain hold that Cosatu has over some of its member unions. Corporatism requires a significant degree of union subservience to tripartite agreements. In fact, the relation between public-sector unions such as Samwu and the other 'social partners' is particularly complicated because the state also has the role of employer in relation to them.

Support and disagreement between unions do not run along straight lines, however. While there might be divergences between unions about process, policy and specific sets of bilateral relations, there is also unexpected agreement on some issues. Not the least of these was the general thrust of the 1995 LRA. The mass action campaign on the LRA was interpreted by a labour-supporting journal as signalling

> ... a quite unprecedented unity between the three major labour federations.
> During the 1980s Cosatu and parts of Nactu engaged in joint action against the amended LRA. In 1991 Fedsal played a prominent role in the anti-VAT coalition

spearheaded by Cosatu, but stopped short of participating in the stayaway. However, this year not only have Fedsal put forward a common position on what they want to see in the new LRA, but the former two have come out in support of the mass action campaign initiated by Cosatu. (Von Holdt, 1995: 32)

The significance of this lies in the fact that the Federation of South African Labour Unions (Fedsal) is a federation of predominantly white, and white-collar, unions. Another important aspect of the campaign is that it was not only one about relations between state, capital and labour, but also about relations *within* trade unions:

There is a surge of militance among shop stewards and union members on the ground. This is partly because Cosatu affiliates have re-focused their energies on collective bargaining programmes after three years of intense political activity. But militancy is also being driven by concern about the gap between the grassroots and the leadership.

The involvement of union and federation leaders in increasingly complex interactions and negotiations in industry forums, Nedlac and other institutions has widened this gap and produced a sense of disempowerment at the base. Grassroots activists are keen to assert their militancy and their demands ... For leadership, the campaign provides an opportunity to forge stronger links to their mass base, demonstrating their willingness to engage in struggle. (Von Holdt, 1995: 32)

Organized business is generally much less unified than the trade union movement. Labour representatives in Nedlac can also claim to speak as elected officials of umbrella bodies of democratically organized unions, with democratic practices which extend down to the shop floors of various industrial and commercial sectors. Business representatives can at best claim the dubious democracy of annual conferences. And it is always debatable whether a negotiator like Bobby Godsell represents his home corporation, Anglo American, or the ostensible voice of organized business, BSA.[15] Baskin has provided a list of the deficiencies which would make organized business a dubious partner in attempts to establish corporatist interest intermediation. Organized business is dominated by large corporations, employers in important commercial sectors are not organized or are weakly organized, the peak associations of business lack the ability to 'present a united, disciplined front' and to discipline their corporate members. (Baskin, 1993c: 61–62; see also Von Holdt, 1995)

Baskin concludes that:

Within a laissez faire system the union movement can benefit from division among

---

15. BSA's membership structure is designed to incorporate as many of South Africa's wide array of business associations as possible, but the dominant members are Sacob, Seifsa, the Chamber of Mines and the AHI. It also incorporates the two major black associations, Fabcos and Nafcoc, but their relationship with the large, primarily white, organizations tends to be, at best, uneasy. Not the least of the difficulties arises over disagreements about the ways in which Fabcos and Nafcoc should be represented in bodies like Nedlac.

employers. But as soon as labour moves toward greater concertation, the very opposite
becomes true. Labour, within the corporatist paradigm, needs a cohesive and relatively
united employer counterpart. (Baskin, 1993c: 62)

While the apparent measure of unity among trade union federations
could begin to approximate some of corporatism's defining features, namely
sectoral monopoly and hierarchical control of members, the employees'
organizations have always had difficulty in agreeing with each other and in
obtaining mandates from their members. The fragmentation of both organized and corporate business was to some extent alleviated by the creation
of BSA in 1994. BSA was presented as putting business 'in the same position
as organized labour in respect of mandated representation on tripartite
bodies' (BR, 1994: 51). BSA's Godsell has claimed that 'business has never
been so united' and that the negotiating team on the LRA

has functioned more cohesively and more unanimously than at any time in 20 years (of
organized business activity) . . . Business is absolutely unified in our sense of the issues,
in our sense of the strategy. (*Financial Mail*, 7 July 1995)

Despite these assurances, the agreement on the 1995 LRA was soon
followed by rumours that some business organizations were readying themselves for direct lobbying in opposition to the agreement. By October 1995
this 'second bite of the cherry' option had not yet surfaced publicly. There is,
nevertheless, little doubt that Godsell's judgements were correct only in a
relative sense.

For the unions the difficulty is somewhat different. They claim strong
democratic traditions and must consequently strive to maintain at least a
symbolic balance between hierarchy and democracy.

Concluding Comments

The corporatist trend is far from institutionalized in a sociological sense of
the word. In September 1995 the weakness of the trend was vividly illustrated by a widely supported series of 'illegal strikes' among health workers.
The strikes were condemned by the relevant trade union, the National
Education, Health and Allied Workers' Union (Nehawu), and other major
health employees' organizations. The nurses' strikes were opposed by the
government, although government spokespersons evinced sympathy for the
'cause' (*The Citizen*, 7 September 1995). The events point to the possible
absence of a vital dimension for successful corporatist interest intermediation: the ability of organizational elites to ensure their followers' compliance
with corporatist pacts. However, it also highlighted the unresolved issue of
relations between state, capital and labour in situations where the state itself

employs a significant component of labour.

The trend towards corporatism could, furthermore, be delayed, if not arrested, by the structural differences between organized business and labour which were previously noted in this paper. Another possible impediment is disagreement with regard to the way in which tripartite bargaining processes should be conducted. For example, business tends to see the unions' proclivity to mass action as inimical to structured and productive interactions. For unions, however, mass action is part of the process of defining positions and mobilizing support. Specifically, the unions view mass demonstrations as vehicles for the enhancement of union power and the reduction of distance between leaders and masses. Organized business's condemnation of mass action, and the disingenuous recent threats to embark on an 'executive strike', reflect both its traditional stance on strikes and its lack of understanding for union political culture and the structural differences between labour and capital's respective power bases. On the other hand, the unions' insistence on taking to the streets in order to make their points does endanger an essential instrument of corporatism: negotiation.

Despite the impediments, the trend could persist simply because the major 'social partners' seem to believe that some form of tripartite bargaining is essential to resolve conflicts in the economic arena. Beyond, and in support of, this arena there is the evolving and thus far relatively successful modus operandi of negotiated political settlements between political party elites. It needs to be noted that inter-party negotiations stemmed not so much from the preferences of the elites, as from the fact that the major parties, the ANC and the NP, have found themselves in a conflictual balance of power. To the extent that labour, capital and the state remain in a similar situation, corporatism may continue to expand. However, the ANC's growing hold over the instruments of state may well shift the balance of power between itself, labour and capital. Moreover, the ascendance of a Parliament rooted in regular elections and the rise of an African bureaucratic class, many of whom are drawn from the union leadership, may well diminish government's need and support for corporatist arrangements. If, and to the extent that, an ANC government responds to its broad electorate rather than its union allies, the unions may turn more insistently towards corporatism. Capital, in turn, is likely to persist in viewing corporatist intermediation with suspicion, although it will also continue supporting quasi-corporatism.

The unknown factor in any assessment of future systems of interest representation and interest intermediation is the vast population of people who are not organized into coherent interest organizations: the poor, the unemployed and the homeless. Despite Nedlac and Parliament, these people are not yet effectively involved in policy-making. The exclusion of the poor is, however, not particular to any specific set of political arrangements. When they are a majority, as they are in South Africa, more than corporatism and parliamentism might be needed to consolidate democracy.

REFERENCES

Adam, H. (1979) 'Interests Behind Afrikaner Power', in H. Adam and H. Giliomee (eds) *The Rise and Crisis of Afrikaner Power*, pp. 177–95. Cape Town: David Philip.
Adam, H. and H. Giliomee (eds) (1979) *The Rise and Crisis of Afrikaner Power*. Cape Town: David Philip.
Baskin, J. (1991) *Striking Back: a History of Cosatu*. Johannesburg: Ravan Press.
Baskin, J. (1993a) *Corporatism: Some Obstacles Facing the South African Labour Movement* (CPS Social Contract Series, Research Report No. 30). Johannesburg: Centre for Policy Studies.
Baskin, J. (1993b) 'The Trend Towards Bargained Corporatism', *SA Labour Bulletin* 17: 3.
Baskin, J. (1993c) 'Time to Bury the Wiehahn Model?', *SA Labour Bulletin* 17: 4.
BR (1992) 'National Economic Forum', *Bilateralism Review* 1: 1.
BR (1993a) 'The National Economic Forum – a Perception from Labour and Capital, Interview – P. Richer with J. Naidoo', *Bilateralism Review* 1: 3.
BR (1993b) 'The National Economic Forum – a Perception from Labour and Capital, Interview – L. Douwes Dekker, B. van Rensburg and G. Bezuidenhout', *Bilateralism Review* 1: 3.
BR (1994) 'Employers' Associations. Establishment of Business South Africa', *Bilateralism Review* 3: 1.
De Villiers, R. (ed.) (1994) *Forums and the Future*. Johannesburg: Centre for Policy Studies.
Edmunds, M. (1995) 'Parliament's New Opportunists', *Mail & Guardian*, 4–10 August.
Fine, A. (1987) 'Trends and Developments in Organized Labour', in South African Research Service (ed.) *South African Review 4*, pp. 219–31. Johannesburg: Ravan Press.
Friedman, S. (1986a) *Building Tomorrow Today: African Workers in Trade Unions, 1970–1984*. Johannesburg: Ravan Press.
Friedman, S. (1986b) 'How to Assist Change, Case A: Labour Relations', unpublished research report, South African Institute of Race Relations, Johannesburg.
Friedman, S. (1994) 'Having Sanco at the Table Could Be Bad for Digestion', *Business Day*, 14 November.
Giliomee, H. (1979) 'Afrikaner Politics: How the System Works' in H. Adam and H. Giliomee (eds.) *The Rise and Crisis of Afrikaner Power*, pp. 196–250. Cape Town: David Philip.
Lambert, R. (1985) 'Political Unionism and Working Class Hegemony: Perspectives on the South African Congress of Trade Unions, 1955–1956', *Labour, Capital and Society* 18: 2.
Lambert, R. (1987) 'Trade Unions, Nationalism and the Socialist Project in South Africa', in South African Research Service (ed.) *South African Review 4*, pp. 232–52. Johannesburg: Ravan Press.
LaPalombara, J. G. (1963) *Interest Groups in Italian Politics*. Princeton, NJ: Princeton University Press.
LaPalombara, J. G. (1974) *Politics Within Nations*. Englewood Cliffs, NJ: Prentice-Hall.
Malloy, J. M. (ed.) (1977) *Authoritarianism and Corporatism in Latin America*. Pittsburgh: University of Pittsburgh Press.
Maree, J. (1985) 'The Emergence, Struggles and Achievements of Black Trade Unions in South Africa from 1973 to 1984', *Labour, Capital and Society* 18: 2.

Naidoo, J. (1994) 'Transcript of Address on "Forum/Government Interface in the Transition"', in R. De Villiers (ed.) *Forums and the Future*, pp. 57–64. Johannesburg: Centre for Policy Studies.

Naidoo, J. (1995) Interview with L. Stack, *TransAct* 2: 7.

Patel, E. (1993) 'Going in With Confidence', interview, *SA Labour Bulletin* 17: 1.

Pretorius, L. (1979) 'Aantekeninge by die Studie van Belange-intermediasie in Suid-Afrika', unpublished paper, Conference of Lecturers in the Governmental and Related Sciences, Johannesburg (August).

Pretorius, L. (1982) 'Interactions Between Interest Organizations and Government in South Africa', *Politeia Unisa* 1: 1.

Pretorius, L. (1994a) 'The Head of Government and Organized Business', in R. Schrire (ed.) *Leadership in the Apartheid State. From Malan to De Klerk*, pp. 209–44. Cape Town: Oxford University Press.

Pretorius, L. (1994b) *Relationships between State and Society in South Africa*, inaugural Lecture, Unisa, Pretoria.

Schmitter, P. C. (1979) 'Still the Century of Corporatism?', in P. C. Schmitter and G. Lehmbruch (eds) *Trends Toward Corporatist Intermediation*, pp. 7–52. Beverly Hills, CA: Sage.

Schmitter, P. C. and G. Lehmbruch (eds) (1979) *Trends Toward Corporatist Intermediation*. Beverly Hills, CA: Sage.

Shubane, K. and M. Shaw (1993) *Tomorrow's Foundations? Forums as the Second Level of a Negotiated Transition in South Africa*. Johannesburg: Centre for Policy Studies.

Skocpol, T. (1979) *States and Social Revolutions*. Cambridge: Cambridge University Press.

Slabbert, F. v. Z. (1975) 'Afrikaner Nationalism, White Politics, and Political Change', in L. Thompson and J. Butler (eds) *Change in Contemporary South Africa*, pp. 3–18. Berkeley: University of California Press.

South African Institute of Race Relations (SAIRR) (1992) *Race Relations Survey 1991/92*. Johannesburg: SAIRR.

South African Institute of Race Relations (1993) *Race Relations Survey 1992/93*. Johannesburg: SAIRR.

South African Institute of Race Relations (1994) *Race Relations Survey 1993/94*. Johannesburg: SAIRR.

Stack, L. (1995) unpublished notes on a Centre for Policy Studies Conference September, Johannesburg.

Von Holdt, K. (1993) 'The Dangers of Corporatism', *SA Labour Bulletin* 17: 1.

Von Holdt, K. (1995) 'LRA Negotiations', *SA Labour Bulletin* 19: 3.

Webster, E. (1984) 'New Force on the Shop Floor', in South African Research Service (ed.) *South African Review* 2, pp. 79–89. Johannesburg: Ravan Press.

Webster, E. (1988) 'The Rise of Social Movement Unionism', in P. Frankel, N. Pines and M. Swilling (eds) *State, Resistance and Change in South Africa*. Beckenham: Croom Helm.

12. THE POLITICS OF AFFIRMATIVE ACTION IN THE OLD AND THE NEW SOUTH AFRICA

Pierre Hugo

Introduction

The South African debate on affirmative action has, unsurprisingly, assumed a greater sense of urgency since the country's first full adult suffrage election in 1994. In the process, reformism in the garb of colour blindness is increasingly being eclipsed in favour of policy interventionism reaching beyond what proponents of affirmative action have criticized as the ineffective termination of apartheid which leaves its heritage of racial employment inequity largely undisturbed. Judge Albie Sachs (1992: 204), a long-standing legal critic of apartheid and now a member of the Constitutional Court, has referred to those who reject affirmative action out of hand for taking account of race as people who are less colour blind than totally blind to South African realities. It is, however, as well to register the point that while affirmative action is being driven by an awareness of reversing the heritage of apartheid injustices it is equally and probably more immediately spurred by policy-makers who perceive the need to pacify new black constituencies and their potentially disruptive reaction to the non-redress of their political demands for a better life after apartheid.

Prior to the election of the new Government of National Unity little was done by the previous government to advance affirmative action in the civil service even after the unbanning of the African National Congress in 1990, from which date it was plain to see that the civil service's traditional racial profile would not long endure. The main reason for the government not taking a lead in this regard was concern that white civil servants would transfer their political support en masse to white right-wing parties should they perceive their employment interests to be under threat. As a result of this inaction a situation of long-term total untenability was allowed to continue with little effort being made to recruit blacks into positions of managerial responsibility.

More serious political contingency planning did, however, take place in the private sector where by the end of the 1980s most of the larger business corporations had some form of affirmative action programme. With few exceptions these programmes did not include quotas in favour of blacks. Special efforts were, however, made to recruit at black university campuses and high schools. White managers by and large saw it as being in their own interests to take on black trainees and turn them into success stories. In the same vein, entry standards for such trainees were relaxed and special in-service programmes were often created with a view to bringing blacks up to levels where they could compete on merit for specific jobs while not necessarily being the best applicants. In most companies blacks who showed promise were placed on accelerated promotion paths.

Despite what white-owned corporations would describe as their best efforts to advance black employees, the results have not been encouraging. By 1993, for example, only some 3 percent of middle-management positions were held by blacks (meaning Africans, Coloureds and Indians) while the figure for those in top management was under one percent. Organizations such as the Black Management Forum (BMF) (1993), which claims to be the legitimate voice of black managers, have, predictably, reacted angrily to this state of affairs which they have attributed to a lack of commitment on the part of the white business elite. In a detailed policy document on the subject of affirmative action the BMF proclaims its allegiance to the goal of transforming South African business organizations from discriminatory structures to ones which reflect the 'demographic composition and values of South African society as a whole'. In order to achieve this goal all South African companies should have the following percentages of blacks in their employ by the year 2000: 80 percent of all trainees; 70 percent of all supervisors; 50 percent of junior managers; 40 percent of middle managers; 30 percent of senior managers; 20 percent of executive directors and 30 percent of non-executive directors.

The BMF, no doubt, reflects a general opinion among blacks when it argues the above-mentioned quotas will remain a chimera unless they are driven by legislative enforcement. To this end the organization is actively engaged in lobbying government to introduce such legislation. In addition it has pushed for other measures to facilitate the implementation of affirmative action. These include keeping official statistical records which reflect race and gender codes; and creating a Manpower Commission which would conduct an audit of available human resources by race and gender as well as assessing all the areas in which the government contracts out services. On this latter score the lobbying strategy has already borne fruit with the Department of Public Works having in August 1995 announced its intention of changing a system whereby about 5 percent of consulting, engineering and architectural firms – all white – have traditionally won some 80 percent of the contracts awarded by the department. Henceforth this department would assess firms who tendered for its contracts on the basis of their track record in such areas as affirmative action hiring, their alliances with black firms, their programmes for bursaries, in-house training, and mentorship schemes for blacks. Black firms would also be paired with 'established' (i.e. white) firms in the awarding of contracts while smaller black contractors would be helped to draw up tenders (Department of Public Works, 1995).

The BMF has also recommended the establishment of an Affirmative Action or Equal Opportunities Commission which, in line with the American precedent, would be administratively empowered to require employers to submit to it their affirmative action employment targets as well as steps being taken to achieve such targets. These steps would have to include a firm commitment to the company's affirmative action programme by its chief executive who would assume overall accountability for its success or failure and who would in turn require his or her executives to do the same. A racially and gender-mixed affirmative action committee would, moreover, be required to monitor progress, and appropriate penalties or rewards for failure or success in complying with company affirmative action policy should be firmly entrenched. The appointment of a senior manager responsible for the day-to-day working of this policy is also recommended by the BMF. These latter recommendations have now, to all intents and purposes, become standard operating procedure in most large South African companies. These companies appreciate the seriousness of the new black political power-wielders in changing the racial profile inherited from the policy of apartheid, which, in effect, was little more than a white job reservation system guaranteed by successive governments to a white electorate in exchange for their support. This was especially true in the civil service where Afrikaners who formed the main constituency of the previous government which came into power in 1948 eventually constituted 80 percent of whites in civil service employment (Giliomee, in Gilomee and Adam, 1979: 224). The racially polarized occupational structure of the civil service outside the old so-called homeland or Bantustan territories is clearly reflected in Table 1.

White Advancement

Given the consistency with which previous South African governments have passed racially exclusive legislation encompassing most activities, the *de*

Table 1. Senior Employment in the Civil Service by Race and Income, 1989

	White	Coloured	Indian	African	% White
R165,001+	29	0	0	0	100.0
R120,001–R165,000	3	0	1	0	75.0
R100,001–R120,000	91	1	0	0	98.9
R87,001–R100,000	720	5	5	2	98.4
R74,001– R87,000	1945	17	55	12	95.9
R49,001– R74,000	13,596	1509	1055	397	82.1
R38,001– R49,000	21,809	2147	1952	814	81.6
R29,001– R38,000	42,048	4974	3389	3119	78.6
Total	80,241	8653	6457	4344	80.5

Source. Hansard, 14 March 1990, cols 483–91.

jure non-discriminatory legislation pertaining to employment in the civil service presents a curious anomaly. In the field of industrial employment, for example, laws such as the Industrial Conciliation Act 1924, the Wage Act 1925 and the Mines and Works Act 1926 explicitly disadvantaged blacks in terms of government policy to protect white interests. And yet neither the Public Services and Pension Act 1912, the Public Services and Pensions Act 1923 nor the Public Services Act 1957 incorporated any formal racial disbarment. In fact, section 11 (3) of the latter act stipulates a number of non-racial attributes based on qualifications, merit and efficiency which should be applied in making appointments and promotions. In practice, however, the apparent anomaly has belied a reality every bit as racially exclusive as in the field of industrial employment; in point of fact, more so.

In industrial employment the colour bar (until its final scrapping in the early 1980s) was applied selectively to certain categories of employment while economic imperatives and pressures from organized employers acted as a partial brake on its proliferation. Despite its own supposed functional imperatives in the interests of the efficient delivery of services, no such selectivity constrained the operation of the colour bar in public sector employment. In this sphere the logic of racial separatism and exclusivity reigned supreme. Other than in menial and non-permanent employment and with the exception of the Department of Defence (particularly after the outbreak of hostilities in Angola in 1975 and the subsequent conflict in Namibia) and the police force, blacks were, throughout this century, consistently excluded from the civil service. Policy in this regard, especially since 1948, was based on the ideological raison d'etre that the political destiny of blacks lay in 'their own homeland areas'. Any departure from this principle, particularly in regard to black participation in organs of state, was deemed to imply an irreparable compromising of the separatist principle.

To give an inch (see further on) on this principle would be tantamount to seeding unacceptable black expectations of a political future alongside white South Africans.

The pristine application of this principle in the case of the civil service is amply demonstrated by the costs which its proponents were willing to inflict on the body politic in order to exclude blacks. Nowhere was this more glaring than in officialdom's approach to the critical historical shortages of personnel which plagued all ranks of South Africa's civil service. As early as 1946 the Social and Economic Planning Council of the Union of South Africa pointed out that understaffing had seriously jeopardized the ability of the public service to perform its existing tasks as well as ruling out any prospect of its undertaking essential additional functions. By 1950 nearly 15 percent out of a total of 106,956 public service posts were vacant and the situation continued to deteriorate. By 1955, excluding the Department of Defence, the South African police and the Department of Prisons, the vacancy rate had grown to nearly 26 percent including 8097 vacancies out of a total of 24,055 posts in the clerical division. Over the period 1972 to 1975 the number of vacancies for whites in entry grades doubled to 14 percent with the clerical and technical divisions being worst affected. During 1978 to 1981 the number of vacant white posts continued to spiral with increases of 183 percent in the clerical division and 88 and 72 percent, respectively, in the professional and technical divisions.

The government response to these recurrent personnel shortages took on a variety of forms, all of which operated on the politically motivated assumption that the problem was one of a white public service whose requirements were to be met exclusively by whites. To this end, a host of racially exclusive stop-gap and ultimately ineffectual remedies were attempted. These included more vigorous recruiting and widespread advertising; short, intensive training courses; relaxing entry-grade and promotion requirements; employing (white) women on a part-time basis; enhanced salaries and fringe benefits; the employment of pensioners; raising the retirement age from 60 to 65; mechanization; the introduction and extension of study bursaries; intensified overseas personnel recruitment; and, as a final mark of the dictates of racial policy, the curtailment of the functions of the public service to accord with the dwindling pool of available qualified whites.

Later official pronouncements continued to emphasize that the government was committed to the concept of a 'white' public service where integration would not be tolerated and in which 'non-whites' would accordingly not be trained for employment. In so far as their participation in administration and in public service activities was concerned Coloureds and Indians were limited to their own areas (*House of Assembly Debates*, 1969, cols 7233, 7234 and 7254), a principle which was to be reaffirmed in the wake of the creation of the 'own affairs' dispensation introduced in the 1980s. In the case of black Africans their role in public service was to be limited to the separate ethnic homelands. There is no gainsaying the frank admission in 1986 by the then chairman of the Commission for Administration that the 'whole structure [of the civil service] is imbued with the apartheid policy – it has become a way of life' (De Beer, 1986: 48.)

The history of white advancement in the public service of South Africa illustrates the theory of social closure propounded by Parkin (1979) who argues that social closure constitutes a mechanism by means of which social groups seek to maximize rewards by restricting access to resources and opportunities to a limited circle of eligibles. Such groups justify this exclusion on the basis of certain social or physical attributes. In turn, a class of outsiders is created who, because vertical mobility is denied to them, may use their collective strength to usurp the privileges of the upper class. Exclusionary social closure makes use of educational certificates as a means of monitoring entry to key positions in the division of labour. In the South African case, race was also used as a primary exclusionary device.

The Afrikaner first entered public service in substantial numbers in the lower grades. This took place initially under the Pact government's so-called 'civilized labour' policies in the 1920s and continued after the Second World War in the wake of the National Party victory in 1948, when the state sector further expanded, with preference for jobs thus created being accorded to the dominant Afrikaner ethnic segment of society. The Pact government under General Hertzog's leadership consisted of both the then Nationalist Party and Colonel Cresswell's Labour Party. The policy of this new government, which came into power in 1924 having unseated General Smuts's South African Party, was explicitly focused on catering for the needs of the poor whites in the cities.

A new Department of Labour was created in 1924 with a specific view to establishing areas of employment in which whites would be protected from black competition. Inducements included tariff concessions to firms whose labour policies entailed demonstrable efforts to employ whites even at the expense of existing black workers (Davenport, 1985: 361). Local government and other public bodies were also encouraged by the government to employ more whites. Statistics attest to the success of these policies. In 1921, for example, there were 4705 white unskilled employees in the state railway system. By 1928 the number of such white workers had expanded to 15,878 (De Kiewiet, 1957: 234). Not only were policies followed which gave racial preference in job access to whites, but a major effort was devoted to educating and training whites to participate in a society which was undergoing rapid transformation away from a rural-based economy. This effort at mass upliftment was not extended to blacks. Thus, in 1937 some £8,147,211 was spent on the white minority's education and £677,518 on black education (De Kiewiet, 1957: 234). As a result the whites as a group were launched on the road to universal literacy giving them a long headstart over blacks. In addition, whites were able to back up their claims on the state by means of their voting power which was denied blacks.

Adam and Moodley (1986: 44–5) have placed the economic development of the Afrikaners in context and noted that their advances were 'directly linked to the expanding prosperity in South Africa ... and that for blacks, only a growing bureaucratic, rather than entrepreneurial, bourgeoisie can be realistically envisaged ... [but that] the careers of this group are blocked by racial control of the central civil service'. Race, educational qualifications and political clout, then, were the exclusionary measures exploited to ensure the social closure of the white sector of the population.

Black Advancement

The question of institutional legitimacy must loom large in any considera-tion of black advancement in the civil service, or in any field of activity in which blacks are consumers of services rendered. As Maphai (1987: 9–10) has noted in the context of black advancement in the private sector, South Africa can ill afford to alienate large numbers of blacks from key economic institutions for fear that these institutions will then be undermined by them. Adam and Moodley have also pointed to the social and political significance of incorporating blacks through recruitment in the civil service (1986: 142–4) and of locating efforts at re-education for a deracialized society in the civil service (1986: 209).

In the present context the issue of legitimacy is at heart one involving the degree to which people feel themselves assured of a reasonable and sym-pathetic response to their interests on the part of the executive organs of government. As an Indian commission of inquiry into the role of the so-called 'backward' or 'untouchable' classes in government employment has stated: 'Having men [sic] belonging to their own fold at different levels, gives the people a sense of confidence that they will get a fair deal, they will be treated with consideration and no officer will scorn them as people of no consequence' (cited in Galanter, 1984: 85).

Given the ubiquitous role of white public servants in enforcing the panoply of punitive apartheid measures over long years, the possible corrective effect of an affirmative action intervention of this kind in the South African civil service can hardly be disputed and there is, moreover, every likelihood that legislation will be enacted within the next year or two to provide for such intervention. For the time being, the African National Congress appears to have settled for the inclusion of an affirmative action dimension in the interim constitution; a dimension which it will undoubtedly insist is included in the final constitution.

Although not referred to by name, affirmative action principles do, in fact, find reflection in the interim constitution. If one has in mind a conscious effort assertively to expand the opportunities open to those to whom they were previously denied on ascriptive grounds such as race, then affirmative action principles are first encountered in chapter 3 of the constitution under the general heading 'Fundamental Rights'. Here one finds:

8. (1) Every person shall have the right to equality before the law and to equal protection of the law.

(2) No person shall be unfairly discriminated against, directly or indirectly, and, without derogating from the generality of this provision, on one or more of the following grounds in particular: race, gender, sex, ethnic or social origin, colour, sexual orientation, age, disability, religion, conscience, belief, culture or language.

(3) (a) This section shall not preclude measures designed to achieve the adequate protection and advancement of persons or groups or categories of persons disadvantaged by unfair discrimination, in order to enable their full and equal enjoyment of all rights and freedoms.

As is apparent, section 8(3)a authorizes the constitutionality of 'measures' which take account of race or gender but do so for the specific purpose stated. Similar constitutional provisions are to be found in countries such as Namibia, Australia, Sweden, Canada and India. In India, for example, the constitution (in article 16) guarantees non-discrimination on the basis of religion, race, caste, gender and descent but goes on to specify that this article will not prevent the state from making 'any special provision for the advancement of any socially or educationally backward classes of citizens' or from making 'any provision for the reservation of posts in favour of any backward classes of citizens which, in the opinion of the State, is not adequately represented in the services under the State'. The interim South African constitution also refers specifically to the case of the civil service and in article 212(2) states that the civil service shall be 'non-partisan, career-orientated and function according to fair and equitable principles; [and] promote an efficient public administration broadly representative of the South African community'.

The 'new South Africa' will not part company with Murphee's (1979: 119–20) observation that new black governments in Africa have wanted to be seen as

... accelerating black placements at points in the occupational spectrum conceived (either correctly or incorrectly) as being 'power positions'. In this regard the public interface is particularly important. Pressure for 'Africanization' ... have therefore been particularly great in the public service and in positions of public prominence.

The outcome of this political imperative is dramatically illustrated in Zim-

babwe, where, in 1980, whites occupied over 90 percent of senior and middle
management positions in the public service. In the years immediately after
independence this situation was very swiftly reversed and by 1989 over 90
percent of these positions were occupied by black Zimbabweans (Bennell
and Strachan, 1992: 26–7).

What remains to be seen is not whether South Africa will see the
implementation of affirmative action but whether it will escape the down
side of such government-driven employment policies, a subject which will
be discussed in the rest of this chapter on the basis of the African experience.

Lessons from Africa

National resources in Africa have been engulfed by civil service payrolls
which have, more often than not, been supply driven. This situation has led
the African scholar Balogun (1991: 31–3) to refer to 'predatory' government, characterized by a civil service which collects taxes merely to pay its
own salaries as against one which 'gives back to society more of the good
things than it takes'. The point is simply that sound reconstruction and
development strategies can be designed ad infinitum but unless financial
resources are available to back them up they will remain condemned to a
life on the drawing boards. Developmental governance in this sense is
fundamentally concerned with generating and husbanding scarce financial
resources. This is not to discount other standard 'good governance' indicators such as political participation, public accountability, a vigorous civil
society, respect for the rule of law and so on. But, seen from a developmental point of view, all of these lofty principles cannot generate the
development sine qua non of economic recovery and growth in the form of
the sound management of a country's financial resources, the antithesis of
which is reflected in the manifest historic imbalance between the role of the
public and private sectors in post-independence Africa.

The empirical record on this score is typified by the experience in Ghana,
a pacesetter of African independence and a paradigm case of massive state
interventionism. Faith in the prospects held out by independence in Ghana
was vividly portrayed by Nkrumah's declaration that with the demise of
colonialism 'we'll transform the Gold Coast into a paradise in ten years'
(quoted in Rimmer, 1992: 5). Socialism in the form of expanded state
ownership and centralized economic planning and control was to be the
mobilizing banner under which this transformation would occur.

The key element of the new socialist ideology of development was
therefore the growth of the public sector with the rapidly increased 'proportion of resources which were publicly used, of output that was publicly

produced and employment that was publicly provided' (Rimmer, 1992: 7). The envisaged route to Nkrumah's socialist paradise was enthusiastically applauded by mass public sentiment which was resentful of the domination of the economy by whites, a situation which Nkrumah depicted as neo-colonialism, i.e. the continuation of colonialism by economic means. The veritable flood of state-owned enterprises (and the concomitant expansion of state employees) which mushroomed under Nkrumah was, moreover, deemed to be an appropriate entrepreneurial response to the inability of private enterprise and private capital to provide the required acceleration of productive forces in society. It was held that the new parastatals would succeed in supplying goods to the people more cheaply than the private sector.

These were some of the openly stated premises in favour of the state eventually creating or acquiring some 235 economic enterprises before the advent of structural adjustment divestiture programmes in Ghana in the early 1980s (Gyimah-Boadi, 1991: 195). Less prominent in the socialist discourse of the day, but in practice extremely salient, was the desire by the government to reward its followers in the form of wage-earning employment both within the civil service and in the parastatals. By the time of Nkrumah's demise in 1966 no less than 70 percent of wage-earning employment was located in the public sector. Successor regimes in the country continued to expand the role of the public sector within the economy until, after some 25 years of independence, the Ghanaian experiment in state hegemony culminated in a society on the brink of complete collapse with fully one-fifth of its total population and the bulk of skilled professionals having been forced to take economic refuge outside its borders (Sandbrook, 1991: 109). Commenting on the overstaffing and overall dismal failures of the Ghanaian public sector, Rimmer (1992: 10) observes that state employment was used as a political tool to reward loyalty or to secure support.

The malaise described in the previous paragraphs is accurately captured by Clapham's (1991: 4) comment: 'Socialist ideologies [in Africa], which nominally justified the use of state power on behalf of the exploited masses, could be seen instead as serving the interests of the class which most heavily depended on state employment.'

When one talks of the overstaffing record of African civil services the impression gained is that these state employees constitute a privileged sector of society. This is certainly true of the elite whom Ben Turok (1992: 25), the Gauteng ANC politician, in the case of Zambia, describes as a 'parasitic' element which 'uses every opening to increase its share of the national cake without increasing the productivity of the economy' (a distortion which he warns may lurk in wait for a future South Africa 'though it is rarely referred to for fear of alienating the middle level Africans supporting the liberation struggle'). This elite, often derogatively referred to as the 'bureaucratic bourgeoisie', has largely succeeded in maintaining its privileged position even during the downward African spiral into economic crisis. The impression of all civil service incumbents as a privileged sector of society will, however, only hold true in comparison with the most wretched and downtrodden. The vast bulk of civil service employees have not been able to weather the storms of economic collapse, a collapse which has gone hand in hand with radically reduced flows of patronage. Their early perceptions of the blessing in having found stable salaried employment have evaporated in the wake of harsh realities inflicted on them by economic decline in their societies.

Faced with existing levels of mass unemployment, most African governments have found themselves hoist by their own petard of having initiated bloated civil service payrolls and being unable or unwilling to accept the political costs of major retrenchments. The compromise solution adopted in most African countries has been to retain the bulk of the civil servants while shrinking their salaries and benefits. The result, exacerbated by high levels of inflation, has been to devastate the socio-economic status of civil servants. By way of example, starting salaries in the Sudan plummeted by four-fifths in the 1970s; in Ghana and Uganda real starting salaries have fallen below subsistence levels, while in Guinea the average civil service salary in 1985 was $18 per month. In a number of other countries including Somalia, Nigeria, Sierra Leone and Tanzania, even middle-level officials have been unable to feed, let alone adequately house, clothe and educate their families on their salaries. The outcome of this situation in the form of rampant graft and declining efficiency has become a way of life reaching pandemic levels in countries such as Zaire and Nigeria. In Uganda the poor levels of official remuneration have had the effect of putting public employees on sale to the highest bidder (Sandbrook, 1991: 108). 'Moonlighting' (or more accurately 'daylighting', given the absence of officials during working hours who are engaged in informal-sector activities) is also prevalent. And the end result of this overstaffing, particularly in general administrative or clerical ranks, is to penalize society as a whole by making a mockery of the concept of public service.

The lessons for South Africa on this score are dramatic. In one expert's view:

> In a great many [African] countries the state grew so large that it collapsed in on itself. The numbers of new employees exceeded the ability of the state to pay them and utilize their services meaningfully ... Thus majority rule Africa has found itself over the last fifteen years faced with expanding civil services providing less and less benefit to society. (Leonard, 1991:1–2)

The danger in a future South Africa lies in confusing state policies designed to achieve a necessary improvement in the quality of the lives of the underprivileged with the added absolute numbers of officials employed to do so.

It is as well to recognize that potential outcomes of this nature in South Africa need not, as in Africa, necessarily be equated with or driven by a political leadership which professes an adherence to socialist ideology. Here Rimmer (1992:14) reminds us that socialism was long officially professed in a country like Ghana compared to the absence of such ideological espousals in places like Nigeria and Cote d'Ivoire. In the event and notwithstanding ideological rhetoric, the proliferation of the public sector in the latter two countries far outpaced equivalent developments in Ghana during certain periods when the state happened to find itself in a financial position (in Nigeria's case via its soaring oil revenues in the middle 1970s) to support the growth of the public sector. Leadership ideology, therefore, is neither a necessary nor a sufficient condition to explain actual state behaviour in Africa or elsewhere, as amply demonstrated in the former USSR, not to mention the rise of the state sector in a South Africa governed for decades by anti-socialist leadership rhetoric.

The African lessons, in respect of a skewed relationship between the productive and less or non-productive sectors of society and the concomitant overstaffing of civil services, are now loud and clear. It would be ironic if South Africa aimed itself in a direction from which its sister states on the continent were moving away. It must, however, be admitted that the lessons of the African experience could be waved aside by the politics of unreason. The same lessons, already on display in 1980 when Zimbabwe achieved its independence, were largely ignored, giving rise inter alia to civil service numbers (excluding teachers) rising from 40,000 to 90,000 in the space of nine years (Bennell and Strachan, 1992: 27) and to the expansion of parastatals which, to prevent them from collapsing, have had to be subsidized from public funds by as much as 14 percent of total annual budgets or the equivalent of twice the expenditure on health services (Herbst, 1989: 72).

Conclusion

There is every indication that affirmative action will remain in place as a feature of the much heralded transformation of the apartheid state. However controversial this process, particularly among the white minority, popular moral perceptions of equity and the resultant politically driven policies will ensure its continuation.

Knee-jerk reactions by whites against the notion of affirmative action, dismissing it out of hand as apartheid in reverse, will not be helpful in dealing with the reality of a heritage of oppression, dispossession and denial of opportunity. A sulking withdrawal from the challenge of dealing with this legacy will only compound the problem. Withdrawal by disaffected whites, moreover, could be counterproductive. The participation of *all* sectors of the population is needed in order to minimize any risk of an uncritical adoption of inappropriate policy ends and means, and to maximize attempts to design what Murphree (1979: 124), writing of the impending political transition in Zimbabwe, calls a 'constructive balance between political exigencies and economic realities, between sectional interests and common good'. Murphree, himself one of the more thoughtful students of the affirmative action debate, was not unmindful of the potentially disruptive and even hazardous course which a lack of such balance could inflict on society. Such concerns would not be misplaced in respect of South Africa's own transformation process.

The success of affirmative action in South Africa will be closely linked to the extent to which it operates under clearly defined terms and conditions and is subject to continual critical monitoring. The role of the courts as final arbiters will be crucial.

It can be anticipated that certain traditionally accepted standards or requirements for access to the civil service will be revised. Experience (which blacks outside the 'homelands' have been precluded from obtaining) will be one such requirement. The African National Congress has made it clear that it does not envisage that white civil servants will be removed from their jobs. At the same time this organization is wedded to achieving greater racial representation within the civil service. These two considerations, which (as in the case of affirmative action regimes elsewhere) will no doubt be driven by majoritarian political imperatives, are likely to move South Africa further in the direction of the bloated bureaucracy syndrome, an affliction from which it already suffers. Policy planners who oversee this process would be wise to measure their actions against the broader consideration of the national interest in which the resources devoted to creating salaried civil service employment need to be judged against the use of such resources for other more developmentally productive purposes. Affirmative action, in other words, should not become a policy aimed exclusively at the alleviation of short-term unemployment without consideration of the national cost involved.

While affirmative action, in one form or another, will remain in place for some time as a compensatory principle, enhancing equality of opportunity on behalf of blacks, every effort should be made to move the debate away from what the Americans like to call 'race-conscious' action towards a programme in which race per se (as opposed to objectively assessed deprivation) is no longer a defining criterion of affirmative action.

Difficult though it may be, South Africa should learn that those situations in which affirmative action no longer operates as a temporary expedient, encompassing a broad notion of eventually achieving its own demise, but has become a system of power-driven permanent quotas and preferential entitlements. In such circumstances the brightest and the best of the non-beneficiaries, at great national cost in the loss of skills and expertise, simply leave, while their less endowed compatriots turn to other and often more disruptive forms of protest at what they perceive as the illegitimate looting of their interests. While such concerns are no doubt more prevalent among white South Africans, it is as well to recognize the signs of a reaction among other black groups such as Coloureds and Indians who complain that under apartheid they were discriminated against because they were too black, and are now seen by the African majority as not black enough!

Politicians, by the nature of their profession, find it difficult to prescribe longer cures in the face of popular clamours. The temptation to seek a 'quick fix' for institutionalized and racially linked inequity in South Africa will be enormous. The judicious management of affirmative action in the successor South African state will therefore impose near-superhuman demands on the country's leaders. As the African experience demonstrates, using the civil service as the employer of last resort is not among the most promising of available policy options.

REFERENCES

Adam, H. and K. Moodley (1986) *South Africa Without Apartheid*. Cape Town: Maskew Miller.

Balogun, M.J. (1991) 'The African Civil Services Within the Context of Structural Adjustment and Structural Transformation', *African Management Development Forum* 2(1): 22–36.

Bennell, P. and B. Strachan (1992) 'The Zimbabwe Experience: Black Occupational Advancement', in Pierre Hugo (ed.) *Redistribution and Affirmative Action: Working on South Africa's Political Economy*. Halfway House: Southern.

Black Management Forum (1993) *Affirmative Action Blueprint*. Johannesburg.

Clapham, C. (1991) 'The African State', paper presented at a Conference of the Royal African Society on Sub-Saharan Africa, Cambridge University, April.

Davenport, R. (1985) *South Africa: A Modern History*. Cape Town: Maskew Miller.

De Beer, J. (1986) Interview in *Leadership Magazine*, pp. 43–7.

De Kiewiet, C.W. (1957) *A History of South Africa*. Oxford: Oxford University Press.

Department of Public Works (1995) *Business Report*, 21 August. Johannesburg: DPW.

Galanter, M. (1984) *Competing Inequalities: Law and the Backward Classes in India*. Berkeley: University of California Press.

Giliomee, H. and H. Adam (1979) *The Rise and Crisis of Afrikaner Power*. Cape Town: David Philip.

Gyimah-Boadi, E. (1991) 'State Divestiture: Recent Ghanaian Experiences', in D. Rothchild (ed.) *Ghana: The Political Economy of Recovery*. Boulder, CO: Lynne Rienner.

Herbst, J. (1989) 'Political Impediments to Economic Rationality', *Journal of Modern African Studies* 27(1): 607–22.

Leonard, D.K. (1991) 'Issues of and Problems in Public Sector Management in Sub-Saharan Africa', paper presented at a conference of the Newick Park Initiative in England on

African Participation in Public Administration and Public Sector Economic Activity in South Africa, April.

Maphai, V. (1987) 'Affirmative Action: Are There Moral Dilemmas?', paper presented at a seminar on affirmative action, University of South Africa, July.

Murphree, M.W. (1979) 'Africanizing Employment in Zimbabwe: The Socio-political Constraints', *Zimbabwe Journal of Economics* 1(3): 118–36.

Parkin, F. (1979) *Marxism and Class Theory*. London: Tavistock.

Rimmer, D. (1992) 'Redistribution and Economic Growth: Lessons from Tropical Africa', in Pierre Hugo (ed.) *Redistribution and Affirmative Action: Working on South Africa's Political Economy*. Halfway House: Southern.

Sachs, A. (1992) 'Affirmative Action and Good Government' in Pierre Hugo (ed.) *Redistribution and Affirmative Action: Working on South Africa's Political Economy*. Halfway House: Southern.

Sandbrook, R. (1991) 'Economic Crisis, Structural Adjustment and the State in Sub-Saharan Africa', in D. Ghai (ed.) *The IMF and the South: The Social Impact of Crisis and Adjustment*. London: Zed Books.

Turok, Ben (1992) 'Africa for Africans: Plan it Now', *The Weekly Mail*, 4 June.

13. THE RECONSTRUCTION AND DEVELOPMENT PROGRAMME

Robert Cameron

The Reconstruction and Development Programme (RDP) is the major policy initiative of the Government of National Unity (GNU). The African National Congress (ANC) initially released a document entitled *The Reconstruction and Development Programme. A Policy Framework* as part of its election manifesto. This was a general base document which listed the aims and principles rather than the details of the RDP. The RDP was accepted by all parties in Parliament. After the election, the GNU approved the release of a more detailed White Paper. This White Paper formed the basis of RDP policies which have been approved and are being implemented.

Goals of the RDP

The RDP is an integrated, coherent socio-economic framework. It attempts to integrate development, reconstruction, redistribution and reconciliation into a unified programme. The programme will attempt to meet basic needs and open up previously suppressed economic and human potential in urban and rural areas. This is intended to be a vision for the fundamental transformation of South African society (RDP White Paper, 1994: 9). Five key RDP programmes were identified: meeting basic needs; developing human resources; building the economy; democratizing the state and society; and implementing the RDP (RDP White Paper, 1994: 7).

Six basic principles underpin the RDP: integration and sustainability; a people-driven process; peace and security for all; nation-building; linking reconstruction and development; and democratization. The RDP aims to eradicate poverty in the same way that the Marshall plan did in western Europe after the Second World War.

The Government and the RDP

To ensure the successful implementation of the RDP, the government committed itself to the transformation of the way in which the government itself operates. The White Paper envisaged that every office of govern-ment, from the smallest village council to the largest national department, would be restructured to take the RDP forward (RDP White Paper, 1994: 12).

At national level, the RDP ministry was set up under the Minister Without Portfolio, Jay Naidoo, and located in the President's office. The national government sets the broad objectives of the RDP and, together with provincial and local governments, facilitates its implementation at provincial and local level.

The RDP is implemented through the programmes of national line departments, particularly those at provincial and local governments. The RDP office is not intended to be an implementation agency. It is intended to be responsible for the effective management of this process (RDP White Paper, 1994: 15). Fitzgerald et al. (1995: 54) argue that the RDP office is best concerned as an instrument of strategic change management within the office of the President. The following structures, among others, are intended to facilitate and coordinate the RDP: Special Cabinet Committee on the RDP; Core Committee on the RDP; Standing Committee on the RDP; Intergovernmental Forum; Ministerial Forum and Interdepartmental Task Teams (RDP White Paper, 1994: 16).

The RDP Fund

The RDP fund was established in terms of the RDP Fund Act of 1994 and is administered by the Minister of Finance. However, allocation of funds is controlled by the Minister Without Portfolio. The sources of RDP funds are:

• money appropriated by Parliament. In the 1994/95 budget, R2.5 billion was allocated to the RDP fund. This amount increased to R5 billion in 1995/96. These are funds which have been removed from departmental allocations and can be reassigned to them, subject to compliance with new priorities;

- the government's receipt of international and domestic grant aid;
- interest earned from the investment of money in accounts;
- the proceeds from the sale of state assets. The government subsequently approved, in principle, the privatizing of certain assets as part of a six-point plan (*Sunday Times*, 30 October 1994);
- other sources of funds including revenue from lotteries and gambling;
- the redirection of funds by local government by projects within its area of jurisdiction (RDP White Paper, 1994: 16–17).

What is clear in the White Paper is that the RDP is to be financed primarily through the shifting of national, provincial and local budgets to RDP priorities. It was also announced, as part of the six-point plan, that the onus is on each department to go through its budget to assess whether it is fulfilling the objectives of the RDP. If not, the item is scrapped from the budget (*Sunday Times*, 30 October 1994). The RDP office assigns money to departments on the basis of whether such budgets conform to new initiatives in line with the RDP vision. .

Consultation, Participation and Capacity Building

The RDP has to be implemented by line functions of national government, by provincial and local government and by parastatals, but through the widest possible public consultation and participation. Provincial and regional local forums have been established for this purpose. The National Economic Development and Labour Council (NEDLC), consisting of labour, business, civics and the government, is also a key mechanism for consultation and coordination (RDP White Paper, 1994: 48–9).

Capacity building is required in civil society to ensure effective participation in RDP implementation. The government is expected to assist non-governmental organizations (NGOs) in civil society to gain access to information and to participate effectively in the RDP (RDP White Paper, 1994: 49–51).

Provincial Government and the RDP

The White Paper states that each province should develop a strategy for implementing the RDP in the context of its particular circumstances (RDP White Paper, 1994: 20). Provincial governments are supposed, *inter alia*, to carry out RDP activities in accordance with their constitutional responsibilities, introduce the necessary reforms to meet the conditions for the implementation and devolution of RDP programmes, restructure provincial governments to reflect the priorities of RDP, develop institutional capacity to implement the RDP and engage civil society in a meaningful process to implement the RDP (RDP White Paper, 1994: 21).

Provincial governments can only assume responsibility for their functions once the central government is satisfied that they have adequate capacity to undertake these responsibilities. A number of provincial powers are RDP-related functions. These functions are concurrent powers such as health services, housing, urban and rural development, education and welfare services. The central government, in consultation with provincial governments, drew up a checklist to facilitate the development of RDP programmes to provinces. Negotiations on devolution are intended to take a number of factors into account including provinces' capacity to implement people-centred government, major development roles for NGOs and maximum local area assessment of needs and capacities (RDP White Paper, 1994: 22).

Local Government and the RDP

The White Paper noted that local authorities are key institutions for delivering basic services, extending local control, managing local economic development and redistributing public resources (RDP White Paper, 1994: 22). Local government is the level of government which interacts most often with the population through the delivery of basic services. Many of the functions which the RDP aims to upgrade are local government responsibilities such as water, electricity, transport and health. It is therefore the key implementing agency of the RDP, and has been described as the 'hands and feet' of the RDP. The conclusion in the RDP White Paper states:

> Daunting challenges face government in implementing the programme set out in this paper. Perhaps the most crucial is the establishment of credible and effective local government in both urban and rural areas. Without this, implementation of development programmes will be seriously hindered. (RDP White Paper, 1994: 53)

Given that most local government is the only level of government where elections have not taken place, there are certain strings attached to RDP funding. RDP funding will be made available only if:

• amalgamation of different local authorities proceeds effectively;
• single budgets are adopted for a single municipal area;
• the local government electoral process is under way (RDP White Paper, 1994: 22).

In addition, a transitional local authority would gain access to increased resources only if it became developmental in orientation (RDP White Paper, 1994: 23).

In the pre-interim period, the RDP office is operating on a 'carrot and stick' approach. Local authorities which democratize and become development-oriented are eligible for funds. Conversely, local authorities which do not democratize are not eligible for funds.

The Performance of the RDP

The government was obviously keen to start the RDP as soon as possible in order to deliver tangible benefits to its constituency. The first projects were announced by President Mandela during the first budget debate. A number of pilot schemes were identified which could be started within 100 days of the election. Among the Presidential Lead Projects that were announced were free health care to children under 6 years and pregnant women, supplementary nutrition schemes for primary school children, urban renewal projects aimed at rehabilitating townships and stabilizing communities savaged by political violence as well as overcrowding. This would involve integrated provision of infrastructure, housing, electrification, transport, job creation, community and recreational facilities. Other projects include water and sanitation projects in rural areas (Turok, 1995: 311).

How can the RDP be assessed? Jay Naidoo claimed in his first year-long RDP report that the RDP was a 'major success'. The PLP had been a 'major success in transforming government and ensuring delivery'. He cited a number of these 'major successes':

- *Free health care*: Four times as many patients were being treated in rural areas since the inception of the programme.
- *Clinic building*: 172 clinics would be built or upgraded by April 1996.
- *Electrification*: A total of 378,171 houses were electrified in 1994, exceeding the target of 300,000.
- *Primary school nutrition*: Over 5 million children in 12,800 houses benefited against a target of 6.8 million.
- *Urban renewal*: Major development projects were being set up in the most crisis-ridden areas and R1.6 billion had been allocated from the RDP fund over a five-year period.
- *Rural water provision*: the RDP fund had helped the Department of Water Affairs and Forestry to launch several water projects, and 1.3 million people would benefit from this in 1995.
- *Housing*: 196 housing subsidies had been approved (*Cape Times*, 25 April 1995).

However, it soon became obvious that this optimism was misplaced. It was revealed that of the total RDP funds of R2.8 billion allocated for the

1994/95 financial year, only R1.1 billion was spent (*Cape Times*, 18 July 1995). The RDP office responded by pointing out the major logistical and capacity problems associated with transforming government departments to reflect new priorities (Ewing, 1995: 24).

A number of projects that Jay Naidoo referred to were planned projects which had not yet delivered tangible benefits. The only tangible coherent seemed to have been the primary school nutrition programmes. Even the free health care programme had not been a major success because it led to already overstretched clinics and hospitals being swamped with patients. There was also scepticism about doctors and nurses being prepared to work in remote rural areas. Housing projects were extremely slow in getting started due to technical and legal obstacles (*Financial Mail*, 7 April 1995).

The RDP office was subsequently shaken by further revelations. The Eastern Cape nutrition programme had been riddled by corruption; 3.1 million children were fed in August as opposed to 5.4 million at the end of March (*Financial Mail*, 18 August 1995). Also one of the showpiece PLP projects, that of urban development in violence-ridden Katorus, was facing failure after floundering in bureaucratic red tape for 10 months (*Sunday Times*, 23 July 1995). Also, very little RDP activity appeared to be happening in the violence-racked KwaZulu-Natal, the most populous province in the country (*Financial Mail*, 18 August 1995).

There was widespread speculation that a powerful faction within the ANC wanted the removal of Jay Naidoo as head of the RDP. The criticisms of him included the lack of delivery, the creation of unnecessary bureaucratic structures, the introduction of red tape and his inability to communicate the RDP in an understandable way. There was also concern that the RDP Office was becoming a 'super ministry'. He had become unpopular with some ANC ministers because they could either not justify how they would spend the RDP money that they had applied for or had not reprioritized their budgets (*Sunday Times*, 2 July 1995). President Mandela also admitted that red tape was holding up the RDP (*The Argus*, 4 September 1995). Independent observers such as Independent Development Trust chair of trustees Mamphela Ramphela also warned that red tape could kill the RDP (*The Argus*, 20 September 1995).

The ANC's National Executive Committee (NEC) assessed its first 15 months in office and concluded that the RDP would not succeed without concentrating first on stimulating growth, an area which had been neglected. The NEC also decided that a powerful Economic Cabinet Committee was needed to implement the new priorities and coordinate the delivery of programmes by various ministries. This new initiative also demoted Jay Naidoo from his pivotal role of overseeing the reprioritization of government spending and responsibility for coordinating economic policy (*Financial Mail*, 18 August 1995; *Sunday Times*, 30 July 1995). This was a clear indication that without economic growth, the RDP could not be successfully implemented. However, it remains to be seen whether the Economic Cabinet Committee can produce a more coherent economic growth strategy.

Evaluation of the RDP

(i) Institutional Deficiencies

Smith (1985: 135–7) argues that policy implementation is more of a major impediment to the success of public policies in the third world than in developed countries. There are a number of reasons for this, including lack of financial resources, trained staff, poorly framed policies, target group opposition and underdeveloped bureaucracies which are unable to formulate and plan properly.

More specifically, one of the potential RDP problems that had been identified was the lack of skilled staff able to formulate and implement policy (Cameron and Stone, 1995: 99; Wallis, 1995: 92–3). The RDP has been called strong on vision but weak on the institutional mechanics for implementation (Fitzgerald et al., 1995: 14).

These predictions turned out to be prophetic. Jay Naidoo, in response to these criticisms, agreed that the government had been slow to deliver RDP projects. This was because government departments did not have the capacity to implement projects once they had been approved. Departments were having trouble spending their own money, let alone RDP funds (*Sunday Times*, 2 July 1995).

One problem is that the government is trying to introduce affirmative action at the same time as the rapid delivery of services. It has been pointed out that these are contradictory objectives. Many new appointees have not yet acquired necessary skills (*Financial Mail*, 18 July 1995; Wallis, 1995: 90). Furthermore, even large components of the old public service had no experience in large-scale delivery (Ewing, 1995: 26). It has also been argued that the capacity of the old public service has been overrated (Personal communication, P. Fitzgerald, Chair, Gauteng Provincial Service Commission).

Certain provinces lack sufficient capacity due to the problems of the integration of 'homelands', many of which had highly inefficient and corruption-riddled bureaucracies. Other provinces such as the Northern Cape have lacked capacity because they have had to start largely new administrations (Cameron and Stone, 1995: 99).

(ii) Local Government and Implementation

It has already been pointed out that legitimate, viable local governments are essential for the successful implementation of the RDP. However, a major problem is that local government, the 'key implementing agency' of the RDP, is in a state of disarray in many parts of the country. A report, 'The state of local government finance', was drawn up by a technical committee set up by the Departments of Provincial Affairs and Constitutional Development in 1994. It said that black local authorities (BLAs) had all but collapsed. Some BLAs were operating on monthly cash budgets, unable to plan and barely surviving. It warned that if the instability of local governments in the townships spread to white areas, it could lead to a deterioration in basic services with devastating consequences.

What was of fundamental importance was the need to break the back of the rent and services boycott which at the end of 1993 amounted to R1.8 billion (*Hansard*, 22 December 1993, Cols 10041/2). Jay Naidoo said that this boycott could torpedo the RDP and vowed that no RDP money would go to the writing off of arrears (*Cape Times*, 24 September 1994). Furthermore, R709.9 million was allocated in inter-governmental grants to local authorities in the 1994/95 financial year, but, unlike previous years, none of the money was allocated for the writing off of arrears.

The Masakhane campaign was launched among much fanfare in 1995 by the GNU. Its aim was to end the nonpayment of rent and services as well as the nondelivery or poor delivery of services (*Cape Times*, 24 February 1995). This has led to the increase of service payment in certain (but not all) areas. Also, BLA service capacity in certain areas such as Ikapa is improving due to the efforts of neighbouring white local authorities (WLAs). This is likely to be accelerated once formal integration of WLAs and BLAs occurs.

On the negative side there is the concern that the culture of nonpayment is so widespread in some areas that even substantial political changes will not break the back of the campaign. There is also evidence that township dwellers will not pay because they cannot afford to (Mguli, 1995).

Furthermore, the lack of democratically elected local government structures remained a fundamental obstacle. One of the reasons given by Jay Naidoo for the slowness in the RDP was the lack of legitimate local government structures to drive the development process (*Cape Times*, 18 July 1995). This made it essential for successful local government elections to occur on 1 November 1995.

Finally, many local authorities in former homeland areas and rural areas are very weak, with little finance and capacity. Technical assistance and financial support from higher levels of government are imperative to improve this lack of capacity (Cameron and Stone, 1995: 100).

(iii) Community Participation

The RDP places great emphasis on community participation. The White Paper proposed a cooperative framework between the state and civil society when it came to formulating policy. This is a laudable aim. International experience has suggested that development projects are more likely to succeed if they involve community participation (Rondinelli et al., 1984). However, there are certain practical problems which have yet to be overcome. First, the concept of community participation is very vague. Who exactly is the 'community'? There are often competing civics in the same area all claiming to represent the community (Cameron and Stone, 1995: 100). In fact, one of the reasons for the delay in the Katorus PLP project was the plethora of community groups that had to be consulted (*Sunday Times*, 23 July 1995). A similar point is that RDP forums in the Western Cape are largely controlled by the minority ANC which sees it as a way of influencing policy disproportionately through the back door.

Second, concern has been expressed that RDP forums could become a 'new bureaucracy' which could delay projects (see 'Kriel Warns of Red Tape in RDP Forums', *Cape Times*, 24 July 1995). A related point is the criticism that there is excessive community consultation which has delayed RDP projects (see the Western Cape MEC for Housing, General Morkel, 'Criticism in Red Tape May Kill the RDP', *The Argus*, 25 September 1995). Third, the RDP office is being flooded with applications by communities, yet they are not being processed because there is no real framework for community participation (Ewing, 1995: 26). Fourth, previous local forums have been unable to reach consensus (Turok, 1995: 316) and there is evidence that similar infighting in local RDP forums is delaying projects (see 'Rumpus over RDP Red-Tape Bungle', *Weekend Argus*, 23 April 1995). Finally, the RDP attempts to be both a top-down programme forcing agencies to reprioritize and a people-driven process. This is contradictory and is causing tension (Nattrass, 1995).

(iv) Centralization

The centralist tendency of the RDP office vis-a-vis community participation has just been described. A similar point can be made in respect of intergovernmental relations.

Many of the RDP PLP projects are concurrent provincial functions such as health services, housing, urban and rural development, education and welfare services. It is clear that, while there is room for local adaptation, the government expects provinces and local authorities to implement RDP policies in accordance with the RDP framework. The process already described through which provinces and local authorities have to go to obtain

RDP funds is centralized, with the RDP office allocating resources on the basis of applicants having fulfilled certain uniform national conditions (see Cameron and Stone, 1995: 96–7). As Fitzgerald (1995: 55) points out, the RDP 'inevitably represents a period of centralising allocations and initiatives within the state' (within the RDP office).

The centralist imperatives of the RDP are understandable in that the GNU wants public-sector bodies to redirect its priorities and policies. However, if the major function of provinces and local authorities is to implement RDP policies, this could affect the autonomy of subnational government substantially. Concern has been expressed in the two opposition-controlled provinces about the centralist thrust of the RDP.

(v) Budgetary Delays

One of the major concerns was that the RDP undermines sound budgeting. At one level, it created red tape in that departments were forced to apply to the RDP funds for funding which they previously received. This was time-consuming and led to delays. Gill Marcus, chair of the Standing Committee on Finance, argued that this created parallel lines of authority and impeded proper budgeting. The Minister of Finance should have overall responsibility for the budgeting process and all other departments should feed into the appropriate structures within that Ministry (*Financial Mail*, 1 September 1995). A similar point is made by Nattras (1995). She argues that if the entire cabinet supports the RDP, why shouldn't the allocation of funds be left to the Minister of Finance and various departmental ministers? She also suggests that this parallel process is a costly and unnecessary piece of bureaucratic musical chairs.

Conclusion

Despite the failure of the RDP to perform according to expectations, it cannot be dismissed as a total failure. The RDP programme has only been going for about 15 months and many of the effects of the RDP programme will be felt in the medium to long term. In many senses, the RDP is, as Ewing (1995: 27) suggests, a long-term development programme involving community participation, job creation, education and training rather than a rapid service delivery programme.

Also, this paper has focused largely on the PLPs which were the initial RDP projects. More recent RDP projects which have been approved have been applications for line departments. These projects are often mainstream functional activities which are less grandiose than some of the PLP projects and accordingly may stand a better chance of success, particularly if viable local government is set up in much of the country.

It also needs to be noted that R2.5 billion was voted to the RDP fund out of a total expenditure figure of R60 billion, a mere 1.5 percent in the 1994/95 financial year. It would therefore be confusing to conflate the RDP with the GNU's total development efforts.

However, there is no doubting the enormous expectations placed on the government to deliver tangible benefits soon. Given the political demands upon the GNU to redress the inequalities of apartheid, it is a case of too much being expected too soon. The RDP is the most prominent feature of the GNU's policy and if it fails to perform in the next couple of years, the government's image will be badly tarnished.

REFERENCES

African National Congress (1994) *The Reconstruction and Development Programme. A Policy Framework*. Cape Town.

Cameron, R. G. and Stone, A. B. (1995) *Serving the Public. A Guide for Practitioners and Students*. Pretoria: J. L. van Schaik.

Ewing, D. (1995) 'Is the RDP Working?', *Towards Democracy* (Second Quarter).

Fitzgerald, P., A. McLennan and F. Munslow (eds) (1995) *Managing Sustainable Development in South Africa*. Cape Town: Oxford University Press.

Hansard (1983) *Debates of Parliament*. Cape Town: Government Printer.

Mguli, T. (1995) 'The Culture of Non-payment of Rent and Service Charges in Khayelitsha. A challenge to Post-apartheid Local Government', unpublished. Master of Administration thesis, University of the Western Cape.

Nattras, N. (1995) 'The RDP. What Is It and Do We Want It?', unpublished manuscript, University of Cape Town.

Republic of South Africa (1994) *White Paper on Reconstruction and Development. Government's Strategy for Fundamental Transformation*. Pretoria: Government Printer.

Rondinelli, D. A., J. R. Nellis and G. S. Cheema (1984) 'Decentralization in Developing Countries. A Review of Recent Experience', Staff Working Paper No. 581. Washington DC: World Bank.

Smith, T. B. (1985) 'Evaluating Development Policies and Programmes in the Third World', *Public Administration and Development* 5(2): 129–44.

Turok, I. (1995) 'Restructuring or Reconciliation? South Africa's Reconstruction and Development Programme', *International Journal of Urban and Regional Research* 19(2): 305–18.

Wallis, M. (1995) 'The Problems of Bureaucratic Administration', in P. Fitzgerald, A. McLennan and F. Munslow (eds) *Managing Sustainable Development in South Africa*, pp.86–100. Cape Town: Oxford University Press.

14. SOUTH AFRICA'S CONSTITUTIONAL DEVELOPMENT

André Louw

The basic thesis proposed here is that the South African state moved from being monarchical, to republican, to constitutional. In historical terms this can be related to the development from monarchy to aristocracy to democracy. In concrete terms the analysis tries to relate the preambles of South Africa's key constitutions (i.e. the doctrinal justification of the constitution) to the role of the heads of state (i.e. the practical realization of the constitution).

In what follows an attempt is made to analyse the South African constitution in terms of these considerations. What, if any, is the link between the individual as subject and the individual as object of political power in the South African constitution?

Approach

'All states, all powers, that have held and hold rule over men have been and are either republics or principalities,' according to Machiavelli in Chapter 1 of *The Prince*. This is a very important insight if we understand it in terms of the spirit rather than the letter of the law, i.e. in terms of intent rather than effect. It represents a focus which directs all political thinking and is a useful term to analyse any constitution.

The problem can of course be formulated in many idioms but the implications remain the same. Grotius' divisions of sovereignty into proper and common in the *De Jure Belli ac Pacis*, and Oakeshott's division of states into either partnerships or corporations are examples of expressing the same idea in another idiom (Oakeshott, 1975: 199). This dichotomy is evident throughout the history of political philosophy and can be traced back to attempts to see political society in either natural or rational terms. Should the state, in other words, be seen in subjective or objective, material or formal terms: should it operate in terms of power or principle, descent or consent? In philosophical terms the first is perhaps best exemplified by Locke, the second by Kant. In historical terms the Roman Empire illustrates the first, the Holy Roman Empire the second, albeit in rather hybrid versions. Unchecked, the first leads to imperialism, the second to absolutism.

Does society create the state or does the state create society? In what sequence should the concrete and the abstract be related? In the final analysis the state operates in terms of either fact or value and the monarchy/republic dichotomy reflects this reality as archetypes. They represent the alternatives of basing society on either status or contract, and authority on either selection or election. Either the moral is derived from the material or vice versa. The first (i.e. deriving the moral from the material) is achieved in terms of precedence, while the second (i.e. deriving the material from the moral) is achieved in terms of coherence. The first is often expressed in terms of myth, the second in terms of fiction and the leadership expressing the particular approach will reflect this. Monarchies tend to see political power in evolutionary terms, republics in revolutionary terms, not in intent but in effect. For present purposes this is important because the monarchical state merely recognizes and organizes authority, while the republican state creates authority. It follows that in a monarchy society precedes the state, while in a republic the state precedes society.

Above all, however, this dichotomy reflects the confrontation between the personal and the communal, between the subjective person and objective person; between acting and thinking. The individual can act but not judge without society; society can judge but not act without the individual. The individual acts in terms of identity, society in terms of unity. It is important in this regard to keep in mind the Latin roots of the concepts 'monarchy' and 'republic': *monarchia* means 'rule by one' and *respublica* means 'public concern'. All constitutions try to balance the personal and the communal, and it is stressing the one at the expense of the other that determines the character of a given constitution (Kelsen, 1961: 283).

In analysing constitutions it is thus useful to see them in terms of sovereignty, i.e. in terms of the distribution of power. Sovereignty in this sense can be personal, communal or constitutional depending on whether the distribution of power is determined by birth, association or allegiance; on culture, class or consent. In each type of state there should be a link between the status of the citizen and the authority concerned, i.e. between the role of the citizen and the role of the head of state.

Constitutional Path

South Africa, as a united country, was established in 1910 as a monarchy under the British crown. The preamble to this constitution read as follows:

> Whereas it is desirable for the welfare and future progress of South Africa that the several British Colonies therein should be united under one Government in a legislative union under the Crown of Great Britain and Ireland:
>
> And whereas it is expedient to make provision for the union of the Colonies of the Cape of Good Hope, Natal, the Transvaal, and the Orange River Colony on terms and conditions to which they have agreed by resolution of their respective Parliaments, and to define the executive, legislative, and judicial powers to be exercised in the government of the Union:
>
> And whereas it is expedient to make provisions for the establishment of provinces with powers of legislation and administration in local matters and in such other matters as may be specially reserved for provincial legislation and administration:
>
> And whereas it is expedient to provide for the eventual admission into the Union or transfer to the Union of such parts of South Africa as are not originally included therein:
>
> Be it therefore enacted by the King's most Excellent Majesty, by and with the advice and consent of the Lords Spiritual and Temporal, and Commons, in this present Parliament assembled, and by the authority of the same, as follows ... (Quoted in May, 1955: 579)

Several features of the monarchy in particular and the constitution in general can be discerned in this preamble. The monarchy precedes, predates and indeed transcends the constitution. The same applies to the British constitution except that in the case of Britain the monarch personifies rather than transcends the constitution. Power and privilege, also of citizens, is determined more by history than ideology. The power of the monarch is indeed material and not formal, but in this material sense quite extensive and amounts to an almost limitless scope for political influence, i.e. to 'advise, encourage and warn' (Wade and Phillips, 1970: 177). The monarch can, for instance, influence the choice of prime ministers, the constitution of cabinets and the dissolution of parliaments. Since, in the sense of Locke (rather than Kant), the status of the monarch predates the constitution, his or her powers are determined more by convention and prerogative than by statute (Wade and Phillips, 1970: 177). His or her sovereignty is thus personal and flexible. The sovereignty of the state is indeed material as well, and its range is determined by its reach. The law organizes rather than creates power. The role of the monarch is thus determined more by status than contract.

What is important about this personal sovereignty of the monarch is the opportunity it creates to play a political role behind the scenes. As head of the executive the monarch's influence is so personal that it becomes un-traceable in a legal sense. Two instances in South African constitutional history illustrate how pervasive this influence can be. The Governor-General, Lord Gladstone, acting on behalf of the monarch, in 1910 appointed General Louis Botha prime minister before any election; and in 1939 the then Governor-General, Sir Patrick Duncan, appointed General Jan Smuts prime minister without any election. The role Botha and Smuts played in South African history, i.e. South Africa's participation in both world wars, was thus the indirect result of the exercise of the royal prerogative.

The weakness of the monarchy in the South African situation, however, was that it could never relate directly to the community it was meant to personify, i.e. that its mythical character was revealed. All monarchies are in fact mythical in the sense that they all try to project the historical as the universal. The British monarchy could never play the same role outside as inside Britain. This is reflected in South Africa's whole political and institutional development from 1910 to 1950. The status of the Union Act of 1934, for example, translating the statute of Westminster of 1931, tried to establish South African sovereignty as being totally divorced from that of Britain and the monarch in that sense as being the monarch of South Africa as such. The person of the monarch was intended to relate to the South African community directly instead of indirectly (May, 1955: 631–41). The theory was that the crown was divisible; but the British crown proved to be so personal and material in character that it could relate only to communities that in their totality could relate to the same historical tradition. Personal sovereignty crowded out communal sovereignty.

The problem with personal sovereignty is that in order to assert itself it has to become inclusive, and since there is no principle underlying it this tends to escalate into imperialism. In what follows we will consider the alternative, i.e. communal sovereignty.

The problem with communal sovereignty is that in order to assert itself it has to become exclusive in order to mobilize the community and this easily degenerates into absolutism. Personal sovereignty lacks legitimacy, communal sovereignty lacks mobility.

The South African constitution made the transition from personal sovereignty to communal sovereignty only gradually, but the most convenient cutoff date is 1950. From 1950 onwards South Africa was materially, albeit not formally, a republic: in intent if not in effect. In 1950 the South African parliament abolished appeals to the Privy Council, thus ensuring the total autonomy of the South African legal process. From that date on there was a gradual shift in legislation and policy formulation from the sovereignty of the crown to the sovereignty of the state, culminating in the 1961 Republican Constitution. Kahn summarized the legal significance of this shift:

The legal personality of the State and its executive organ. Under the South Africa Act both the Union as a State and the Governor-General-in-Council were by implication given legal personality. But there was a slurring of the identities of the two bodies, which must have arisen through influence of the shunning by English law of the personality of the State. Thus, for instance, section 117 spoke of revenues vesting in the Governor-General-in-Council: and sections 122–5 of Crown lands, rights to mines and minerals and ports, harbours and railways so vesting. The new Constitution continues the process mirrored in the legislation of the past decade of openly avowing the personality of the State as distinct from its executive arm, and, so far as possible with the existing state of the Statute Book, these early inelegancies have been eliminated. (Kahn, 1962: 27)

Here is a shift from the empirical and subjective approach to the state to the rational and objective approach to the state or, differently put, from the English approach to the Continental approach (South Africa knows both traditions). The preamble to the 1961 Republican Constitution read:

In Humble submission to Almighty God, Who controls the destinies of nations and the history of peoples;

Who gathered our forebears together from many lands and gave them this their own;

Who has guided them from generation to generation;

Who has wondrously delivered them from the dangers that beset them;

We, who are here in Parliament assembled, Declare that whereas we are conscious of our responsibility towards God and man;

Are convinced of the necessity to stand united;

To safeguard the integrity and freedom of our country;

To secure the maintenance of law and order;

To further the contentment and spiritual and material welfare of all in our midst;

Are prepared to accept our duty to seek world peace in association with all peace-loving nations; and

Are charged with the task of founding the Republic of South Africa and giving it a constitution best suited to the traditions and history of our land:

Be it therefore enacted by the Queen's Most Excellent Majesty, the Senate and the House of Assembly of the Union of South Africa, as follows ... (Kahn, 1962: 39)

Just as the monarchy assumed a common loyalty, so the republic assumed a common purpose. All monarchies are based on the myth of a common loyalty (i.e. a common origin) and all republics on the fiction of a common purpose (i.e. common values). Locke's myth of the state of nature confronts Kant's fiction of pure reason.

In an attempt to turn fiction into fact a concerted programme was initiated to restrict South Africa to one community by systematically excluding all other communities from Parliament. The aim was to achieve communal sovereignty and not national sovereignty. Although the 1984 Constitution was a belated and half-hearted attempt to rectify this, the result was inevitable. The partial legitimacy of 1984 was as counter-productive as the partial sovereignty of 1934. Just as the South African state was from 1910 to 1950 based on the myth that the material can determine the formal, so it was from 1950 to 1990 based on the fiction that the formal can determine the material (Hosten et al., 1977: 357).

As in the case of the monarchy, this was true of the head of state as well as the state. To the extent that he or she had personal status the monarch was more sovereign than legitimate, and to the extent that the president had communal approval (albeit selective) he was more legitimate than sovereign.

Under the 1961 Constitution the powers of the State President were almost completely formalized in the sense that all prerogative powers were transformed into statutory powers. Not only the powers, but also the authority of the State President became formalized. This authority would henceforth be shared by the Cabinet, and through the Cabinet by Parliament, and ultimately thus by the electorate. This was also true of the monarch, of course, but in his or her case personal status and hence sovereignty was totally independent of the political process and as such guaranteed much greater discretion. Power exercised in terms of circumstance obviously grants more discretion than power in terms of principle.

All power, in fact, is essentially circumstantial in the sense that it is always material. The monarchy used myth to turn power into principle, while the republic ended up using fiction to turn principle into power. The final result of the first was domination, and of the second, stagnation. The legal basis of all this was innocent enough:

> An end has been put to the complex situations that previously obtained, under which the only important prerogative power that was directly conferred by the King on the Governor-General was that of mercy, but the Cabinet could ensure through having recourse to the Status Act and the Royal Executive Functions and Seals Act, the operation of all prerogative powers through the Governor-General. Now it is envisaged that all prerogative powers shall be exercised by the State President on the Cabinet's advice. (Kahn, 1962: 28)

The personal yielded to the communal but at the price of flexibility and innovation. By trying to create power rather than merely organizing it the republic sacrificed the practical for the doctrinal. The 1961 Republican Constitution thus not only formalized the shift in power that started in 1948; it also stamped it and froze it by making it selective and exclusive. In the same way as the monarchy did not realize that loyalty had to be justified, the republic did not realize that purpose had to be negotiated and thus shared.

Fact and value, loyalty and purpose have to be related to each other but not derived from each other. The state is neither brute fact nor mere idea but a moral commitment, i.e. it should be neither material nor formal but both, i.e. legal. What is required is thus neither personal nor communal sovereignty but constitutional sovereignty. What is required, in other words, is a head of state with the status of a monarch and the legitimacy of a president. Unlike the British monarch he or she should thus be elected, and unlike the republican president, elected by all the different communities in the country. Further, the election should be by Parliament to stress the constitutional nature of the head of state and to deny sovereignty in any personal or communal sense. Unlike the monarch the head of state should be South African, but unlike the President he or she should represent everybody.

This dichotomy was resolved by F.W. de Klerk when in 1990 he unbanned all the banned political parties and created the opportunity for all the communities in South Africa to express themselves in constitutional terms. The preamble to the resultant 1993 Constitution, implemented in 1994, reads:

In humble submission to Almighty God,
We, the people of South Africa declare that –

Whereas there is a need to create a new order in which all South Africans will be entitled to a common South African citizenship in a sovereign and democratic constitutional state in which there is equality between men and women and people of all races so that all citizens shall be able to enjoy and exercise their fundamental rights and freedoms;

And whereas in order to secure the achievement of this goal, elected representatives of all the people of South Africa should be mandated to adopt a new Constitution in accordance with a solemn pact recorded as Constitutional Principles;

And whereas it is necessary for such purposes that provision should be made for the promotion of national unity and the restructuring and continued governance of South Africa while an elected Constitutional Assembly draws up a final Constitution ... (Basson, 1994: 1)

From this preamble it is clear that the aim was to create a sovereign as well as a legitimate (i.e. democratic) state, i.e. to create a constitutional state. There is to be no personal or communal sovereignty, since all persons and all communities are presumed sovereign. Sovereignty should therefore be neither material nor formal, but legal. Law in this sense is of course also formal, but the assumption is that it has broad material backing, i.e. it is the union of nature and reason.

The remaining question is what sort of head of state a constitution like this requires. Article 81 of the constitution provides that answer:

Responsibilities of President

81. (1) The President shall be responsible for the observance of the provisions of this Constitution by the executive and shall as head of state defend and uphold the Constitution as the supreme law of the land.

    (2) The President shall with dignity provide executive leadership in the interest of national unity in accordance with this Constitution and the law of the Republic.

    (3) The President shall not hold any other public office and shall not perform remunerative work outside the duties of his or her office. (Basson, 1994: 113)

The role of the President thus mirrors the constitution very closely. His or her role basically is to assert and promote constitutional sovereignty. This means that the state should function at all times in terms of the law and not in terms of sectional or personal considerations. This is stressed by the fact that the President must provide executive leadership to promote national unity and not communal interests, i.e. communal sovereignty is rejected. Added to this the article stipulates that he or she 'shall not hold any other public office and shall not perform remunerative work outside the duties of his or her office'. This implies that status as President must be determined by the constitution and nothing else, i.e. he or she will be allowed no trace of personal sovereignty. The President thus combines the discretionary power of political leadership with the statutory constraints of elected leadership. He or she is thus neither personally nor politically sovereign but constitutionally sovereign, i.e. linking sovereignty and legitimacy.

This dichotomous nature of the presidential office is perhaps best understood by contrasting article 81 (Responsibilities of President) with article 82 (Powers and Functions of President). Article 81 stresses the discretionary and therefore material side of the role, while article 82 stresses the statutory and therefore formal side. A careful scrutiny of article 82 reveals that the President's formal powers entail endorsing, activating or consulting other organs of state, i.e. the deputy presidents, the Cabinet, Parliament or the Constitutional Court, the Supreme Court, the diplomatic service or the army.

The link between the two is at all times the constitution, never personal or political considerations. The sovereignty of the monarch is joined to the legitimacy of the President.

Two aspects of this constitution need stressing to illustrate this analysis: (1) the Government of National Unity, i.e. no part or community in isolation can be sovereign; and (2) the deputy presidents, i.e. the President is not meant to be sovereign in any personal sense. Should the final constitution abandon these principles we may well see a regression to communal sovereignty (i.e. one-party rule) or even to personal sovereignty (i.e. a president for life). South Africa has an opportunity to break out of the cycle of African constitutional development, but may not recognize it.

Conclusion

Monarchies are based on the myth that power can be objective, hence sovereignty. Republics are based on the fiction that principles can be subjective, hence revolution. Because these positions are untenable the monarchies tried to solve the problem by depriving the monarch of direct political power, while the republics, many of whom started as aristocracies, tried to solve the problem by linking power to the majority. Monarchies thus gradually turned into republics with the prime minister as a *de facto* president, while republics gradually turned into monarchies with the president as *de facto* monarch. Effect thus belied intent.

The solution to this problem is to realize that although power can never be objective it can be harnessed, and although principles can never be subjective they can be shared.

Neither the individual nor the community can ever be sovereign; only the law can. Ritual can never bestow power and circumstance can never generate principle. Ritual can only confirm power and circumstance can only realize principle.

The historical and the universal, the subjective and the objective, should interact with but not imitate each other. On a practical level this entails giving all major segments of society representation in all major organs of government. Representation, also in the cabinet, is the key to the constitutional state since it aims at the qualification and not the quantification of power. The essence of the constitutional state is that all authority requires consent, and thus even the authority of the majority, i.e. the principle of majority authority, requires consent. Consent or contract remains the only possible rational link between power and principle.

If it is wrong for one or a few to dictate then it is wrong for the majority to dictate, since the problem is not the number of those who dictate but the fact that they dictate. Constitutions themselves require consensus, therefore, even if the constitution stipulates that elections and therefore governments do not. This is the meaning of constitutional sovereignty as opposed to personal or communal sovereignty. People relate in terms of myth, fiction or contract.

Although both myth and fiction have played important roles in the historical evolution of society, they imply a certain degree of isolation: tribal in the case of myth, doctrinal in the case of fiction. In a global world where cultures can neither dominate nor ignore each other, they must either relate to each other or destroy each other. The dialectical evolution from tribal to doctrinal to constitutional society seems to imply, albeit on varying time scales, a broad historical pattern (cf. Weber, 1964: 328, for his three types of legitimacy).

Europe developed in extended cycles in this way from the tribal (i.e. the

Roman Empire) to the constitutional (i.e. the modern state). In this sense a tribal concept of the state often develops into a system of domination justified in terms of myth, while a doctrinal concept of the state often develops into a system of stagnation justified in terms of fiction. The aim of the constitutional state is not to suspend these two dimensions of the state but to integrate them.

REFERENCES

Basson, D. (1994) *South Africa's Interim Constitution*. Cape Town: Juta.
Hosten, W.J. et al. (1980) *Introduction to South African Law and Legal Theory*. Durban: Butterworth.
Kahn, E. (1962) *The New Constitution*. Cape Town: Juta.
Kelsen, H. (1961) *General Theory of Law and State*. New York: Russell & Russell.
May, H.J. (1955) *The South African Constitution*. Cape Town and Johannesburg: Juta.
Oakeshott, M. (1975) *On Human Conduct*. Oxford: Clarendon Press.
Wade, E.C.S. and Phillips, G. (1970) *Constitutional Law*. London: Longman.
Weber, M. (1964) *The Theory of Social and Economic Organisation*. London: Collier-Macmillan.

15. THE NEW PARLIAMENT: TRANSFORMING THE WESTMINSTER HERITAGE

Hennie Kotzé

Introduction

At different times in South Africa's history, political leaders have faced different choices regarding parliamentary structures. This chapter focuses on the outcome of one such choice: the nature of the interim Parliament entrenched in the transitional constitution of 1993. The final choice still has to be made early in 1996 when the final constitution will have to be ratified by a two-thirds majority of both houses of the interim Parliament. To put this choice into a historical context and to understand better the motivations for the choice, a brief survey of the options available since the establishment of Union is provided.

One of the most important features of the South African state that came into being at the time of Union in 1910 was the exclusion of the majority of the population from the parliamentary decision-making process. As the name indicates, the Union was a unitary state negotiated only by white political leaders at the National Convention of 1909–10. Parliament and the whole governmental structure was based on the familiar British Westminster system. In a united response to their exclusion, black leaders established the South African Native National Congress in 1912 – later renamed the African National Congress (ANC) which became the majority party in the country's first democratic election in 1994.

More than 80 years were to pass before complete parliamentary democracy was established in South Africa. During this period Parliament was used on several occasions to entrench the unequal treatment of individuals in legislation. After the National Party's (NP) victory in 1948 the unitary type of constitution made it relatively easy to establish parliamentary supremacy. This led to unconstrained treatment of constitutions. For instance in the early 1950s the NP government bypassed the constitution in order to disenfranchise coloured voters; in 1983 it scrapped the existing constitution and a tricameral constitution was introduced. Parliamentary procedures and functions, however, were still based on the Westminster model.

The route South Africa travelled towards democracy was tortuous and full of pitfalls. South Africa's politics underwent more dramatic changes in the period from 1983 to 1993 than in any decade since Union was established. After the implementation of the tricameral Parliament in 1984 (separate assemblies for whites, Coloureds and Indians) with a state president as executive head, the inherent contradictions in the apartheid policy forced a new direction on the government. In addition, increased resistance from the disenfranchised African majority, and the socio-economic challenges which urbanization, unemployment, housing and education posed, compelled the de Klerk government to open the way in 1990 for a democratic settlement with the unbanning of the black resistance movements and the subsequent release of Nelson Mandela.

In the four years that led to the final acceptance of South Africa's new interim constitution late in 1993, the most important agents in the South African transition were the political leaders – one group in Parliament and the other outside – negotiating together in a multiparty forum, the Convention for a Democratic South Africa (Codesa). The ANC and the NP were the main components in the negotiation process involving up to 26 parties. The ANC and the NP reached a compromise between, on the one hand, the view of the ANC that normal democratic principles should apply, namely, that the majority should have the right to make decisions with a 50 percent plus one majority, and, on the other hand, the view of the NP that the country should be a constitutional state in which minority rights are protected by special procedures. The NP also accepted the principle of an elected constituent assembly which, as an interim Parliament, would draw up the final constitution. An astonishingly inclusive compromise was reached whereby South Africa would be governed by a Government of National Unity (GNU) for the first five years. The composition and procedures of this Parliament do not differ much from those of states which have strong federal features. (For an extensive discussion of the negotiations on the form of the central government see Atkinson, 1994: 92–102.)

The new interim constitution, The Constitution of South Africa Act, 1993 (Act 200 of 1993) was adopted in December 1993. This constitution came into effect on 27 April 1994 with the first democratic election. It is ironic that the illegitimate South African Parliament was used to create, through legislation, a constitutional state in which the constitution is the highest and

most important law in the country. The new Parliament was empowered in
the 1993 Constitution to function as the Constitutional Assembly as well
and as such to write a new constitution to be completed by 26 May 1996.

The new South African Parliament is one of the most important products
of the negotiated transition of the period 1990–4. As the process of regime
change moved from a transitional phase to the consolidation of democracy,
so Parliament has also become a 'central site' in democratic consolidation.
This chapter focuses on this Parliament and its characteristics, with specific
reference to the composition of Parliament, its working, its influence in
public policy-making and its administrative component.

The Composition of Parliament

According to the constitution (Constitution Act, chapter 4, section 37)
Parliament is the legislative authority of the Republic empowered to make
laws in accordance with the constitution. Parliament consists of two houses,
the National Assembly and the Senate. This composition is also the result of
a compromise between the ANC and the NP. The ANC initially favoured a
unicameral system, while the NP proposed a second house in which all
political parties with a certain percentage of support would have equal
representation (De Villiers, 1994:10).

National Assembly

The National Assembly consists of 400 members. Of the 400 members, 200
were elected on a national list and 200 on provincial lists by a system of
proportional representation. Each party thus has a number of seats based
on the share of the votes gained by that party in the elections that took place
on 27 and 28 April 1994. On Monday 9 May the members of the National
Assembly were sworn in by the Chief Justice at the Houses of Parliament in
Cape Town. They comprised members of the following parties:

African National Congress (ANC)	252
National Party (NP)	82
Inkatha Freedom Party (IFP)	43
Freedom Front (FF)	9
Democratic Party (DP)	7
Pan Africanist Congress (PAC)	5
African Christian Democratic Party (ACDP)	2

Every citizen who is qualified to vote for the National Assembly (all
citizens over 18 years) is eligible to be a member of the Assembly. The
normal disqualifications to voting apply, such as unrehabilitated insolvents,

persons declared of unsound mind by a court, or anyone who has been
convicted of an offence and sentenced to more than 12 months' imprison-
ment without the option of a fine (Constitution of South Africa Act, section
42).

One of the most interesting phenomena is the high percentage of women
who have seats in the National Assembly – something which is exceptional
in developing states. There are now 117 women in Parliament (101 out of
400 in the National Assembly and 16 of the 90 senators). The Speaker of the
National Assembly, Dr Frene Ginwala (ANC) is a woman and three of the
27 ministers are women. These figures place South Africa seventh on the list
of representativeness of women in Parliament (Davis, 1995:17). It is especially in the ANC that a large percentage of women is found. It was the
determination of the ANC Women's League, which has more than 700
branches countrywide, to fill at least one-third of the ANC election list with
women that is to a large extent responsible for this high percentage of
women in Parliament (Kotzé and Greyling, 1994: 82–3; Badat, 1995: 22).

If one looks at the 'representativeness' of the National Assembly it is
clear that this body does not reflect the features of the general public.
Putnam's (1976: 33) view is relevant here: 'The disproportionate advantage
of male, educated, high-status elite recruits increases as we move up the
political stratification system.' Apart from the more salient features such as
gender, it is difficult to determine the level of experience, age and other
social characteristics of MPs. The official register of Parliament in which
these details are recorded is still incomplete. Furthermore, because of the
'sensitive nature' of the information, most MPs refused to respond to these
background questions in the National Parliamentary Survey conducted by
the Institute for a Democratic South Africa (Idasa) (*Parliamentary Whip*, 15
September 1995: 3).

The fact that more than 79 percent of elected MPs were new to parliamentary politics, and that most of them had never even been in Parliament,
meant that they had no knowledge of the rules and orders in connection
with the conduct of its business and proceedings. A series of information
seminars for MPs was presented during June 1994 by the parliamentary staff
under the Secretary to Parliament. In addition to procedural and related
matters, information about the building complex and administration and
services was also included (Secretary to Parliament, 1995).

Vacancies. A member of the National Assembly has to vacate his or her seat
if he or she does not satisfy the requirements laid down to be a member, for
example through insolvency, official resignation from Parliament, becoming
a member of the Senate, provincial legislature or local management, or
ceasing to be a member of the party that nominated him or her as a member
of the National Assembly (Constitution of South Africa Act, section 43).

The last requirement, section 43B, led to considerable unhappiness among MPs. Its implication is that party representation is 'frozen' for the duration of Parliament – this means no party switching, coalition formation, or even taking a seat as an independent member is possible. It was argued in Codesa that one of the most important reasons for this provision was that it was necessary to ensure stability during the transition process. A much stronger argument is that candidates are elected on party lists, which makes party interests much stronger than the mandate candidates received from voters. It is especially the MPs of the NP and the DP who are opposed to this provision. They argue that the provision holds MPs 'hostage', while the ANC and the PAC support the provision because they feel that the party has drawn up the list and that its interests should therefore have priority (Esterhuyse, 1995: 19).

A further provision, which created considerable embarrassment particularly among ANC members, is that MPs may not be absent from Parliament for more than 15 consecutive days. In a review of the 1994 session a respected political journalist, Hugh Roberton, expressed the problem as follows: 'Why is it that so many of the new crop of MPs are so dysfunctional, or uninterested in their work, that they cannot fulfil the primary role which the constitution, and the voters, have given them – to attend debates of the National Assembly?' (*Daily News*, 18 November 1994). The parliamentary attendance register showed that ANC MPs were absent for 4348 working days out of a possible 14,652; NP MPs missed 1126 days, the IFP 782, the Freedom Front 159, the Democratic Party 114, the PAC 75 and the ACDP 9. Eight ANC MPs attended the Assembly for 20 days or fewer, and 13 were absent for 40 days (*Cape Times*, 28 November 1994).

In 1995 one ANC MP, James Mahlangu, was expelled from Parliament for failing to attend on 15 consecutive working days (*Natal Witness*, 25 August). This vacancy was immediately filled. According to section 44 of the Constitution, if a person vacates his or her seat or is expelled, the party is entitled to fill it with a person whose name appears on the party list of candidates in order of preference or the next qualified and available person.

The ANC was subjected to considerable press and public criticism in 1995 after the media revealed the degree of 'absenteeism' of MPs. The DP's chief whip, Douglas Gibson, insisted that 'urgent action be taken to rectify the situation to preserve the image of Parliament and to prevent the government from becoming a laughing stock' (*Natal Witness*, 25 August). The ANC then instructed the chief whip of the party, Bulelani Ngcuka, to fine MPs if they were absent without good reason.

To a large extent the forward planning and scheduling of the day-to-day agenda of the National Assembly is the responsibility of the party whips and parliamentary officials. Without strong party discipline it is difficult to ensure the smooth running of operations – but it is true that there was little initial experience in this field. There was already a noticeable improvement in the effectiveness of Parliament towards the end of 1995.

Quorum. One of the consequences of the high rate of absenteeism has been that there is not always a quorum in the House of Assembly. Section 47 of the Constitution Act provides that at least one-third of the members of the National Assembly, excluding the Speaker, must be present – and at least half of the members if there is to be a vote on a draft bill. On at least two occasions the absence of a quorum was widely publicized and created an embarrassing situation for MPs. On one occasion the Minister of Water Affairs could not table the 'hugely important' Water, Laws and Rationalisation Amendment Bill in the Assembly because only little more than a quarter of MPs were present (*Daily News*, 18 November 1994). Furthermore, the debate during the second reading of the Appropriation Bill in August 1995 had to be stopped twice because there was no quorum (*Natal Witness*, 29 August). At the division of votes the Appropriation Bill could not be approved because there was no quorum – only 166 of the minimum 200 members were present. At that stage only the FF had more than 50 percent of its members in the Assembly, while only 33 percent of the NP and 48 percent of the ANC members were present. The vote on the budget was postponed for a week (*Sunday Independent*, 3 September 1995).

Some of the reasons given for the absenteeism of MPs in the Assembly include:

- The party list system according to which MPs are elected removes their accountability towards the voters.
- The relatively large distances between the place of residence of some MPs and their voters necessitates long journeys that make it difficult to be present in the House on a regular basis. As there are no fixed geographical constituencies, most parties made informal divisions of regions to which MPs should devote special attention; however, linkage has yet to develop for the majority of MPs (see Marcus [ANC] in *Saturday Star*, 27 May 1995).
- The large number of parliamentary committees and the lack of coherence in the management of Parliament's programme, which keep the members of especially the smaller parties busy full time.
- Some members find it difficult to adapt to the routine of life as an MP after the excitement of the 'struggle' against apartheid.
- A large number of MPs are not mature enough and have not attained the necessary level of education required to be an effective MP.
- Due to lack of experience, party whips find it difficult to cope with forward planning and the scheduling of the day-to-day agenda of Parliament.

In short, the most important problems arise as a result of a lack of parliamentary experience among the largest group of MPs. Yet after almost two years of on-the-job training there is already a substantial improvement in the operation of the National Assembly.

The Senate

The Senate consists of 10 senators for each of the nine provinces – 90 in total – irrespective of differences in population, size and economic power. Each provincial legislature elects senators in proportion to the party's support in that province (Constitutional Act of South Africa, 1993: section 48). Senators comprising members of the following parties made and subscribed to the oath or solemn affirmation before Chief Justice Corbet on 20 May 1994 in Cape Town:

African National Congress	60
National Party	17
Inkatha Freedom Party	5
Freedom Front	5
Democratic Party	3

Kobie Coetzee (NP), a former Minister of Justice, is the presiding officer (president) of the Senate and he is assisted by the deputy president of the Senate, Govan Mbeki (ANC). Both officials are elected by the Senate. They are both elected unopposed because the two strongest parties, the ANC and the NP, concluded agreements in advance on the election of office-bearers – this was also the case with the officials in the National Assembly.

Precisely the same requirements as apply for membership to the National Assembly apply in the nomination of senators.

Vacancies and quorum. As far as the vacation of seats and the filling of vacancies are concerned the same requirements apply to senators as to MPs. An additional requirement is that if a provincial legislature is dissolved, the senators of the province concerned vacate their seats in the Senate; the seats remain vacant until an election is held and a new set of senators is appointed (see Constitutional Act of South Africa, 1993: section 51).

The presence of at least one-third of the senators is required to constitute a meeting of the Senate – or at least half the senators when there is to be a vote on a draft bill (section 53). The Senate has not experienced the same problems as the National Assembly as far as absenteeism and the lack of quorums at debates are concerned. The probable reasons are, first, that it is a smaller group for the whips to control and, second, that there is greater accountability as a result of the indirect way in which senators are elected.

Parliament at Work

Apart from the legislative process, one of Parliament's functions is to write a new constitution. This has to be done by the Constitutional Assembly (CA).

The Constitutional Assembly

The 1993 Constitution provides that the National Assembly and the Senate shall in joint sittings constitute the CA, which has as its purpose the writing of a new constitution. The new constitution must be written in accordance with the 34 Constitutional Principles laid down in the interim constitution of 1993 (see Schedule 4, Constitution Act of South Africa, 1993).

At the first joint sitting on 24 May Cyril Ramaphosa (ANC) and Leon Wessels (NP) were elected as chairman and vice-chairman, respectively.

In adopting a report by the all-party Constitutional Steering Committee (46 members with parties represented on a proportional basis), appointed to devise a constitution-writing structure and process, the CA decided on 15 August 1994 that the constitution-making process should be transparent, inclusive and encourage participation by members and the public. Six all-party theme committees, each consisting of not more than 30 members, were appointed to deal with specific aspects of the Constitution, such as fundamental rights, judiciary and legal systems, the character of a democratic state and specialized structures of government, and the relationship between levels of government. The task of these theme committees is to consider and reduce submissions from the public and political parties so that they can be expressed in a more technical form. These drafts, which reflect the areas of agreement and differences, are referred to the Constitutional Committee, to which the CA has delegated certain powers of negotiation (see Secretary to Parliament, 1994: 4).

An all-party Management Committee, consisting of 12 members, coordinates all the activities of the CA. In addition a seven-member panel of independent constitutional experts has been appointed as specified in the constitution (section 74) to advise the CA.

Because of the emphasis on public participation as well as the extensive constitution-making structure that has been developed, a substantial administrative support system has been appointed on contract. A series of public meetings took members of the CA to the furthest corners of the country, and almost 2 million submissions including petitions were received by the CA before it released the working draft of the new constitution in November 1995 (*Constitutional Talk*, 1995).

A Transformed Committee System

Although the workings of Parliament were to a large extent initially based on the tricameral Parliament, the parliamentary committee system has undergone fundamental changes. These changes in the committee system were predominantly initiated and carried through by the ANC MPs. According to Saki Macozoma, a prominent ANC MP, the changes are aimed at operationalizing two principles in particular of the ANC's Reconstruction and Development Programme. First, they must empower the population concerning their rights and institutions, and second, they have to do with the modernization of the government and its structures. Macozoma (1996:89) adds that these principles, 'if applied to the parliamentary system, mean that parliament will have to be organised in a particular way. In effect it means the parliament must organise its work such that both elected representatives and the citizenry are enabled to be involved in a legislative process that fosters participation, accountability and transparency.' According to the ANC, therefore, there should be more rapid progress towards participatory democracy.

Whereas the tricameral Parliament had only 13 standing committees that, in terms of the rules, dealt mainly with legislation, after April 1994 26 standing committees (called portfolio committees) were appointed, corresponding to the number of state departments. The Senate has only 12 such committees. In addition to the internal committees, committees on private members' legislative proposals and the pensions committee, both houses have appointed different ad hoc committees to deal with specific bills on aspects such as abortion and sterilization and the report of the SA Law Commission on surrogate motherhood. In terms of the constitution, portfolio committees in Finance, Defence, the Public Protector and the Human Rights Commission have also been appointed. In all, there are 63 committees: 38 appointed by the National Assembly, 20 by the Senate, and five joint committees (see Secretary to Parliament, 1994:16). This large number means that some meetings take place simultaneously. This makes it extremely difficult for the MPs of the smaller parties to attend all the sessions.

An informal survey was conducted by Idasa's Parliamentary Information and Monitoring Service (*Parliamentary Whip*, 18 August 1995: 8) to get an idea of how many committees individual MPs and senators sat on. Table 1 gives an indication of how seriously overstretched some representatives, particularly of the smaller parties, are.

The smaller parties in particular advocate a rationalization of the large number of committees. Hennie Bekker (MP, IFP) had the following to say about the number of committees: 'The ideal situation is one where a member of parliament serves on one particular committee and specialises in

Table 1. Multiple Committee Membership

Party	No. of Committees
ACDP	
L.M. Green	13
ANC	
Ms P. Govender	7
Mr P. Dexter	5
Mr S. Macozoma	4
Mr S.P. Makwetla	3
Mr G. Rockman	2
DP	
Sen. W. Mnisi	12
FF	
Mr J. Chiole	10
IFP	
Ms L. Singh	14
Dr D.R.B. Madide	7
NP	
Ms S. Camerer	9
Mr N.J. Gogotya	7
Mr N.G. Rameremisa	4
Dr P.J. Steenkamp	3
PAC	
Ms P. de Lille	15

Source: *Parliamentary Whip* (18 August 1995).

the domain of that particular committee. As far as the smaller parties are concerned, it is a matter of impossibility to serve on all the committees unless a process of rationalisation is implemented' (Bekker, 1996:90). It is clear that the committee system sacrifices effectiveness as a result of the large number of committees, but the situation could improve once the activities of the CA have been finalized and a measure of rationalization is introduced. Although parties such as the NP and the IFP, both represented in the cabinet, put up considerable resistance to the restructuring of the committee system – due especially to the fact that the vast majority of committee chairpersons were ANC members – after two sessions there was a greater acceptance of the system.

Parliamentary committees have not increased in number, but they have acquired relatively significant powers. The interim constitution (section 234[6]) provides that as a transitional arrangement the rules and orders of the tricameral Parliament would apply *mutatis mutandis* to the new Parliament, until amended or replaced. But section 58 of the interim constitution authorizes Parliament to make new rules and orders in connection with the conduct of its business and proceedings. In this respect a significant number of amendments were made by the Rules Committee to the Standing Rules of Parliament and adopted on 15 November 1994 (see Secretary to Parliament, 1994: 13). Some of these changes were:

• Types of committee: there are two broad categories of committee, namely, portfolio committees and ad hoc committees. Whereas portfolio committees continue to function for the duration of the session, ad hoc committees are established by resolution to carry out a particular assignment. Portfolio committees (previously called standing committees) are appointed on the basis of proportional representation: 15 members from the ANC, 5 from the NP, 2 from the IFP, and one each from the PAC, FF and DP. There are 26 portfolio committees.
• Presence of non-members of committees: all members of both houses who are not appointed committee members may participate in the discussion, but not vote. All committee meetings are open to the public and the press, unless a committee decides proceedings are private.
• Functions of portfolio committees: committees investigate not only bills but any aspect of departmental budgets relevant to their work. This function has been summed up as follows: 'They may monitor, investigate and make recommendations on any aspect of the legislative programme or any matter relating to government departments, including budgets, rationalisation, restructuring, organisation, structure, function, personnel and policy formulation' (*Transact*, October 1994: 9).
• Chairpersons of portfolio committees: the chairperson is elected by the members of a committee with a simple majority.

In spite of teething problems, the committee system has increased the effectiveness of Parliament enormously. A prominent NP MP, who had also served in the tricameral Parliament, sums up the usefulness of the committee system as follows: 'these committees play a vital role in the democratic process' (Jacobsz, 1996: 93).

The restructuring and extension of the committee system has important advantages for the legislative process. First, it creates a more informal space where members can debate with one another and test ideas. Second, MPs in the committees have a great degree of political independence. Third, submissions from independent experts create the opportunity to test the views of civil servants who serve on the committees. Fourth, the activities of the cabinet – especially its policy-making function – are thoroughly investigated and there is a check on such activities. Finally, it creates an opportunity for the broader public to participate more directly in the legislative process in an individual way or through interest groups.

It seems that the executive authority and the bureaucracy have not yet fully accepted the new paradigm of effective parliamentary supervision, which includes significant public cooperation. This creates visible tensions between certain portfolio committees and the executive authority as well as certain state departments. In most cases, however, departments have adopted the guidelines laid down by the committees concerned (Macozoma, 1996: 91).

Legislating Public Policy

The principles of a government of national unity as laid down in the constitution are much more in evidence in the functioning of the executive authority (the cabinet) than in the two houses of Parliament. The principle of a 'consensus-seeking spirit' (Constitution of South Africa, 1994: section 89) prescribed for the cabinet does not apply to the committee system nor in the formal sessions of Parliament. Against the background of the principles underlying the renewal of the committee system, it is to be expected that clashes will arise between the committees and the cabinet and between the different parties at the level of policy-making.

Parliament had a limited influence on legislation in the tricameral Parliament and 'rubber-stamped decisions emanating from the executive' (for a discussion see Kotzé, 1989: 170–200). The ANC has changed this situation in the new Parliament, and has in this way not only dramatically reduced the influence that the NP can exert in the cabinet, but has also made the policy-making function of the cabinet more controllable.

The new legislative process in respect of public bills other than money bills was adopted by the houses on 15 November 1994, and has the following important features:

- Bills are published in the *Government Gazette* before they are tabled in Parliament. Two memoranda must be published with the bill: one states the purpose of the bill as well as the people and organizations consulted in drawing it up, and the other is a notice inviting the public to make submissions to the relevant portfolio committee. Although bills usually originate in the cabinet or a state department, individuals and portfolio committees can also initiate legislation. Copies of the bill must be made available to each MP at least one day before its first reading.
- The party that tables the bill can deliver a speech of 15 minutes at its first reading. Other parties may each make a 3-minute statement; no amendments are permitted.
- The public has at least three weeks after the bill is published to make representations to the relevant portfolio committee.

- After the first reading the bill is referred to the portfolio committee. It can summon people to the committee, receive written or verbal submissions from interested persons or interest groups and can also appoint sub-committees to investigate certain aspects. The committee can deliver a substantive report on the bill and it can even be referred back to the minister for rewriting – this happened three times in 1994.
- Once the committee has finalized its work, the original or amended bill can be tabled in the Assembly with a memorandum. The committee chairperson can also address the house on the bill. No debate is permitted.
- Debate on the second reading may commence only three days after the portfolio committee's report has been tabled.
- Once a bill has been adopted or rejected in one of the houses of parliament, the other house is notified of the decision and the bill is referred to the relevant committee of the house – where the process is then repeated. The Senate does not have to refer to a portfolio committee, but the National Assembly must always do so.
- If only one house adopts the bill, or different versions of the bill are adopted, the bill must be sent to a joint committee of the two houses for the necessary amendments. After this another vote is taken on the bill in both houses and if it is then adopted with an ordinary majority, it is sent to the president for signing. After that it is promulgated in the *Government Gazette* (see Secretary to Parliament, 1994: 11–12 and *Transact*, October 1994).

In addition to co-responsibility for ordinary legislation, the Senate also has exclusive responsibility for the approval of the central budget (see Constitution of South Africa, 1994: section 64; see also McBlain, 1994: 8 and *Budget Watch*, September 1995). As far as the national budget is concerned the Committee on Finance has only 'post-budget involvement' when the budget is discussed and it can make no amendments (Marcus, 1996: 120).

As far as legislation in 1994 is concerned, Idasa's Parliamentary Information and Monitoring Service comes to the following conclusion: 'Of the 61 Acts passed since the first sitting of the National Assembly on 26 May 1994 most can be commended for being clear, articulate and well drafted, and for their careful use of non-sexist, inclusive language' (*The Statute Book*, May 1995: ii). It is interesting to note that the National Assembly had to vote on only five of these acts. In 1995, 89 laws were placed on the statute books.

There have been no noteworthy changes in other parliamentary procedures. Question time, interpellation and parliamentary privilege have been retained. In essence parliamentary 'case law' – 'the precedents arising from the decisions of successive Speakers in interpreting traditional practice and standing orders' (Laundy, 1989: 62) – is also applied in the same way.

It is clear that policy-making has moved into a new dimension in South Africa. Members clearly have a new conception of the role of Parliament in the creation of legislation. The important role of the parliamentary committee system in the legislative process has meant that the process has been brought much closer to the citizens. It also creates more work for back-benchers of all parties, most of whom have significant intellectual and other skills.

In a new democracy which is receptive to the influence of rapidly changing factors, the level of Parliament's influence in the policy-making process can fluctuate as new institutions and relationships develop. In the case of South Africa, however, it seems as if the new Parliament has developed strong policy-making powers over a short period (see Mezey, 1990:155–6 for a discussion of the influence of parliaments on public policy).

The Administration of Parliament

The changes in the procedures and functions of Parliament have also had an impact on its administration. Many of the changes were also necessitated by the longer sessions – on average eight to nine months, while the tricameral Parliament sat for only five months a year. Some of the most important changes can be summarized as follows:

- Translation services have had to be extended. All of South Africa's 11 official languages may be used in debates in both houses and plenaries of the CA – translations of all the official languages are available in English and Afrikaans. Hansard (the verbatim report of debates), however, is available only in English and Afrikaans.
- The technical services division has had to be extended to keep pace with the information explosion – for example, the activities of the CA can be monitored on the Internet.
- A more informal approach to Parliament has been created. An outstanding feature is a relaxation of the dress code – the Speaker no longer wears formal attire during sessions and it is not compulsory for male members to wear jacket and tie. The old and obsolete legacy of the Westminster type of Parliament to the effect that visitors may not make notes in the visitors' gallery has also been abolished. Seeing that Parliament as a whole has become more accessible, staff have been engaged to run a special public education department; a parliamentary public relations section has also been established. At the end of a long period of

international isolation an international relations section has also been created to develop growing international parliamentary relations.

- A special educare centre has been built for the children of MPs and parliamentary staff.
- Steps had to be taken to reduce MPs' administrative and research burdens. Up to the end of 1995 MPs had almost no secretarial and research support services – for example, ANC members had one secretary for every 12 MPs and no researchers; for the NP there was one secretary for every 4 MPs and 4 researchers (*Parliamentary Whip*, 19 June 1995). Various non-governmental organizations (NGOs) and nearby universities, however, did provide assistance in this regard. (This situation will change in 1996 as a budget of almost R120m has been approved for additional administrative and research staff for parties in Parliament.)

Against this background the Secretary to Parliament reports that more than 470 new staff members were appointed in 1994 and that a policy has been adopted to ensure that staff composition reflects 'demographic composition' as far as possible (Secretary to Parliament, 1994:19). This expansion of staff in Parliament, the high salaries of MPs (about R190,000 per year) and ministers (R450,000 per year), inefficiency and the management crisis in Parliament have given rise to a general perception among the public that Parliament has become a 'gravy train' for politicians (see *The Argus*, 15 September 1994; *City Press*, 20 November 1994). Portfolio chairman Joseph Chiole (FF) summarized this accusation as follows: 'Members of Parliament, facing accusations that they had climbed aboard a "gravy train", had been discredited, insulted and degraded to such an extent that MP bashing had become a favourite sport' (*The Citizen*, 15 November 1994). According to him this perception has been erroneously created among the public by the media.

That the position improved a great deal in 1995 may be ascribed to the fact that everyone has acquired more experience. Although Parliament is only one of the institutions of the GNU, it remains the most important component and it is therefore essential to note that the legitimacy of the GNU has been strongly positively evaluated by the majority of South Africans. After a series of surveys the Human Sciences Research Council (July 1995: 10) came to the following conclusion: 'All the findings . . . appear to indicate that the very high level of legitimacy that the GNU had shortly after the election in May 1994 tailed off to a certain degree by February 1995, whereafter there was a slight improvement in a positive evaluation of legitimacy.' In June 1995 the indexed responses to six dimensions of legitimacy indicated that 69 percent of the more than 2000 respondents evaluated the GNU positively while 24 percent evaluated it negatively.

Eight percent were uncertain.

Yet Parliament still faces its most important challenges. The real legitimacy and consolidation of the democratic process can only be confirmed if MPs apply the 'problem-solving capacity' of Parliament with even greater vigour to resolve the urgent social and economic redistribution issues.

Concluding Remarks

The transformation of Parliament has not yet been completed. What is clear, however, is that the Westminster model of the previous dispensation is making way for a distinctively South African model. One can already deduce from the important role played by a committee system that the new Parliament will shortly become the centre of political power – as is appropriate in a democratic state. In contrast to some other democratic states, it seems as if the power of the legislature is becoming stronger relative to the executive branch of government. But it is too early to gauge clearly the success of attempts to create a greater degree of direct democracy at the cost of representative democracy.

In contrast to the greater degree of public participation in the policy-making process, the strong party control with respect to policy issues among some parties, which restricts the freedom of choice of the individual representative, is a source of concern. The fact that a member must resign if he or she changes party is an example of this. Among the largest parties there is also no question of a 'free vote' on contentious policy issues such as abortion. As far as party discipline and control over policy issues is concerned, the new Parliament has taken a step closer to the Westminster model or even the former eastern bloc parliaments.

Given the large majority of the ANC in the present Parliament, it is possible that opposition parties may in time be marginalized – a tendency which has become familiar in the African context. If this happens, the consolidation of democracy might be subject to great pressure because opposition parties could increasingly resort to extra-parliamentary politics. All indications, however, are that the democratic 'rules of the game' are becoming more firmly entrenched as the new Parliament becomes increasingly institutionalized.

It seems as if the proposed changes in the new constitution are not going to affect the functions and procedures of the present Parliament significantly. As the experience of the parliamentary management team increases – this applies to politicians as much as to administrative staff – so the legitimacy of Parliament as an institution will increase. In this way Parliament, as a strong institution, can play a central role in the consolidation of a democratic regime in South Africa.

REFERENCES

Atkinson, D. (1994) 'Principle Born of Pragmatism? Central Government in the Constitution',
     in S. Friedman and D. Atkinson (eds) *South African Review 7: The Small Miracle of South
     Africa's Negotiated Settlement*. Johannesburg: Ravan Press.
Badat, S. (1995) 'Women "better equipped" ', *Democracy in Action – Journal of the Institute
     for Democracy in South Africa* 9(3):22–3.
Bekker, H. (1996) 'The Role of Standing Committees: An IFP Perspective', in H. Kotzé (ed.)
     Parliamentary Dynamics, pp. 123–4. Stellenbosch: Centre for International and Compar-
     ative Politics.
Budget Watch (1995). Cape Town: Idasa Budget Information Service.
Constitution of the Republic of South Africa (1993) *Act 200 of 1993*. Cape Town: Government
     Printer.
Constitutional Talk (1995), Official Newsletter of the Constitutional Assembly, working
     draft.
Davis, G. (1995) 'Women MPs Report Progress … of a Kind', *Sash* 37(3):17–20.
De Villiers, B. (1994) 'The New Constitution: Framework and Protection of Human Rights',
     Konrad-Adenauer Stiftung: Occasional Papers, Johannesburg: July.
Esterhuyse, E. (1995) 'Om te bedank as LP' [To Resign as an MP], *Finansies en Tegniek*, 20
     October.
Human Sciences Research Council (1995) *Perceptions of Current Sociopolitical Issues in South
     Africa*. Pretoria: HSRC.
Jacobsz, F. (1996) 'The Role of Standing Committees: An NP Perspective', in H. Kotzé (ed.)
     Parliamentary Dynamics, pp. 117–22. Stellenbosch: Centre for International and Compar-
     ative Politics.
Kotzé, H. (1989) 'Aspects of the Public Policy Process in South Africa', in A. Venter (ed.)
     South African Government and Politics. Johannesburg: Southern Book Publishers.
Kotzé, H., ed. (1996) *Parliamentary Dynamics: Understanding Political Life in the South
     African Parliament*. Stellenbosch: Centre for International and Comparative Politics.
Kotzé, H. and A. Greyling (1994) *Political Organisations in South Africa A–Z*. Cape Town:
     Tafelberg.
Laundy, P. (1989) *Parliaments in the Modern World*. Aldershot: Dartmouth Publishing Co.
McBlain, L. (1994) 'The Senate – Not a Rubber Stamp', RSA *Review/Oorsig* 7(5):7–18.
Macozoma, S. (1996) 'The Role of Standing Committees: An ANC Perspective', in H. Kotzé
     (ed.) *Parliamentary Dynamics*, pp. 145–9. Stellenbosch: CICP.
Marcus, J. (1996) 'Drafting the Budget', in H. Kotzé (ed.) *Parliamentary Dynamics*, pp. 111–15.
     Stellenbosch: CICP.
Mezey, M. (1990) 'Classifying Legislatures', in P. Norton (ed.) *Legislatures*. New York: Oxford
     University Press.
Parliamentary Whip (1995). Cape Town: Idasa (Institute for a Democratic South Africa)
     Parliamentary Information Service.
Putnam, R.D. (1976) *The Comparative Study of Political Elites*. Englewood Cliffs, NJ: Prentice-
     Hall.
Secretary to Parliament (1995) *Information Seminars for Members of Parliament*. Cape Town:
     Parliamentary Service.
Transact (1994) *A Monthly Analysis of Law-making in South Africa's Transitional Parliament*
     1(1), October. Johannesburg: Centre for Policy Studies.
The Statute Book (1995). Cape Town: Idasa (Institute for a Democratic South Africa)
     Parliamentary Information Service.

INDEX

Name Index

Strydom, H., 113

Templar, Sir Gerald, 165
Thompson, G., 90
Thompson, L., 107
Tilly, Charles, 179
Turok, Ben, 225
Turok, I., 235, 239

Urquhart, B., 144

Van Aardt, M., 126
van der Westhuizen, J., 78, 79, 86
Van Nieuwkerk, A., 143, 145
van Riebeeck, Jan, 1
van Tonder, J., 65
Van Vuuren, D.J., 109, 112, 139, 141

Van Wyk, David, 38, 78, 132
Venter, Albert, 25, 26
Verwoerd, H.F., 60, 199
Von Holdt, K., 203–4, 207, 209, 211
Vorster, B.J., 60, 70

Wade, E.C.S., 244
Wallis, M., 237
Weber, Max, 250
Webster, E., 196
Welsh, D., 25
Wessels, Leon, 259
Wiechers, M., 79
Wilkens, I., 113
Williams, Rocklyn, 165

Zartman, I.W., 13

Subject Index

accountability, 187–8
Active Citizen Force, 157, 158
actor-oriented approach, 124–38
ad hoc committees, 262
administration of Parliament, 265–7
administrative action, 184–6
administrative justice (in public service), 181–9
affirmative action (politics of), 216–29
Africa (relations with South Africa), 126–7
African Christian Democratic Party, 4, 51, 95,
  116–18, 254, 256, 261
African Muslim Party, 118
African National Congress, 3–4
  affirmative action, 216, 222, 228
  armed forces, 151, 166, 172, 174, 176, 179
  Constitutional Court, 76, 78, 80–1, 83–7
  corporatist trend, 93, 202, 205, 207, 213
  electoral system, 91, 95–6, 99
  executive, 59, 61, 63–74
  external relations, 121, 128–30, 134, 136,
    139–41, 143–4
  interim constitution, 12, 17–18, 24–5, 28
  new constitution, 35–7, 43–56
  new Parliament, 252–63, 266–7
  in party system, 106, 109–12, 114, 116–19
  Reconstruction and Development Programme,
    231, 236, 239
Afrikaans Commercial Institute, 197–8
Afrikaner Broederbond, 113, 198
Afrikaner nationalism, 111, 112, 179, 197–200
Afrikaner Rebellion, 163
Afrikaner South African Party, 179
Afrikaner Weerstandsbeweging, 174

Agreement for Reconciliation and Peace, 48–50,
  53–4, 55
Alvor Agreement, 160
Anglo–Boer War, 153, 154, 156, 157
Anglo–Zulu War, 153, 155
Angola, 130, 154, 160–2, 164, 219
apartheid, 14, 16, 71, 216
  corporatism and, 192, 194–8, 200
  foreign relations and, 122–3, 129–30, 133
  new Constitution, 37, 40, 56
  party system and, 106, 108, 114, 117
Appellate Division, 77, 78, 79, 85
Appropriation Bill, 257
Arab League, 131
armed forces, 151–80
arms control, 122, 140–1
ARMSCOR, 161
Asian-Pacific Economic Cooperation, 137
Association of Chambers of Commerce, 194
Association of South-east Asian Nations
  (ASEAN), 145
Auditor-General, 17
Australia (relations with), 134–5
Aviation Corps, 157
Azanian People's Liberation Army, 37, 151, 166,
  169–72, 178
Azanian People's Organization, 109, 111, 115, 117,
  174

ballots, 93–4, 97–8, 101
Bantustans, 107
basic freedoms, 20
basic human needs, 12, 13